Unrelated Kin

Race and Gender

in Women's

Personal Narratives

Unrelated Kin

Race and Gender
in Women's
Personal Narratives

edited by

Gwendolyn Etter-Lewis

and Michéle Foster

Routledge
New York and London

Published in 1996 by

Routledge
29 West 35th Street
New York, NY 10001

Published in Great Britain in 1996 by

Routledge
11 New Fetter Lane
London EC4P 4EE

Printed in the United States of America
Design: Jack Donner

Library of Congress Cataloging-in-Publication Data available from the Library of Congress

In memory of

Coralie Franklin Cook

and Miss Ruby

Acknowledgments

Michéle and I talked about this book long before it became a reality. It has been both difficult and rewarding to work on a project for almost five years and finally see its fruition. We are sincerely grateful to all of those who made our book possible. We are particularly indebted to the scholars included in this volume who offered their work for publication and patiently waited for the outcome. In addition, we are especially thankful to those women who shared their most private thoughts and experiences with us in order that their stories be told.

Personally I would like to express my appreciation to the following people: co-editor Michéle Foster for her vision and expertise; our Routledge editor, Jayne Fargnoli, for her patience and support; artist Jana Pyle; photographer Mary Whalen; the Western Michigan University students who posed for the cover photos; my student assistant, Aquilla Bell; Dr. Charles Davis who graciously offered a strong shoulder when the going got tough; and our respective families and friends who have survived yet another bout of the craziness we call "writing a book."

—G.E.L.
September 1995

Introduction

Gwendolyn Etter-Lewis

The axes of the subject's identifications and experiences are multiple, because locations in gender, class, race, ethnicity, and sexuality complicate one another, and not merely additively....
Nor do different vectors of identification and experience overlap neatly and entirely.[1]
—Sidonie Smith and Julia Watson, *De/Colonizing the Subject*, 1992

Unrelated Kin is a text that breaks with "custom" by exclusively focusing on women of color. It places women from First World[2] countries/ancestry at the *center* of discussion/analysis and presents their intimate views in a unique mosaic of personal narratives. Traditionally, it has been convenient for researchers and educators alike to regard women as an undifferentiated collective. However, as Smith and Watson suggest, this mistaken assumption is unproductive and misleading. No single group can represent adequately the whole of women, nor can one voice speak for all.

Scholars included in this collection of essays acknowledge the sisterhood of all women, but their primary purpose is to identify and describe distinct life experiences of women of color. Specifically, each chapter explores the significance of race[3] and/or gender[4] as factors which impact women's lives across a diversity of non-Western cultures. Words of women from Tewa and Shoshone societies, from Cambodian refugees, from Latina, African American, Chinese American, and other cultures testify to the particulars of their circumstances/status, both within and outside their respective communities.

As a whole, this book challenges the "status quo" in research and pedagogy as it grapples with controversial issues in the study of life histories. Conceptual, theoretical, and applied research from multidisciplinary perspectives refine and clarify ideas previously unexplored or unexplained in detail. Ultimately, in this text readers will find innovative ways of reconceptualizing the complexities of women's lives.

DENIAL

Coupled with issues of race and gender is the question of denial. That is, the public's tendency to ignore unequal treatment of different races of people and women in the work place, in educational settings, and in social situations.[5] Blinded by the timeworn myth that the U.S. is a genderless "melting pot,"[6] society takes solace in the false security such an illusion creates. It is both easier/safer to say that skin color and sex do not matter in the scheme of American life, than to question the contradictions induced by such a noble concept.

In spite of this convenient fiction, Toni Morrison has observed that the U.S. is a "race-conscious culture" and asks:

> What happens to the writerly imagination of a black author who is at some level *always* conscious of representing one's own race to, or in spite of, a race of readers that understands itself to be "universal" or race free?... How do embedded assumptions of racial (not racist) language work in the literary enterprise that hopes and sometimes claims to be "humanistic"?[7]

In other words, what is the impact of an audience/nation assuming itself to be racially neutral when, in fact, it is acutely conscious/aware of race and also of gender? On the other hand, are there universals that really apply to the non-Western world? Marimba Ani (Donna Richards) answers this question when she suggests that:

> Once individuals are persuaded that universal characteristics are the proper human goals, European patterns and values can be presented as universal, while others are labelled as "particular." Then European ideology can be proselytized without the appearance of imposition, invasion, conquest, exploitation, or chauvinism.[8]

She maintains that what we know as "universalism" is really a disguise for "European cultural imperialism" informed by self-interest and oriented toward conquering inferior "others." In sum, both Morrison and Ani propose that certain ideologies not only promote a naïve and unsympathetic view of human relations in the U.S., but also mask more important issues of race, and by extension gender, that tear and warp the basic fabric of society.

Denial and ignorance establish a comfort zone or buffer that allows the cycle of neglect to continue. As a result, the illusion of impartiality provides a means whereby important differences among women can be minimized, and unique characteristics of groups of women can be reduced to meaningless generalities. If we continue to believe that all women are alike, then any generic remedy of their alleged problems/issues is sufficient. There is no need to look beyond the "norm."

NAMING: THE POWER OF WORDS

Neither blackness nor "people of color" stimulates in me emotions of excessive, limitless love, anarchy, or routine dread. I cannot rely on these metaphorical shortcuts because I am a black writer struggling with and through a language that can powerfully evoke and enforce hidden signs of racial superiority, cultural hegemony, and dismissive "othering."[9]

—Toni Morrison, *Playing in the Dark*, 1992

Women of color, who by definition experience the double bind of racism and sexism, tend to be underrepresented in research and literature alike. In those rare instances where we[10] are included, we are likely to be at the periphery rather than at the center, added extras for the purpose of political correctness. Our experiences and contributions usually are subsumed by a norm/model that marks us as odd exceptions or completely ignores us.

Granted, singling out women of color within the whole of women can be problematic. This approach could lead to stereotyping the very qualities that are most distinctive. Also, there is the additional risk of needlessly restricting (in scope and content) studies of women of color simply because these groups may be regarded as too specific or homogenous to be worth the effort. However, failure to distinguish individual groups promotes a view of "women" as a seamless mass and implies an equality that does not exist.

Consequently, there is a "polite silence" that disguises the significance of cultural variables such as race and social class. Researchers assume that these variables have no direct relationship/connection to gender, that they are entirely separate and only by chance occasionally interact with one another. It is as if women could dissect their bodies (including detaching color from the skin) *and* psyches into individual parts with no overlap and nothing left over. This notion that any woman's life is merely a conglomeration of isolated components that neatly fit into an indivisible whole is as useful as the idea that women should be kept home from work, barefoot and always pregnant.

On a different level, words and terms used to refer to nonwhite women are fraught with controversy and negative connotations. Terms such as wench, Negress,[11] squaw, girl, mammy, auntie, bitch (or color term plus bitch, as in yellow bitch), and others redefine women according to disparaging criteria imposed by the dominant group. Gloria T. Hull, Patricia Bell Scott, and Barbara Smith illustrate the problem in the title of their book, *All the Women Are White, All the Blacks Are Men But Some of Us Are Brave*.[12] The "us" represents black women, who consistently have been omitted from the wholes of "black men" and "women," only to find that there is no word that adequately describes/defines us in our own terms. Alternate choices such as "nonwhite" define by comparison and imply a white norm/standard, while words such as "women of color" may offend those who do not perceive themselves as part of a "colored" and/or historically oppressed subgroup. So there are no easy answers, but it remains clear that, in spite of the limitations of modern English, we must find/create positive terminology for women of all races.

Furthermore, there is the general issue of naming. The power to name is the power to define and control. As most oppressed groups have experienced, one of the first procedures that takes place during initial culture contact is that of renaming.[13] The aggressor/conqueror bestows a "new" name upon the conquered (for instance, "Indian," "native," "savage," and so on) which is usually inaccurate as well as derogatory. Yet the name remains intact until the oppressed group rejects its colonial identity. Hull, Scott, and Smith recognize this process, and argue that "Like any politically disenfranchised group, Black women could not exist consciously until we began to name ourselves."[14]

On the other hand, "minority," a currently popular word applied to people of color, especially African Americans, may have been coined as a neutral and positive means to refer to nonwhite "others" but the inference of low status (minority equals second class) and deliberate miscalculation (people of color are actually a *majority* of the world's population) disqualify it as a viable means of reference. Needless to say, "minority women" is no less offensive. So there appears to be no single term in the English language that is a suitable collective reference for a nonwhite female person.

Recognizing these problems and complications, we use "women of color" as an *interim* or *temporary*[15] term that refers to women who are members of traditionally oppressed groups (and/or their descendants). "Women of color" is not a panacea, and its generalized use frequently sparks debate from various groups of women who raise several important arguments, including the idea that their own ethnic group's uniqueness is obscured by the term. However, since Americans live in what Toni Morrison refers to as a "race-conscious culture," "women of color" is not intended as a euphemism, but rather as a direct means of acknowledging the unlimited variety of women in a constructive manner (a kind of unity in diversity).

RECLAIMING OUR LIVES

Even though women of color have told their individual stories in various forms over time (for instance, slave narratives, spiritual/conversion narratives, diaries/journals, and so on), they rarely have been represented in large numbers in collective studies of women's narratives. Recent research has begun to move away from such limited representation of "women," but inclusive approaches are not yet widely practiced and do not guarantee equitable treatment. Hoffman and Culley's 1985 text, *Women's Personal Narratives: Essays in Criticism and Pedagogy*, focuses on "women's traditional literature" (that is, letters, diaries, and oral testimonies), and argues for inclusion of these materials in the classroom and, by extension, in the literary canon. They suggest that literary creation is a complex interaction "between writer or speaker and audience, each embedded in the specifics of culture. . . . gender, race, and class,"[16] but do not explore this issue to any great extent. The Ward and Donovan essay on Native American oral literature, entitled "Literature in Performance in the Place Where the Partridge Drums," offers the only diversity of the Hoffman and Culley text. The authors describe an oral history course that they taught on the St. Regis Mohawk Reservation. "Although we did not intend to teach a course based solely on Native American materials, we found that our students brought up such materials again and again as we put together scripts for classroom use."[17] Thus, the authors are forced to find and develop primary materials within the Native American community, but they do not specifically address issues of cross-cultural research and pedagogy. In a brief, factual presentation, Ward and Donovan acknowledge the importance of culturally relevant classroom materials, but do not argue for a change in "mainstream" pedagogy or the literary canon.

The Personal Narratives Group edited a collection of essays entitled *Interpreting Women's Lives: Feminist Theory and Personal Narratives*, published in 1989. The volume was an outcome of a conference on "Autobiographies, Biographies and Life Histories of Women" held at the University of Minnesota in 1986. It promised richness and diversity that would increase understanding of the "shared experience of gender and the profound differences among women."[18] Based on the idea that feminist theory generates from and responds to women's lives, the editors list many forms of narration that can be used as resources for interpreting women's lives: diaries, journals, biographies, collaborated life stories, life histories, letters, and autobiographies. This diverse assortment of narrative forms, as well as the international perspectives featured in some of the essays, make the text especially interesting and provocative.

There are several essays on women of color and no attempt to represent any single life history as "the standard" for all women. Nellie McKay, in an essay on nineteenth-century black women's spiritual autobiographies, makes a strong argument for including black women's spiritual writings in the whole of the African American literary tradition. Examining the narratives of Jarena Lee and Rebecca Cox Johnson, McKay points out women's active participation in religious life, and candidly discusses the sexism that black women have experienced inside and outside the black community.

Essays by Marks, Wright, Shostak, and Mbilinyi focus on African women, with some attention to problems of collecting and interpreting collaborative life histories. This is a very important issue, since some of the writers are from cultures different from those of their subjects. Several crucial questions come to the surface, but they are not easily resolved: 1) How can a writer/researcher participate in the collaborative process without imposing her own views and/or preconceived notions? 2) Can an outsider accurately preserve/translate/interpret the experiences of an insider without betraying constraints of her own culture? 3) How and in what way is the collaborative process influenced when the researcher is from a dominant group and the narrator/subject is from an oppressed group? In other words, while gender can be a source of bonding between women,[19] the additional variable of race/ethnicity should not be over-looked as another critical factor in women's interactions. As many of the essays in *Interpreting Women's Lives* suggest, cross-cultural interactions, even between women, are problematic and complex, but potentially transforming.

Women's Words: The Feminist Practice of Oral History[20] (1991), edited by Sherna Gluck and Daphne Patai, assumes a multicultural approach to women's oral histories. Unlike other texts, it undertakes specific philosophical and methodological problems inherent in cross-cultural research: "Most strik-ing in retrospect, were the innocent assumptions that gender united women more powerfully than race and class divided them, and that the mere study of women fulfilled a commitment to do research 'about' women."[21] The honest discussion of these problems in many of the essays is enlightening and thought-provoking. Several different cultures are represented, and there is no dominant model that represents all. Proposing an advocacy approach to the study of women's lives, Gluck and Patai stress the importance of giving some-thing back, of conducting research *for* women.

There is, however, some unevenness in *Women's Words*. The Minister essay, "A Feminist Frame for the Oral History Interview," for example, is especially troubling in its monolithic view of women's narratives, with no particularly insightful vision of issues explored in the collective text. It seems out of place and outdated. On the other hand, some reviewers take exception to Gluck's and Patai's approach as a whole: *Women's Words* indulges in "relentless self-criticism,"[22] lacks a clear definition of feminism, and focuses "too heavily on problematics." While these criticisms may seem justifiable on the surface, clos-er examination calls into question the basic premise of such judgments. Self-critism, for example, is not necessarily a weakness as critics have suggested, but rather a reflexive, internal thought process that can lead to knowledge and transformation. This kind of intellectual self-examination enables researchers to recognize potential biases in their ideology and/or methology and to act/revise accordingly. Undoubtedly, self-criticism is a foreign notion in an arena dominated by male values and where scholars have few incentives to acknowledge the actual limitations of their own research. Gluck and Patai, instead of assuming the stance of researcher as impartial examiner, challenge the myth of objectivity by candidly and publically disclosing their false assumptions. So even though self-criticism in *Women's Words* may be unfamil-iar and even uncomfortable, it strengthens the text and drastically changes the way we conceptualize "scholarly research."

In a different format, women's personal narratives in the form of autobi-ographies offer a potentially fertile source of information. *Life/Lines: Theorizing Women's Autobiography*[23] (1988), edited by Brodzki and Schenck, was heralded as a major breakthrough in women's autobiography studies. Breaching the sterile male tradition that emphasizes autonomy and individualism, Brodzki and Schenck assemble a variety of essays from women scholars who effectively shatter the silence surrounding women's life stories. Many of the essays propose not only that women's self-representation is different from that of men's, but that women must cease to be "framed by the male gaze."[24] There is some cultural variety (African American, Native American, Egyptian, Quebecois, and others), but the major issue is their argument for an expansion of the canon and recognition of a "distinct female tradition in autobiography."[25] This enlightening text goes beyond the conventional, but justifiably limits its scope to literary concerns.

Another text to consider is *De/Colonizing the Subject: The Politics of Gender in Women's Autobiography* (1992),[26] edited by Smith and Watson. The editors argue from a feminist perspective that, due to colonial and neocolonial systems still in existence, women write about their lives in the context of "decolonizing strategies,"[27] or the struggle toward "voice, history, and a future."[28] They discuss the limitations of "traditional" autobiography theory, in that it is clearly Eurocentric, patriarchal, and elitist. In addition, like Patai and Gluck, they emphasize the hazards of conceptualizing women as an "undifferentiated (read normatively white) global 'sisterhood'."[29] Essays in the volume are varied impressively across nations (U.S., Kenya, Egypt, India, the Middle East, and others) and ethnic groups (African Americans, Australian Aborigines, Native Americans, white Americans, Latin Americans, Chinese Americans, and others). The multiple diversities of the book go beyond tokenism by weaving the details of women's lives into a multidimensional whole that is simultaneously individual and collective. Most important, intellectual de/colonization, the overall theme of the text, provides firm scaffolding for understanding differences between women and between systems that oppress them.

Finally, two relatively recent books promise to contribute new information on women of color: *Ethnic Women: A Multiple Status Reality*[30] by Demos and Segal, and *Women of Color in U.S. Society*[31] edited by Zinn and Dill. Demos and Segal focus on the connections between ethnicity and gender in their examination of women of color at home and in the workplace. They also include chapters on myths and socialization. Most impressive is the wide variety of women from different ethnic groups (for instance, Native American, Mexican American, Jewish, Gypsy, Greek, African American, Hmong, and others) and the emphasis on data-based research rather than highly theoretical or personal studies. Similarly, the Zinn and Dill book treats women of color exclusively, and was generated out of a concern for their lack of representation in feminist scholarship. Zinn and Dill also explore a variety of issues, including women of color at work, in prison and in the home. The last section, on "Rethinking Gender," offers ways to reconceptualize the impact of race, class, and gender on women's lives, and the social conditions that are involved in their oppression.

Both of these texts have the potential to change the way we think about and research the lives of women of color. However, neither text uses oral life histories exclusively. Neither concentrates on women's own words. The researcher continues to be the intermediary between the audience and the subject. So we are still deprived/removed from the intimacy of first-person perspectives.

LIFE HISTORY RESEARCH

Documentation of women's lives has tended to be difficult due to a variety of factors, including women's relatively low social status and marginalization within society. According to Gerda Lerner, the types of sources used to record women's lives "depend to a large extent on the predilections, interests, prejudices, and values of the collectors and historians of an earlier day, which in this case reflect the indifferent attention given to women in history."[32] The situation is further complicated by Westerners' preoccupation with the printed word, and associated beliefs that written records are more honest and reliable than oral accounts/reports (even though written words can and do lie as much as spoken ones).

In the midst of this prescribed quagmire of minimal existence we find yet another serious deterrent to women—literacy. In most societies ("developed" *and* "undeveloped") women tend to be the last to acquire literacy skills. Jessie Bernard concluded that:

> Throughout most of human history, the female population has not been a literate one, nor, worldwide, is it very literate today. Even in civilized societies much culture has been created and transmitted orally and its skills passed on by example. Thus today two-thirds of the 800,000 illiterates in the world are female. . . . And when educational training programs are brought into developing countries today, they are often preferentially targeted on males. . . .[33]

Thus, we find that due to certain societal conditions, some women lack the authority that written language bestows upon the literate. Instead, "as-told-to accounts" often have been used as alternatives to first-person narratives. Many slave narratives were told to others who subsequently wrote and published the texts. Extending this example to contemporary African American women, we find that, excluding some autobiographies, many personal narratives are collaborative efforts.[34] Most of these projects yield valuable information; however, the interviewers tend to be whites and/or males. Very few of the interviews are conducted by interviewers of the same gender and/or from the same racial/ethnic background. Although matching interviewers and interviewees by gender and race does not guarantee a bias-free interaction,[35] such a match is more likely to create an empowering environment for the narrator and a more reliable finished product.

Although researchers naturally vary in their elicitation techniques, efforts to adapt interview methods to the needs of the informant are neither consistent nor widespread. "How-to" or instructional manuals are written as if all people are alike. Yet differences between women and men in their language use suggests that even within the same culture divergence in communication styles can cause significant misunderstandings. Questions in mixed-sex conversations, for example, do not have the same meaning for women and men. According to Coats, women use questions to maintain conversation whereas men regard questions as simple requests for information.[36] If such contrasts within the same group/culture can persist, then how much greater are differences in cross-cultural communication?

In spite of these findings, oral history interviewing appears to follow an unaltering pattern on "one size fits all." It is assumed that there is no problem with using the same methods for all informants. In the words of David Lance, "the organizational methods on which this section is based have been applied across a wide subject and chronological range.... They can be adapted for much oral history research which is concerned with the history of particular social and occupational groups."[37] Yet unevenness of interviews and quality, length, and content of narrative texts suggest that no single method could possibly suit all speakers, especially with only minimal/superficial adaptations.

The WPA interviews, for example, display a wide range of variation according to interviewer, interviewee, and method of elicitation. The WPA interviewer who made a racist joke during his interview with an ex-slave obtained very little information from the offended informant.[38] The researcher who constantly interrupted and relentlessly probed her female narrator's marital status could not understand why the interview was so difficult:

> Sadly, the clash in cultures is reproduced in the interview process itself. Gender congruity is not enough in this interview to overcome the ethnic incongruity. The bond between the woman interviewer and woman interviewee is insufficient to create the shared meanings that could transcend the divisions between them ... the narrator and the interviewer do not develop a shared discourse. Confusion and misunderstanding ensue.[39]

This "clash in cultures" is not always an inevitable feature of cross-cultural collaboration if the interviewer takes the time to learn about the culture of the interviewee *before* the interview process begins. Furthermore, "standard" procedures typically are not sensitive to cultural differences in social interactions. So the researcher who does not observe distinct rules of particular cultures, and who does not modify interviewing techniques accordingly, cannot hope to conduct a problem-free interview nor to obtain bias-free data.

DIFFERENT VOICES

The essays contained in this book do not represent all women of color. Although it would be highly desirable to offer a comprehensive collection of women's oral narratives, it was not possible for us to do so in a single volume. Instead, we offer an in-depth variety of essays that describe and interpret women's lives in the context of their own respective racial/ethnic cultures. We do not dwell on comparing these women to each other or to white women. However, we try to do what has not been done before—we place women of color at the center of their communities rather than at the periphery. They are the authorities and standard-bearers of their own lives.

The writers included in this volume are from a variety of backgrounds including a midwife, college professors, graduate students, homemakers, community activists, and others. The essays are arranged according to several different themes in order to provide readers with easier access to the data. There are intentional overlap and natural redundancies that reveal common threads in these diverse lives. Our goal is not to create fixed categories or themes, but to explore the abundant variety of women's lives.

These earnest voices move beyond static recitation of facts to critical analyses of theories, methodologies, and research findings. Each essay offers, in its own way, a part of the whole that promises to transform the way we perceive and study the complex, multifaceted lives of women of color.

NOTES

1. Sidonie Smith and Julia Watson, eds., *De/Colonizing the Subject: The Politics of Gender in Women's Autobiography* (Minneapolis: University of Minnesota Press, 1992), p. xiv.
2. Terms like "Third World" and "developing countries" suggest a Western point of reference saturated with negative connotations of unformedness, ignorance, and lack of advancement. Therefore, I refer to people of color or people from non-Western countries and ancestry as *First World* citizens. I also maintain that Africa, the cradle of civilization, is the real First World.
3. The definition of race is problematic and controversial. However, we offer the following descriptions: a) "In its anthropological sense, the word 'race' should be reserved for groups of mankind possessing well-developed and primarily heritable physical differences from other groups. Many populations can be classified, but, because of the complexity of human history, there are also many populations which cannot easily be fitted into racial classification. . . . National, religious, geographical, linguistic and cultural groups do not necessarily coincide with racial groups." In *Racism: Opposing Viewpoints*, revised edition, by Bruno Leone (St. Paul, Minnesota: Greenhaven Press, 1986), p. 221. Also, "As the British Empire spread to exploit more melanated people who could in no way claim Germanic heritage, the lines of 'race' became more clearly attached to the broad cultural/historical lines that separated Europe from the rest the world. The European self-image has always been based on the implicit perception of cultural/racial difference." In Marimba Ani's *Yurugu: An African-Centered Critique of European Cultural Thought and Behavior* (Trenton, New Jersey: Africa World Press, Inc., 1994), p. 265.
4. We offer the following description of gender: "*Sex* refers to the genetic and physical identity of the person and is meant to signify the fact that one is either

male or female. One's biological sex usually establishes a pattern of gendered expectations, though one's biological sex is not always the same as one's gender identity. . . . *Gender* refers to the socially learned behaviors and expectations that are associated with the two sexes. Thus, whereas 'maleness' and 'femaleness' are biological facts, masculinity and femininity are culturally constructed attributes." In *Thinking About Women: Sociological Perspectives on Sex and Gender*, 2nd. ed. by Margaret L. Andersen (New York: Macmillan, 1988), p. 75.

5. Even if we accept the modern version of this myth—the U.S. is a "salad bowl," I would argue that although the vegetables may be identified individually, *all* are *not* in the bowl.

6. "The modern world is still paying the social costs of historical racism. We are only just beginning to understand the extent which the system of racial domination imposed upon millions of non-Europeans by European nations over the past few centuries still governs the conscious and unconscious relationships between whites and nonwhites throughout the world." Richard Thomas, *Racial Unity: An Imperative for Social Progress* (Ottawa, Canada: Association of Baha'i Studies, 1993), pp. 21.

7. Toni Morrison, *Playing in the Dark: Whiteness and the Literary Imagination* (Cambridge: Harvard University Press, 1992), pp.xi–xiii.

8. Ani, *Yurugu*, pp. 551–52.

9. Morrison, *Playing in the Dark*, pp. x–xi.

10. As a woman of color I find that I can no longer use a writing style that alienates me from my community. Therefore, I choose to use inclusive terms like "we" instead of distancing/generic words like "they."

11. This kind of naming or marking did not apply to all women. There were no words like Englishness, Christianess, or Caucasianess used to refer to white women.

12. Old Westbury, New York: The Feminist Press, 1982.

13. Bosmajian, Haig, "Defining the 'American Indian': A Case Study in the Language of Suppression," in *Exploring Language*, Gary Goshgarian, ed., 4th ed. (Boston: Little, Brown, & Co., 1986), p. 279.

14. Gloria T. Hull, Patricia Bell Scott, and Barbara Smith, eds. *All the Women Are White, All the Blacks Are Men, But Some of Us Are Brave: Black Women's Studies* (Old Westbury, New York: The Feminist Press, 1982), p. xvii.

15. We assume that as language and society change we will develop more accurate and positive ways to refer to differences among people.

16. Leonore Hoffman and Margo Culley, eds., *Women's Personal Narratives: Essays in Criticism and Pedagogy* (New York: MLA, 1985), pp. 1–2.

17. Hoffman and Culley, pp. 162–63.

18. The Personnel Narratives Group, *Interpreting Women's Lives: Feminist Theory and Personal Narratives* (Bloomington: Indiana University Press, 1989), p. 4.

19. Riessman in "When Gender Is Not Enough: Women Interviewing Women," *Gender and Society*, Vol. 1, no. 2 (June, 1987), pp. 172–20, has observed that "gender congruence" does not necessarily guarantee successful collaboration, especially if the interviewer is from a dominant social group.

20. Sherna Gluck and Daphne Patai, eds. *Women's Words: The Feminist Practice of Oral History*. (New York: Routledge, 1991).

21. Gluck and Patai, p. 2.

22. Armitage, Lipsitz, and Mormino, "Women's Words: A Review Symposium," *The Oral History Review*, Vol. 20, no. 1 and 2 (Spring–Fall, 1992), pp. 105–11.

23. Bella Brodzki and Celeste Schenck, eds. *Life/Lines: Theorizing Women's Autobiography* (Ithaca: Cornell University Press, 1988).
24. Brodzki and Schenck, pg. 7.
25. Brodzki and Schenck, pg. 12.
26. Sidonie Smith and Julia Watson, eds. *De/Colonizing the Subject: The Politics of Gender in Women's Autobiography* (Minneapolis: University of Minnesota Press, 1992).
27. Smith and Watson, p. xvii.
28. Smith and Watson, p. xvii.
29. Smith and Watson, p. xv.
30. Vasilkie Demos and Marcia Texler Segal, eds. (Dix Hills, New York: General Hall, Inc., 1994).
31. Maxine Baca Zinn and Bonnie Thornton Dill, eds. (Philadelphia: Temple University Press, 1994).
32. Gerda Lerner, *The Majority Finds Its Past* (New York: Oxford University Press, 1979), p. 64.
33. Jessie Bernard, *The Female World* (New York: The Free Press, 1981), p. 203.
34. In addition to slave narratives such as *Six Women's Slave Narratives* and *Collected Black Women's Narratives* in the Schomburg/Oxford University Press series, see also *Telling Memories among Southern Women* (1988) by Susan Tucker, *Motherwit* (1989) by Katherine Clark, *For the Ancestors* (1989) by John Stewart, and *He Included Me* (1989) by Louise Westling.
35. See Catherine Kohler Riessman, "Women Gender Is Not Enough."
36. Jennifer Coates. *Women, Men and Language: A Sociolinguistic Account of Sex Differences in Language* (London: Longman, 1986), pg. 152.
37. David Lance, "Oral History Project Design." In *Oral History*, David Dunaway and Willa Baum, eds. (Nashville: American Association for State and Local History, 1984), p. 117.
38. Jeutonne P. Brewer, "Challenges and Problems of Recording Interviews." Paper presented at the Language Variety in the South Conference (LAVIS–II), Auburn University, April 1–3, 1993.
39. Riessman, "When Gender Is Not Enough," p. 188.

Mothers,

Family,

and Survival

From a Lineage of Southern Women

1

She Has Left Us Empty and Full of Her

Angelita Reyes

> I love you my grandma,
> as you can see.
> I love you. Even though you
> are spiritually with me,
> I love you as much as I would if you
> were physically with me.
> I love you my grandma
> as you can see.
> — "For My Grandma"
>   Alexandria Reyes[2]

The epigraphs to this narrative illustrate my own sentiments: I didn't know how exceptional my mother was until I got older . . . and now I love her more even though she is not physically with me. She has left me so empty and so full of her.

How can I testify to her, with her, and for her? As I began mentally writing this narrative I had the idea that I wanted to move beyond "an analytically driven" or "conceptually grounded" oral narrative. I decided that I, indeed, wanted to have the space to move beyond the tradition of critical analysis on marginal voices and the centered voice in the written context of a narrative of kinship. I knew that I wanted to engage you, dear reader/listener, in a different way; to allow you to come to your own grounded concepts; to tell you a story that is particular, even if it is not spectacular, a story that could be found in any hamlet. I mentally began to write my narrative as a praxis within an oral tradition of "testifyin'" and "testimonia" from the coming together of two black cultures in the New World—African American and Latino—that gave birth to me, shaped my life, my worldview. But please do not be confused: that shaping of my life is meant to be squeezed in between that of my mother's exceptional being coming from a lineage of Southern black women.

I would like to give you an example of a praxis. Every time I have taught Zora Neale Hurston's *Their Eyes Were Watching God* to university students, something new has taken flight from the pages for me—it was always there but I had not been aware of its presence or of Hurston's dynamic use of language. You know how the novel is Hurston's spiritual litany on life and black womanhood. You are also familiar with Nanny's well-quoted lines from the novel, which state that, "the black woman is da mule of da world as far as Ah can see ... " And Janie, Nanny's granddaughter, cries after she hears what her grandmother has to say about the black woman's life, because she has to postpone heading for the horizon and jumping at the sun. She does Nanny's bidding and marries Logan Killicks. But Nanny also tells something else to Janie that many readers gloss over. With as much passion, Nanny says to Janie:

> You know, honey, us colored folks is branches without roots and that makes things come round in queer ways. You in particular. Ah was born back due in slavery so it wasn't for me to fulfill my dreams of whut a woman oughta be and to do. Dat's one of de hold-backs of slavery. But nothing can't stop you from wishin'. You can't beat nobody down so low till you can rob 'em of they will. . . . But all de same Ah said thank God, Ah got another chance. *Ah wanted to preach a great sermon about colored women sittin' on high, but they wasn't no pulpit for me. . . .* Freedom found me wid a baby daughter in mah arms, so Ah said Ah'd take a broom and a cook-pot and throw up a highway through de wilderness for her. *She would expound what Ah felt.* But somehow she got lost offa de highway and next thing Ah knowed here you was in de world. *So whilst Ah was tendin' you of nights Ah said Ah'd save de text for you.* (Hurston 15–16; my emphasis)[2]

Sermon and text. Perhaps more significantly than seeing the black woman's position as the mule of the world, Nanny's dreams go beyond that position of despair. Nanny implies that, at some point in her life after Freedom, she had wanted to be an educator, to help other "colored" women, to help them empower their lives. She did not have the chance to be the orator or the writer—to have a pulpit of her own. She had hoped her daughter Leafy would live the dreams she could only dream. Nanny sees her second chance in Janie. Rather then viewing Nanny as an obstacle to Janie's horizon, you can also see Janie as expounding on Nanny's ambition "to preach the great sermon to colored women." Janie will not only hear the sermon, but also be empowered by it, and eventually become both text and sermon. She will have the power of both sermon and text—long after Nanny has passed on. Her marriage to Killicks merely delays her until she is finally able to pull "in her horizon like a great fish-net."

The sermon, coming out of the African American oral tradition, converges with Hurston's text (Janie's story) in order to underscore what Hurston constructed out of her own experience of private and public passions. Sermons carry power and empowerment (internal energy) because they are first preached—the Word. But they can be written down and intersect with the power of that Word. At the end of *Their Eyes*, Janie has become both sermon and text, fulfilling Nanny's dream of finding a pulpit from which to expound to colored women. *Their Eyes Were Watching God* is what Hurston has left for us from her pulpit on high.[3]

By the time I had again taught *Their Eyes*, my essay had moved from mental paragraphs to tangible ones. I simply wanted to tell you a story as I return to the memories of another Southern lineage.

Alice Walker writes about her "mothers' gardens" and Southern women as the "crazy saints" who could not realize their full potential as creators. Paule Marshall writes about the West Indian women who were the poets and bards and mothers in the kitchen. Very much like those women who had their personal and public survival strategies and triumphs, my own mother was forced to defy adversities in order to create fulfillment through her and around her. Kesho Yvonne Scott calls these modalities going beyond the "habits of survival," and writes that:

> Such habits, first and foremost, are responses to pain and suffering that help lessen anger, give a sense of self-control, and offer hope. They can also be responses to unexpected happiness—ways of keeping "good times" going. They work, so oppressed people use them over and over again to defeat pain or prolong pleasure. People teach these habits to each other, often by example.... Like dance steps, they provide a social etiquette, a way of moving through the world.... [The habits] acquire the status of cultural prescriptions....[4]

Indeed, the crazy saints, the kitchen bards, the mules of the world—all know that they have to triumph by going beyond the habits of survival in order to celebrate and expound for related and the unrelated kin—different lines but connected lineages that have left many of us both empty and full of these mother-women.

Who are the mother-women? Kate Chopin used the term "mother-woman" in her 1899 novel *The Awakening*, where the central character Edna Pontellier lives in a society that sanctifies "women who idolized their children, worshipped their husbands, and esteemed it a holy privilege to efface themselves as individuals and grow wings as ministering angels."[5] In that novel, the biological/reproductive premise essentializes the mother as the affluent "angel in the house." She is the domestic, unsullied angel who administers unabashedly to her husband first, then to her children and household at large. Her husband-centered domesticity essentializes every thing that she does.

Black women in the New World have had to be more than domestic angels. Toni Morrison explains it this way: "Black women seem able to combine the nest and the adventure. They don't see conflicts in certain areas as do white women. They are both safe harbor and ship; they are both inn and trial. We black women do both. We don't find these places, these roles, mutually exclusive. That's one of the differences."[6] Here, my meaning of mother-women testifies to black women as both safe harbor and ship; inn and trail. In some instances the testimony could be similar to what people of African descent would call "traditional family values." Because, however, of partisan political appropriation of the phrase "family values" that, among other things, condemns single parenting and women working outside the home, I want to call it something else: these mother-women are devoted to the *olden ways of kinship*.

Olden kinship includes what Morrison also refers to as memory returning to the "archaeological site."[7] The return provides access to meaning and allows certain truths to surface. This exercise is also critical for any person who is black, or who belongs to any marginalized category, for, historically, we were seldom invited to participate in the discourse even when we were its topic.[8] In further discussing this memory process, Morrison uses the image of the river that is engineered, straightened out, to make room for modern development. "Occasionally," she says, "the river floods these places. 'Floods' is the word they use, but in fact it is not flooding; it is remembering. Remembering where it used to be. All water has a perfect memory and is forever trying to get back to where it was."[9] Morrison speaks about the archaeological site with both a communal and personal intimacy.

My mother's memories and ways of being were so much connected to that part of Mecklenburg County in Virginia where the James River overflows—where the river remembers, never forgetting the source from where it came. Sometimes the re-memory process is arduous, and at other times the process involves the source of events that are very close in time.

It is more like yesterday when she was laid to rest. Our mother is buried in a secluded and lovely cemetery in the little town along the Long Island

Sound of New York that she first came to during the Great Migration of the 1930s. The cemetery is not geographically close to me or the rest of my siblings, but it is near the remaining women-cousins of her generation who had also come up from the South—and if she had known that this quiet and beautiful green spot would be her final resting, it would have been a great comfort to her. In fact, upon leaving the church where she had been a member back in the thirties, when she arrived from the South, the hearse, instead of going straight to the burial site, slowly took the funeral entourage on her last journey around and through the town to the cemetery. We drove past the elementary and high schools that she had attended as a girl-child recently from the South, the once all-white churches, the Knights of Columbus hall, the old stores, the lovely homes and gardens of the white people who had both embraced her and fought her—all her memories and my images of her memories as she used to tell them to me.

My sister and I sat at the kitchen table going through the insurance papers that we had to have before the funeral arrangements could be made. Less than two days ago, our beloved mother had died. It was hard. It was harder than hard. A most beloved parent. And it always seemed to be the women in families—our three brothers were there, but we were the executors—who had to attempt logic and do all the *business* of crisis—not much time for the real grief of mourning. It was a holiday—Memorial Day weekend. From then on I knew the Memorial Day weekends to come would forever be real ones, of personal loss and mother remembrances.

She was the daughter of Virginia farmers who could trace their maternal lineage in Virginia back to the eighteenth century. (The paternal side of her lineage had come from Jamaica in the West Indies.) This we knew from the old handwritten ledgers in the county courthouse. The ancestors were first listed in the ledgers, as property along with the land, farm animals, furniture and other material possessions of the generations of people who had owned them. As the centuries changed and Freedom came, the lineage was eventually able to own some of the land that the earlier ancestors could only slave on.

The land was beautiful and fertile. But too soon the tobacco acreage on the farm did not produce enough. Her family was forced to become sharecroppers next to the land they owned in Mecklenburg County. Grandpa hated sharecropping after returning from World War I; he could not make a living from it, and it was demeaning. He left for a few years, residing and working in New Jersey, and then returned. Eventually the entire family knew they had to pack a few suitcases. They became a part of the migration of blacks during the Great Depression. My tall, feisty, proud, self-educated, ordained Baptist minister, short-story writer, farmer, seamstress, truck-driving, mother of thirteen sets of adopted children grandmother left first. My grandfather followed a few years later with their four young children, of whom my mother was the oldest.

I had never wanted to talk to her about dying. About death itself. Much too painful even to imagine my worlds without her world, my life. She knew, however, when the time was coming for her—as so many elderly black women do know. They possess that ancient spiritual essence that enables them to communicate with the spiritual kingdom. A few weeks before her passing, her aunt, my great-aunt of eighty-nine years, saw the death in one of her dreams:

> I saw your grandmother [my aunt's deceased sister] come to a door, there was lot of light, and she stretched out her hands to your mother. She was smiling.

My breath sucked in when my great-aunt, deaf and partially blind now, told me the dream as she cried. Yes, I am convinced of this ancient spiritual essence that many olden women seem to possess; a spirituality that guides them as they move closer to their own mother-ancestors—who wait for them. But of course, this spirituality is not exclusively limited to women of African ancestry; other cultures also possess it. I have seen this sensibility, for instance, among Persian, Garifuna, and Lakota women—women whose traditions unabashedly embrace old age as a gift to the community. They can become technicians of the unseen. I am blessed to have known my grandmother for a long time, and she loved my mom dearly. My own young daughter is blessed to have known my mother, her grandmother, even though only for five years of her life.

So we worked through the immediacy of funeral arrangements that night in my mother's cozy, high-rise, big-city apartment. Although very religious and spiritual, she had not been an active member of any church for many years. Would the current Baptist minister in the little church she had been a member of when she first came North accept doing the service? We made the necessary calls. "But of course the funeral can be held there," said my uncle, who was a deacon of the church.

The Baptist minister wanted to know the service we were planning. Would he accept an interfaith program?

> "He won't know the difference," I told my sister. Just give him the titles of the Catholic, Baptist and Baha'i prayers. I don't know if Mr. M. will say anything from the Talmud. We'll leave a space for him in case he's able to come. He's so old now, his heart probably couldn't take this loss. I think he's too upset to come.

December. We are going to have a Christmas tree and I want you to come home and help me clean up for Christmas. I have so much to do. I go to school all week long and when Saturday comes I wash and iron. Come home as quick as you can because Christmas is coming on fast and I want you to hurry and come home momma. The teacher house got burned down Friday and she didn't teach but half a day. Be sure to let me know when you coming home don't forget. We all send love. From you daughter Bettie D. Shields. Write soon and let me hear from you.[12]

The ten-year-old girl grew up remembering what it felt like to be left alone. In many ways our mother was determined that what happened to her would not happen to us. Our lives would be different. She would not leave us alone. . . .

I liked hearing the story of how her penmanship was admired whenever she went back to Clarksville. The Southern white postmaster wished he could hire her because of her distinguished handwriting. He would say in his Virginia drawl, "I declare you got a pretty handwritin', I shur wish I could hire you heah. But I can't hire no colored gal." Every time he saw her during the early years when she went back, he would tell her this.

Mom stayed in high school, and celebrated with her high school diploma in 1940. She was extremely proud—in her quiet way—of that diploma. For a black woman to have actually completed high school on time in those days was a special achievement. As it was to many black people of her generation, education was the cornerstone of racial progress and dignity. In the senior class book, *The Trawler*, they wrote of her: "Domestic . . . artistic . . . capable . . . soft spoken . . . rarely explosive . . . Damecon Club member." Her motto was: "A soft voice turneth away wrath."

As I read her testimony with tears blurring the remembrances of the collected memories, I envisioned all her struggles—at least the ones that I knew about—and her girlhood Virginia stories, her "Northern" triumphs, her challenges in being married to a foreigner whose language she did not learn, all wrapped up with the little treasures of achievements which, in those days of racism and sexism, were like mountains that had been leaped or tossed aside. She went on to reminisce about attending Goldwater School of Nursing in New York City (how many stories I had heard about her experiences as a psychiatric nurse in a state hospital) and her short venture at a business school, but most of all, she wrote about her love for being a mother and for her five children:

Misfortune overtook me. Since graduating from high school in 1940 I have obtained different jobs plus raising a family. Many regrets have confronted me due to the fact that opportunity to carry out my desired nursing career was neglected. Little satisfaction has been achieved while employed in factory jobs and in hospitals as an aide. Working with the sick and the aged,

I would be more satisfied with being skilled in this line of duty by becoming a nurse.[13]

Her life, however, was empowered through the will not to give up "just because things do get a little hard." Education was the avenue to different kinds of achievement and success, she told us. All five of us would go to college. How many times did I hear how she and

> brother Joe, we had to fight to go to Babylon High School. I had to fight for and protect Joe since he was younger than I. The white boys would wait in ambush for us on the way to school—we had to walk to school, you know. They didn't want us there . . . getting an education. I would put rocks in my lunch pail, and when they came out to attack us, I would yell to Joe to run and start throwing the rocks at the boys. Whenever a boy was hit very badly with a rock and bleed, I would be called to the principal's office. Joe turned to amateur boxing. But finally, Joe, he couldn't take it anymore . . . he dropped out of high school and went into the army."[14]

My Uncle Joe, whom I knew only from the handed-down stories, was killed in the army, even before he went to overseas to fight in World War II. He was handsome, carefree, the spoiled baby of the family, an invulnerable boxer until:

War Department, The Adjutant General's Office, July 16, 1942

The report of the board of officers which investigated the death of Private Joseph Shields showed that he died June 9, 1942. Shortly after supper that evening, he had an argument with another soldier concerning some cigarettes. The point of contention was apparently forgotten after a few remarks were made by both parties. However, a short while later the other soldier approached. . . . and after making a few remarks concerning the cigarettes drew an opened knife out of his pocket and without warning cut Private Shields in the neck, severing the internal carotid artery and the internal jugular vein. He was immediately rushed to the station hospital where he died a few minutes later after all efforts to stop the hemorrhage failed.

Because of that, when your Uncle Paul had to go war, I kept him supplied with enough cigarettes. We all kept him supplied with enough of whatever he needed and wanted—because of what had happened to Joe.[15]

Twenty-five years had passed since those high school days and the war years. She had moved away. A letter came one day inviting Mother to the reunion of the 1940 graduation class. They had found her address and wanted her to come. She was hesitant, nervous and afraid. Why did they invite her? She had been one of two blacks in that graduating class—the other one, a black male, did not associate with her because "our family, we're part Indian and are better than you people from blip." All the memories came rushing back for her: she had had no true friends during those four years. With whom would she sit? What would they talk about? Some of them had become wealthy professionals, and even nationally known names. The late radio and TV commentator, William B. Williams, had been in her graduating class. Tapping into her courage and pride, she went to the reunion.

> I can't believe that the very boys who I had to fight and those white girls who never said anything to me only to call me names, now hugged me and each one wanted me to sit at his table. I sat at the class president's table with the girl who had been voted most beautiful and likely to succeed. They acted as if none of what had happened had happened. Did they mean it? I don't know. Maybe. Times are changing. But I had a good time! We even danced! And the food was good![16]

The younger mother valued education, but had also loved her family too much to venture further out on her own. Some of our talks would go into the very late hours of the night, as I sat up with Mom, watching her sew or bake a glorious cake. During these times I learned some of the things that she did not tell everybody. How did it come about that, after graduating from high school, she had applied to Purdue University in Indiana and been accepted? "What?! You went to Purdue? Are you serious? *Really?*" "I did." "But you never told me." Silence. And then:

> I went out there to start school in the fall of that year . . . I had been accepted. I couldn't stay there—there was no place for me to live. We weren't allowed to live in the dorms. No family. I missed Mama. I got back on the train to New York.[17]

She did not talk about the humiliation and disappointment she must have felt when the white university first had accepted her, and then rejected her when she arrived because she was—a Negro. Nobody welcomed her. As she told me only pieces of the story, I filled in the parts. Her pain and sadness of long ago became my pain and anger. A black woman in the forties at a Midwestern university. Not totally unheard of, but certainly a challenging, if not lonely feat. I recognized the many ways in which she, too, had jumped at the sun. Our mother existed because her family existed, and because they were, she was. "There was no family out there for me. I knew I couldn't stay even as I thought I could."

I remembered the telling of the Purdue incident. I thought about how, forty years later, another generation went out to a predominantly white, Midwestern university for a degree. I knew that I would have a place to live—anywhere I pleased. And if anyone denied me that right, I would get a civil rights lawyer, a women's rights lawyer, a housing lawyer, the university attorney, the Human Rights Commission, the Women's Resource and Action Center, and so on and so on. In Iowa City, I had met two elderly black women who had housed black students when the University of Iowa also had not permitted students of color to live on campus. I owe my survival and success in Iowa not only to the "new freedoms," but to our mother's insistence on our getting our education to the fullest, regardless of her fear of "no family" in Purdue. Certainly Mom's decision to leave Purdue did not at all alter her belief and confidence in eventually obtaining an education for herself and for the children she would bring into the world. Her relentless work put confidence into me. It would be her relentless work that would allow all of us to have a completely different kind of life. Her relentless work would provide me with the freedom and financial support to travel all over the world, writing back to her about how much I loved her even though I wanted to travel the world.

As we searched and sifted papers that week following my mother's funeral, I saw the essence of my mother's spiritual and emotional prosperity. We found birthday, Christmas, Mother's Day cards—all kinds of holiday cards—that our own friends had sent to "Mom" throughout the years. She had saved the very pretty ones in a ribbon-tied box. Our mother had also been "Mom" to our friends.

May 8, 1983, New York City

Dear Friends,
Thank you for the beautiful Mother's Day card. It was a great surprise and the most outstanding card on my Mother's Day card display table. . . . the picture of the singing birds and the blooming flowers gave notes of love, faith and hope.

It is nice to know that others care especially on this special day for Mothers.

I am so proud to be a Mother. Not only did all my children send greetings and gifts, but many friends far and neighbors near remembered me. The phone calls rang out from across the country with love and greetings. I love each one of you. Truly this was prosperity on Mother's Day.

Love,

Bettie D. Reyes[18]

Mom took care of her own children even as she mothered so many others. Because of our Latino father, of whom the Southern relatives would say, "that Negro who don't speak good English," our growing up was a true bicultural family of Spanish- and English-speaking cousins and aunts and uncles. There was always a welcoming mat at "Auntie Bettie's." When we got older and went to college, our African, Caribbean, and Latino friends recognized Mom as an extended "other mother" with whom they could find a very warm welcome.

When I was still in college and living at home, I answered a telephone call one day, and was surprised to hear the voice of a former South American boyfriend. I righteously wondered why he was calling, since we were no longer seeing one another. He replied, "I'm not calling to talk to you, I would like to speak to *Mom*, I want to know how *she* is doing!" During our college years, for many of our friends who were foreign students away from home, our home was special because of Mom. For her, there was the unspoken need to sustain the way of the family, of the olden kinship.

"How could I ever repay you for what you have sacrificed for us?" "You all could never *repay* me! The only way you could pay me back is to have children of your own."

I used to think that when she told us this, she meant that we had to have children who would give us grief, disappointments, and hardship; that she wanted us to feel what she had endured by having five children of her own as well as taking care of other mothers' children when they could not. No. That was not what she meant. It took me a long time to "grow up" and finally understand what she was telling us: that by having our own children we would, as parents, learn compassion, sacrifice; we could only put into practice the values she had instilled in us by having children of our own. Having a wanted child brings enlightenment, compassion, and hope—despite the ever-present adversities that confront us. There would be the feeling that "I want things to be better for my child—for better tomorrows."

> My leisure hours are spent mostly reading, arts and crafts—that is usually spent with the children. I believe in talking to them and being with them—we all come together for dinner at night. When I listen to their stories of the day, I not only listen to them but I can correct their grammar and there is always a teaching opportunity. A learning time. When they were young I would read to them; now we have all kinds of discussions. I am foremost, a mother of which I very much enjoy being and doing.[19]

Because of her belief in the olden kinship that had sustained her people, she always told us the importance of sticking together as a family. There were the sibling squabbles among the five of us, each vying for her special attention, even when we became adults! But she wanted us to be close to each other, and to find for ourselves another "center" among us after she was gone. "When I am gone, my spirit will be able to be with all of you at the same time."

My mother "had a belief in self that was larger than anyone's disbelief." Of such a belief in self, regardless, Toni Morrison says, "I remember the very real life-threatening obstacles people in my family faced, and whenever I would feel overwhelmed, that's all I had to think about."[20] Whatever I have to endure is not nearly so painful and dehumanizing as what my mother and her foremothers have undergone. And so now, when my own eight-year-old daughter cries and complains because "piano practice is too hard," or whenever I am overwhelmed by life, I begin remembering all over again how Mom, walking miles to school with Uncle Joe, had to carry fighting rocks in her lunch pail because the white kids did not want her to go to school with them. I have told my own daughter the story over and over again:

> It's because of your grandmother and so many others before her that you don't have to fight to go to school; she had to fill her lunch pail with fighting rocks. She had to fight in order to attend school. Whenever it gets to what you think is too hard, young lady, remember you are here with this opportunity to go to any school we want you to attend—and you are going to the best of schools—because of her.
> Mi querida, my precious lamb, I don't want to hear that word "hard." Your grandma's going to school put me where I am now in order to provide for you—to make a better world for you.

Black women have loved their mother-women, and appreciated them, and knew what their mothers and grandmothers (with or without spouses) did for them. Exceptions only prove this to be true. Trinidadian writer Dionne Brand writes, in her short story "Photograph," of the passing of the beloved grandmother, a mother-woman:

> We were all full of my grandmother, she had left us full and empty of her. We dreamed in my grandmother and we woke up in her, bleary-eyed and gesturing for her arm, her elbows, her smell. We jockeyed with each other, lied to each other, quarrelled with each other and with her for the boon of lying close to her, sculpting ourselves around the roundness of her back. Braiding her hair and oiling her feet. . . . We anticipated where she would sit and got there before her. . . . She had left us empty and full of her. (180)[21]

The mother-woman of my archaeological site has left me empty and full of her.

NOTES

1. Reyes, Alexandria. "I Love You, My Grandma." unpublished poem. 1992.
2. For a comprehensive analysis on the sermon and text reading of Hurston's *Their Eyes Were Watching God*, see Nellie McKay's "Crayon Enlargements of Life: Zora Neale Hurston's *Their Eyes Were Watching God* as Autobiography." *New Essays on "Their Eyes Were Watching God,"* ed. Michael Awkward (Cambridge: Cambridge University Press, 1990).
3. Hurston, *Their Eyes Were Watching God*

4. Scott, Kesho Yvonne. *The Habit of Surviving*. New York: Ballentine Books, 1991.
5. Chopin, Kate. *The Awakening*. New York: Putnam, 1964.
6. Morrison, Toni. "The Site of Memory." *Inventing the Truth: The Art and Craft of Memoir*, ed. William Zinsser. Boston: Houghton Mifflin, 1987, pp. 103–124.
7. Morrison, Toni. "The Site of Memory."
8. Morrison, Toni. "The Site of Memory."
9. Morrison, Toni. "The Site of Memory."
10. Shields-Reyes. Manuscripts and letter excerpts are quoted from the Shields-Reyes family papers.
11. Shields-Reyes. Manuscripts and letter excerpts.
12. Shields-Reyes. Manuscripts and letter excerpts.
13. Shields-Reyes. Manuscripts and letter excerpts.
14. Shields-Reyes. Manuscripts and letter excerpts.
15. Shields-Reyes. Manuscripts and letter excerpts.
16. Shields-Reyes. Manuscripts and letter excerpts.
17. Shields-Reyes. Manuscripts and letter excerpts.
18. Shields-Reyes. Manuscripts and letter excerpts.
19. Shields-Reyes. Manuscripts and letter excerpts.
20. Parker, Bettye J. "Complexity: Toni Morrison's Women—An Interview Essay." *Sturdy Black Bridges: Visions of Women in Literature*, eds. Roseann Bell, Bettye J. Parker, and Beverly Guy-Sheftall. New York: Anchor Books, 1979.
21. Brand, Dionne. "Photograph." *Her True-True Name: Anthology of Women's Writing from the Caribbean* London: Heinneman, 1989, pp. 179–182.

"You Don't Live Just for Yourselves"
Stories from a Chinese Woman in Atlanta

2

Jianli Zhao

In Chinatown Square Shopping Center in Chamblee, northeast Atlanta, a Chinese woman whom we call Zhuang-Tse used to own and run, with the help of her two sons, one of the seven fast-food services in the food court—"Little Mandarin."[1] When I met them for an oral history interview on May 31, 1992, Zhuang-Tse and her sons were packing up the last few utensils left in what was once Little Mandarin. Their food service was closing, and this was their last day. "Why did you decide to close?" I asked, curious, as their cooking had been the most popular in the food court. Looking at her two sons, who were busy cleaning the kitchen, Zhuang-Tse answered quietly: "I started this restaurant for them, and now it is closed because of them, too."

In the interview that followed, Zhuang-Tse told me the story of her life, and stories of three other Chinese immigrant women who have not only led similar lives, but have also influenced and inspired her in her life in the United States. Since no formal history has been written about Asian American women in general and Chinese American women in particular, stories of Zhuang-Tse and her sister Chinese in America become potentially important. On the one hand, stories of these women deserve to be recorded for their own sake. These women, though seemingly ordinary, have lived extraordinary lives. They don't live just for themselves. On the other hand, gathering oral histories among these Chinese women helps the immigrants deal with the frustrations and challenges they confront in the U.S. In the process of telling their own stories, immigrant women develop and refine their own sense of history, identity, and values. Finally, while many people still consider Atlanta as a city of black and white, a knowledge of lives of Chinese immigrant women in Atlanta can help illuminate discrete aspects of the increasingly multicultural, Southern American mosaic.

Chinese women have lived in the United States since the mid-nineteenth century,[2] but their voice is seldom heard. Written American history has traditionally either denied the existence or distorted the experience of women of color. Chinese women, as a result, have remained an invisible and misunderstood entity.[3] In contemporary times, women of Asian descent have been effectively silenced by the popular media. When seen at all, "they are generally depicted as the exotic prostitute or geisha, the quiet, submissive servant or peasant, the treacherous dragon lady or villain, the comic buffoon, or the industrious model minority."[4] Although Asian American women are found in cities throughout the country today, many people still perceive them through eyes clouded by the false images portrayed in the media. The message from the screen has been that all Asian American women are passive, submissive, and either exotically sexy or totally asexual.[5] They have not been portrayed as ordinary human beings. These perceptions are unrealistic and based on fixed concepts within the perceiver's mind.

The life story of Zhuang-Tse and stories she has told of other Chinese women contradict the commonly held view that Chinese women are passive and submissive. In the real world, Chinese women, especially those who have made their own decisions to come to the United States, can make decisions based on their own perceptions and priorities. Although their lives are very much influenced by their upbringing as Chinese and as women, they are ordinary people who have voices and names of their own. In fact, many of the values Chinese American women held in their life, those of motherhood, of strong family ties, and of sacrifice, are shared values of women of all races, colors, and cultures.

Born on December 12, 1935, in Beijing, China, Zhuang-Tse first visited the United States in 1982. She was one of the many Chinese who benefited from the revised U.S. immigration laws of 1965, which replaced a discriminatory, racially based quota system with a new system that promoted family unification and recruitment of skilled workers and professionals. Zhuang-Tse's elder sister, Zejun, a seventy-year-old U.S. citizen, with whom she had lost contact for almost forty years, wrote in 1980 and invited her to move to America. Zhuang-Tse came in 1982. But she went back after about a year. "At that time, in 1982, I was not used to life here," she recalled ten years later. "Going back was better. I liked what I was doing in China and my job. So I went back after a year and one month."[6] Another reason, Zhuang-Tse recalled, was that her younger son, Xiao-Qi, wanted to come to the United States for school. At that time, Xiao-Qi, twenty years old, had just been assigned to work in the factory she used to work in China. Zhuang-Tse had promised the factory that if Xiao-Qi would leave the country, she would go back. She was convinced that young people would have a better chance in the United States:

> From what I saw, I felt the United States was a good place for young people. I mean, the younger the better. It would be easier. . . . You wouldn't carry any unnecessary cultural baggage with you. It was possible to make developments in your career. He [Xiao-Qi] was young, only twenty. Look at me. I was forty-five What kind of development could I still have?

And more importantly, she liked her job at home as a geophysicist. "I had worked there for twenty-some years, and after I came here, I was not able to do what I wanted to do."

Zhuang-Tse's second visit to the U.S. was brief. It was in the fall of 1986, and, as a senior engineer, she was representing her factory in China on a joint project with Texas Instruments (TI) in Houston, Texas:

> They sent me because I had been in the U.S. before. But most people in our factory thought that I would have stayed in TI company. In fact, I would say that eighty percent of them thought so. The work I was doing at TI was exactly what I was trained for.

But she did not stay. On the one hand, she came on business, and did not feel comfortable staying just like that. "I would feel like I was betraying my country if I took the advantage." More importantly, she said, she did not speak English well, and she was still not used to life in America. The truth was, her term in Texas Instruments would expire in six months and she would have become illegal if she stayed. She knew that, with limited language skills and no legal status, she would have trouble finding another job.

The problems Zhuang-Tse found in her initial experience in the United States correspond to similar problems many immigrants encounter. First she had difficulty adjusting to life in a strange country, from food and clothing to language and social life. During her first visit, Zhuang-Tse spent some time with one of her nieces in California, who was married to a Caucasian-American, thinking she would learn to speak English and the American way of living. Since she lacked the basic communication skills in English and everyone in the niece's family preferred English to Chinese, she was left in an isolated world of her own.

A second problem that confronts all immigrants, especially adults, is the ability to cope with change—not just change of the environment, but a whole worldview. For most of her adult life, Zhuang-Tse had worked for the same factory in China, in the same city, with the same people. The factory was her world. She worked hard, and her promotions served as recognition of her hard work. Like other people in the factory, she ate at the factory cafeteria and lived in an apartment assigned to her by the factory. Most of her friends worked in the same factory, too. She felt comfortable as a respected engineer in China. That was her identity. But when she came to the United States, her identity as a respected scientist was lost, and she was simply another foreigner with no skills to survive the competition in a strange country. She was forced to look at the world from a point of view that was unfamiliar to her. In order to cope in the new country, immigrants are forced to accept change, and change involves loss—the loss of traditional beliefs, attitudes, roles, and lifestyles which the immigrant is used to. Change involves the uprooting of individuals from the cultural values on which their identity is based.

While many immigrants find relief in work, others are tortured by the inability to do what they have been trained to do. College-educated and a geophysicist since 1958, Zhuang-Tse was working as a "director engineer" in one of China's largest petroleum instrument and equipment factories, Xi'an Petroleum Exploration Instrument Complex, located in the northern city of Xi'an. "I started working there after graduation [from college], from 1958 to 1987. Twenty-nine years. Almost thirty years!" She really enjoyed her work:

> Other people may think it was hard work for a woman to go all over the country. I thought it was not bad at all. . . . It was my first choice of major when I went to college. I wanted to study geology and prospecting. I wanted to be able to go here and there. That way I would be able to see all of China.

The quest for a better livelihood may have served as a reason to immigrate for most people, but arrival in this country does not offer any guarantee of an improved life. Many highly trained professionals like Zhuang-Tse are forced to turn to low-income and semiskilled jobs in ethnic markets in order to survive. They find their language barrier overwhelming in looking for a job and, more often than not, their foreign credentials are unacceptable. So when Zhuang-Tse said she was "not used to life" in the United States, she meant more than just the food, or the climate, or the strange signs in the streets. It involved a total mentality of giving up what she was used to as an engineer in China, accepting the fact that in the U.S. her credentials and experience as an engineer would not count, and that she did not have much choice except working in a restaurant kitchen if she wanted to survive.

Zhuang-Tse, however, finally decided to immigrate to the United States in late 1987. Her sister in New York invited her time and again, and arranged for all the paperwork necessary for Zhuang-Tse to legally immigrate and stay with her sister. In the meantime, her son, Xiao-Qi, who had been going to school in Queen's College, would be graduating in 1988. He wrote, Zhuang-Tse remembered, and said that "it would be nice if you could come." He felt lonely and uneasy sometimes living in his aunt's house.

> So I came. I thought this over and over and finally I told myself, maybe it's okay to give up my job and my career. Because by that time, by the time when I was planning to come to this country for the third time, I was already fifty-two years

old. . . . It was actually about time for me to retire in China. Fifty-five soon. You have to retire by fifty-five, even if you want to continue working.[8] So I said, okay, this is it. Therefore I finally moved to the United States.

Zhuang-Tse's decision to immigrate to the United States was not an easy one, as she herself admitted. It was a decision that would cost her more than she was prepared for. She had been quite successful as an engineer in China, and had considered herself "middle class." She started as a trainee, and moved up to become an assistant technician, then technician, engineer, and finally, "director engineer" in 1985. Her salary increased with each promotion. She made Yuan 65.00 a month[9] when she first graduated from college in 1958, but by the time she left China in 1987, she was making Yuan 200.00 a month, definitely "middle class" according to Chinese standards then. "Life was very comfortable," she recalled. "I only needed to pay about Yuan 1.00 a month for rent, less than a U.S. quarter. It was a one-bedroom apartment with a living room, a kitchen, and a bathroom." But after thirty years, Zhuang-Tse decided to give up all these: her job, her career, a well-established home, a comfortable and secure living style, and finally, a seemingly successful marriage. This time, she wanted to bring her other son, Xiao-Hui, to America. From a mother's point of view, she was convinced that in the U.S., Xiao-Hui, like his younger brother, would have a brighter future. And the only possible way for her to do so was to immigrate to America herself.

Zhuang-Tse's decision to immigrate to the U.S. also meant the end of her marriage, which had lasted over twenty years. Divorce, however, was not something that a Chinese woman is willing to talk about. Rather big-framed for a Chinese woman, Zhuang-Tse speaks her mind freely. During our initial interview in May 1992, Zhuang-Tse talked for hours about her life both in China and in the United States. But the issue of divorce was skillfully avoided. Traditional Chinese culture emphasized the subordination of women, and divorce was not permitted. Women without children, in fact, were encouraged to commit suicide at their husbands' deaths. Although women enjoy much more freedom in contemporary China, divorce is still considered shameful and embarrassing. After living in the U.S. for five years, Zhuang-Tse still had difficulty facing the fact and talking about her divorce in front of other people. Although the husband appeared in the conversation from time to time, he was always referred to as "his [Xiao-Qi's] father," or "their [her sons'] father." It was apparent that the husband was still in China, but there was no discussion as to why, whether he would join them later, whether they were temporarily separated, or whether they had filed for divorce. The story did not become clear until much later, about one year after the initial interview, when Zhuang-Tse and I had become friends, not interviewee and interviewer, and when the conversation had become purely woman-to-woman.

Zhuang-Tse admitted that there had been problems in their marriage, and she and her husband had always had their differences. She was a technician and he was a college administrator. She was more interested in her professional work and in doing her job well, while he was more concerned about "political correctness." She wished that he would be more considerate toward her and the children, and would help with the housework. He, on the other hand, believed that a man, the decision-maker in the family, should not worry about household chores, and that the woman was solely responsible for taking care of the household. There were many things they did not agree on, including their views about the United States. But the marriage lasted, like similar marriages in China. A divorce would have been an embarrassment to them and also to their children. Therefore, "I believe we would have remain married if I had stayed in China," Zhuang-Tse commented.[10] "It had been twenty some years," she added, suggesting that in China, people do not divorce after twenty years. But she had been in to the outside world, had seen the United States, and was convinced that their children would have a better chance in the U.S. He agreed to the divorce. He did not want to be the one who stayed in the way to their children's future. As parents, they have made the decision to do whatever is best for their children, because, as Zhuang-Tse explained, "you don't live just for yourselves."

"You don't live just for yourselves" summarizes Zhuang-Tse's life as an immigrant in the United States. It explains her life here, why she came, how she has survived, what has kept her here, and how she managed to adjust to life in a strange country as a woman, a mother, and a Chinese.

Much academic research on Asian Americans tends to underscore their success, a success which is attributed almost always to a cultural emphasis on education, hard work, and thrift. Asian American women, like Asian American men, have been touted as "model minorities," praised for their outstanding achievements. Very few researchers however, have paid attention to the kind of sacrifices those immigrants have to make. One of the things often overlooked is immigrants' personal loss in the process of becoming the "model minority." In her discussion of the gap between "striving and achieving" of the Asian American women, Deborah Woo looked at the significant "downward mobility" among foreign-born Asian American women.[11] While foreign-educated health professionals, for example, are given preferential status for entry into the United States, thanks to the revised U.S. immigration laws of 1965, restrictive licensing requirements deny them the opportunity to practice or utilize their special skills. Consequently, for many, the only alternatives are menial labor or unemployment. An inability to find jobs in their field of expertise has forced many highly educated immigrants to become owner/managers of Asian businesses such as restaurants and grocery stores catering mostly to Asian customers. The same fate confronted Zhuang-Tse, a thirty-year geophysics engineer. Without fluency in English, she spent her first year as an immigrant with her sister in New York's Chinatown, doing unskilled work just to make a living. She could have tried to contact Texas Instruments, where she had worked for six months just the year before. "I did not have the courage to contact them," she admitted. "My English was not good. I was a woman, and I was fifty-two years old." So Zhuang-Tse chose a job that many Chinese professional women as well as men often find themselves in: the restaurant.

On August 8, 1988, Chinatown Shopping Center officially opened for business in Atlanta. At that time, Zhuang-Tse, the former engineer, was working in the kitchen of her sister's restaurant in New York. She had already worked several jobs: she had worked in her sister's restaurant and picked up many of the skills for Mandarin cooking; she had earlier worked as a manager for a social club and lodge for Chinese that her sister and other local Chinese Americans had started; in the meantime, she had been knitting sweaters for a sweater dealer in her spare time, along with many Chinese immigrant women, and made some extra money. By that time, her son, Xiao-Qi, who had been working as a waiter at his aunt's restaurant while going to school, had graduated from college with a degree in computer science and was looking for a job. An invitation to the sister's restaurant came from the newly opened Chinatown in Atlanta for them to start a Mandarin food service in the food court. Zhuang-Tse's sister encouraged her to try out the skills she had picked up in the U.S.: start her own restaurant. "It was a good time for us to become independent and start our own business," Zhuang-Tse explained. "Atlanta was less expensive compared to New York. With what we had saved then, it was impossible to start a business in New York. Everything was expensive there. . . . Plus the competition." So Zhuang-Tse and her twenty-six-year-old son, Xiao-Qi, moved to Atlanta in November 1988, and their food service, Little Mandarin, officially started business on February 6, 1989.

They started with a three-year lease. Xiao-Qi wanted to work in the restaurant for about three years to make some money while looking for a job in computer science. Whether to continue after the three-year lease, Zhuang-Tse recalled, "all depended on the decision of Xiao-Hui, my elder son." At that time, Zhuang-Tse had obtained permanent residency status, commonly known as the "green card," through the help of her sister, and was putting together paperwork for her elder son to immigrate to the United States. Three years was the time period required for all the paperwork to go through.

Xiao-Hui, Zhuang-Tse's elder son, finally arrived in Atlanta on February 8, 1992. Although he did not speak any English, he had a job waiting for him at his mother's fast-food restaurant. Unfortunately, the job his mother created for him was not what he wanted. Xiao-Hui worked for a few months at the restaurant after he arrived and decided he did not want to work there. He was a vegetarian, and working in the kitchen of a Chinese restaurant dealing with meat every day simply made him sick. Besides, Xiao-Hui, the former athlete, complained that the restaurant was like a prison to him because he had to spend twelve hours a day continuously in the kitchen, seven days a week. So Zhuang-Tse had to close down the business after three years and four months. She did not have a choice, as she explained:

> I cannot afford hiring other people to do it. The business we had, about $3,000 a month [profit], I could not afford hiring other people to work here. Hiring a cook costs me about $2,500. I probably have to hire another person doing the dishes. What is left for me?

The mother was disappointed. She was more puzzled and confused. She tried to understand her sons:

> For Xiao-Qi, he finished five years of college in the U.S., and got a degree in computer science. He felt vexed at working in the kitchen all day. I don't blame him. He is young and should go out and do something. I had all my hope on my elder son, hoping that he would be able to relieve his brother and pick up working in the restaurant. That would be ideal. The business was not losing money. If we could go on, it meant we were creating ourselves a job opportunity. But Xiao-Hui would not work in the restaurant.

From her own experience, Zhuang-Tse knew that with no English skills at all, Xiao-Hui could not possibly find a job elsewhere. What she did not think of, though, was that Xiao-Hui, thirty-two years old and college-educated, did not want to settle as a restaurant cook for the rest of his life. Like many young immigrants, he came to the U.S. to seek his version of the American dream of freedom and to improve his life. Working as a restaurant cook did not seem to be any better than his job as a college track and field instructor in China.

Motherhood, the quality and spirit of being a mother, has been a popular topic in writings about women, ethnic or majority. In recent American literature, much has been written about the mother-daughter relationship. Recent women writers of Asian ancestry have also focused on the relationship between immigrant mothers and their American-born or American-raised daughters.[12] Very little literature is available about immigrant mothers and their expectations toward their sons. For Chinese culture, the relationship between mothers and sons is especially important. Traditional Chinese culture assigned women to an inferior and even expendable status. They were placed under control of the male sex from the cradle to the grave. For thousands of years, Confucian thought had taught women to be obedient to the father before marriage, obedient to the husband when married, and obedient to the eldest son when the husband was absent. Although women in contemporary China are no longer subordinate, male children are still the most important part of a mother's life. It is not difficult, therefore, to understand that the wishes of her sons have a deciding effect on Zhuang-Tse, the Chinese mother. She went back to China in 1982 so that Xiao-Qi, her younger son, would have a chance to attend college in the U.S. She decided to immigrate to the U.S. in 1987 when her other son, Xiao-Hui, wanted to come to America. She started a fast-food restaurant with her own savings so that her sons would have a job, and when both of them decided they did not want to work in the restaurant, she closed it down. She is not a weak and dependent woman, but she is a mother and a Chinese.

To say that her sons' wishes have a deciding effect on her does not mean that Zhuang-Tse has no control over her life. Rather, her decisions about what she would sacrifice for the benefit of her sons reflect the importance of "*mudao*,"— the way of the mother in Chinese—in the life of women in China. "All women," wrote one scholar, "gain identity, personhood, voice, by association—somebody's daughter, mother, sister, wife."[13] Chinese tradition placed primary emphasis on the role of woman as wife and mother, dictating that her status, fulfillment, and economic livelihood depended on the men in her life. While it is inaccurate to say that in contemporary China a woman's life is dependent on men, fulfilling her responsibilities as defined by *mudao* helps Zhuang-Tse redefine her identity as a mother, a Chinese, and a woman. Just as fulfillment was achieved by a successful career in China, motherhood provides Zhuang-Tse fulfillment as an immigrant in America. This fulfillment makes up for the downward mobility and dissatisfaction in the job market. It balances her life and gives her purpose in life: "Everyone lives for some kind of purpose," Zhuang-Tse said,

> when I live here, I cannot do that much about my career. I cannot make use of my technical know-how. What can I do? I place all my hope on my children. I want to bring them here, and they will be able to do something in this country, right? They will have a better future. Their children, I believe, will be able to do even better . . . .

It is this belief in the future of her children that gives Zhuang-Tse hope and meaning for life. And striving for this belief gives Zhuang-Tse her identity.

As a mother who is determined to do anything for the benefit of her children, Zhuang-Tse is not without complaints. She sighed over how her sons are not as grateful as they should be toward all the sacrifices she had to make to bring them here, and how they still expect her to do their laundry and to cook for them every day. She missed her life in China, her work, her relatives, colleagues, and friends. Like all immigrant women, Zhuang-Tse has to confront loss. What is lost is the security that comes with the familiar; in its place is a whole set of new and unfamiliar demands and expectations. This unfamiliarity, coupled with rejection in the new community, creates enormous feelings of social incompetence, confusion, isolation, and cultural alienation. Zhuang-Tse has managed to cope with all these losses. She is an optimist, and comforts herself by looking at the bright side of her immigration experience. As a mother and an immigrant woman, Zhuang-Tse actually has many things to be proud of. She has managed to bring both of her children to the United States as they wished; she has owned a restaurant and made more money in three years than she made in thirty years in China; she can afford a brand-new car and was able to pay cash for it. Her immigration experience was not all sorrows, either. She enjoys her life in the United States, and especially the freedom it offers. She does not have to worry about "political correctness" in whatever she has to say about the country or the government; she can still work if she chooses to; and she lives in a big house that she could only dream about in China. She has her complaints, but she is generally happy.

Zhuang-Tse is happy because her immigration experience has redefined her views about herself. While considering herself middle-class in China, Zhuang-Tse's expectations about her life in the United States are just to be able to support herself so that she will not be a burden to her children or the welfare system. After Zhuang-Tse closed her restaurant, her sister called and asked if she would like to go to New York and help with her business there.

> For me, I told her, I would really like to do some office work, or to work in a factory. I told her I wanted to try a factory, something like a electronics plant. Because I did have twenty-nine years of experience working in such a factory. Something such as electronics assembly, testing or adjustment work. I feel like expert in things like those. . . . I told her I am fifty-six years old now, and I want to work for another nine years before I retire. During these nine years I would like to work at a job with good benefits, including retirement benefits and some time for vacation. I want to earn myself a retirement pension when I can still work. I believe I would deserve it if I work for it. . . . I even told her that I don't really need that much money. I believe I could easily make a living for two hundred dollars a month. Honestly. Two hundred dollars a month, that is, [I can live on a job that pays] five dollars an hour, or maybe five and a half. Really. I believe I can find a job like that.

As it turned out, finding a job in this country as a woman at her age was harder than she had expected. Most of the jobs that were available to her were low-paying, with long hours and minimum benefits. Time and again, she was told she was over-qualified for the jobs. The few places that actually hired her would lay her off at the first opportunity. She had to switch from job to job and was left on welfare for weeks.

In telling the story of her life, Zhuang-Tse insisted that I should hear the stories of three other Chinese women who had inspired her in her decision to immigrate to the US. "If you want to write about me, you have to write about them first," Zhuang-Tse told me at the beginning of the oral history interview in May 1992. "They are an important part of my life and whatever I have done for my sons has a great deal to do with these women. They have inspired me." As can be seen in the excerpts of the interview, stories of these women are intertwined with the life story of Zhuang-Tse herself. They are inseparable. Although Zhuang-Tse is proud of what she has done for her sons, she maintains that, compared with these other women, she is not as admirable. They are much more courageous and hardworking then she is herself. She insists that stories of these women deserve to be heard, and was afraid if she did not tell their story, no one ever would.

Including stories of three other Chinese women in the life story of Zhuang-Tse is also a decision of my own. Considering the invisibility of Chinese women in academic disscussion in America, telling the stories of some of these women, even though through the voice of a third person, serves at least to make their stories known. More importantly, stories of these women, as Zhuang-Tse repeatedly emphasized, not only make up some missing parts of the life story of Zhuang-Tse. They are part of her story. Leaving them out would be telling an incomplete story of her. The immigration experience of Chinese women has been a shared experience, and these stories combined help to present a clearer picture of this experience.

The following are excerpts from the original interview with Zhuang-Tse. With a woman's keen observance and a storyteller's accurate memory, Zhuang-Tse's narrative eloquently told the stories; any editing would seem superfluous.[14] Combining her stories of her own life with those of three other Chinese women in America, Zhuang-Tse has narrated a race, class, and gender story that would arouse resonance among many Chinese American women.

Let me tell you about some of my friends, friends I have known since 1982, when I first came to the United States. I was in New York then. There were four of us. We jokingly called ourselves the "Gang of Four,"[15] except that all four of us were women. Let me tell you about the various experiences of the four of us. They were such interesting stories. I guess the most interesting of all is Lao Yang, whom we used to call Sister Yang, since she was the oldest of us all.

She came to the United States to visit some relatives at the age sixty-five. She is seventy-five years old now.[16] She has been here for eleven years now. She came in 1981, one year before I first came. She was sixty-five then. She went to work as a housekeeper for one family in New York, and applied for permanent residency as housekeeper, which is the "Sixth Preference.[17] She got her permanent residency status six years ago, which means that it took her five years to get her residency status, six years ago. She has taken her citizenship test this year. And she has passed! You see, you can only apply for citizenship test five years after you get your green card. Taking her citizenship test at the age of seventy-five! Why does she try so hard to become citizen? She wanted to bring her son to the

U.S. I believe, let me tell you, I was deeply influenced by her. I have to admit that I was. Because, you know, because you honestly have to make sacrifices if you want to bring your son here. Not that I'm selfish. I, for example, spent $2,000 just for applying for the two of them [her two sons]. The first person was $1,200. The second $800. Total of $2,000 [legal fees]. . . .

It is not the money. It is the time and energy you need to put in. You don't know how complicated it was. You don't understand those forms. Being not good in English, and could not read any of those forms. Americans like paper-work. Oh, heavens, those forms, stacks of them. You don't know. . . . Another thing is that it was so much trouble. Right, as I told you about this Sister Yang. I draw great inspiration from her. At her age. She had already retired in China. She used to work as a technician in a textile mill in China, Nantong, Jiangsu Province, not so big a mill in a small city. Her husband had died, and she had only one son. You know what, her husband died a year before she got her green card. What a pity. She was planning to go back and see him after she got the card, but he died just before then. She went back anyway. However, with a green card, she could not bring her son over because he was married. She was already sixty-five and her son could not be very young, right? She was twenty years older than I was. I remember it clearly. I was forty-five when she was sixty-five.

My deepest impression about her was her learning English with all her might. The sole purpose was to take the citizenship test. Five years. She started right after she got her green card, and all she wanted to do was to take her citizenship test five years later and, sure enough, she passed.

Q: It was not because she wanted to stay here herself?

A: Not really. She was already seventy-five years old. What was she staying here for? What did she want? To bring her son here! She believed that her son was still young, in his forties. [Now that she has become citizen,] the whole family of her son could come. That's her. She lives for a purpose. Everyone lives for some kind of purpose. You either live to be famous or to be rich, right? It is hard to imagine anyone living without the desire for name or for money.

It is very hard, though, for a Chinese to achieve fame in the U.S. For me, personally, I don't really want to be famous. I don't really want to be extreme-ly wealthy or famous. I do want make money, through. In this country, as long as you don't mind working, as long as you aren't picky, you can make money. This is one of the things that I like about America. It is this fairness. Really fair. Fairness means that if you work hard, you'll make more, and if you do less, you'll gain less. This is what I like best. I felt that this is something that I could not achieve while I was in China. I worked hard there, too. . . .

That Sister Yang I was talking about. She came here at age sixty-five. She worked as a housekeeper for a family of five. She cooked for them, did the laun-dry, and cleaned the house. Her only hope was to get the green card. Her story made me think: People should not think about themselves only. Selfishly speak-ing, we should at least think for our children; unselfishly, we should think for other people in the world. But my ability is limited, and I do not think I can reach that ideal. Maybe I should start with my own children, right? I have only two sons and now I have brought them here. This is the story of Sister Yang.

The second story I am going to tell you is that of Chen Ai-Di, from Shanghai Jiao-Tong University. She came to the United States a year ahead of me, and was a year older than I was. She was born in 1934, and graduated from college in 1957. We belonged to the same generation, and were of very similar educational backgrounds. She was a lecturer at Shanghai Jiao-Tong University. She came also to visit relatives in the U.S. You know about things in China. Her husband was *Youpai*[18] a rightist, and for years he lived under a lot of pressures, mental pressure, inhibited from expressing his ideas. They were living a very unhappy life. She therefore decided to stay in the U.S. so that eventually her husband could join her in this country. The first thing to do was obtaining legal status. She started working as a tutor for a twelve-year-old girl and was able to apply for permanent residency in the category of the sixth preference. That was the only way for her and it was a relatively fast way. There are a total of six categories according to U.S. immigration law.[19] The first preference does not apply to us. That is for spouses of citizens and their unmarried children. We are not citizens. The second preference is for spouses of permanent residents and their unmarried children. That is like when I applied for the two of them [her two sons]. The third preference is for people with special contributions, technicians. I could have taken advantage of this before, but the factory I used to work in would not let me go. I was advanced technician, and they didn't want advanced technicians to leave the country. That was called "the outflow of technology. . . ." What is the fourth preference? Married children of citizens, those with families, I think. The fifth is for brothers and sisters of U.S. citizens, as in the case of me. My sister applied for me. And the sixth preference is for ordinary skilled workers that are in short supply in the United States. What are some of the skilled workers in short supply? Tutors, housekeepers, and people like that. Chen was able to work as a tutor because she was a teacher in a big university in China.

I believe she taught either chemistry or physics. Maybe physics. Her husband used to work in the Institute of Mathematics. Can you imagine how hardworking she was? You know I have learned different things from each of these people. She worked as an in-house tutor for this little girl and that family promised to help her with her status adjustment. Beside tutoring, she had to take care of the grandmother of the little girl, who was I think maybe in her seventies. That meant that she actually worked both as a housekeeper and a tutor. . . . The family did not pay her very much money because they agreed to help her applying for the green card. That was the deal. For example, if you work as a housekeeper, they usually pay you $800 or maybe $600 a month. They would pay her $400 or $300 because they helped her with the green card. That was intentional. That was their way of controlling you.

So she did not have money to rent an apartment. She ended up living in the basement of a house that had been converted to apartments. She did not have to pay rent, but she was responsible, twice a week, for taking all the garbage out of the building from each apartment. I tell you that she was about my age, forty-five. Came when she was forty-four, a year ahead of me. I should say that it was because of her that I am able to stay in this country, that I have the courage to stay. This kind of influence came almost unnoticed. I believe she exerted an imperceptible influence on my mind. It was from looking at her that I realize that I was not as good as her. I was not as hardworking. That I had been very fortunate. To save rent, she would live in people's basement, had to take care of all the garbage, week after week, bag after bag, from the third to the second to the first floor, and finally outside the gate. . . . Besides, she knitted sweaters at night for my sister's company because she was not paid much for working as a tutor. And that was how I got to know her. I actually met her on my second day in the United States. My sister told me that she was from mainland China and that we may be friends. We realized that we did have a lot in common. . . .

Well, because she had a college degree, she got her green card fairly soon, and now both her husband and her son have joined her in New York, and although all of them have to work hard, they are living a very happy life. . . . For at least five years, though, she seemed to have lived in endless darkness, complete darkness. But her aim was to find a way out for her husband, a *Youpai* in China, so that he could live a happier life. Look at the kind of life she had. For five years. But she clenched her teeth, and endured with dogged will. Why? Because she saw the future! She knew she would have a better future! This is the story of my second friend.

This third friend of mine was also from Shanghai. She used to work, though, in Xian Medical Institute, where I used to live in China. Her name is Wang Ya-Zhen. She was a nurse, about two years younger than I was, born in 1938. No, 37. She was never married. Oh, she was such a nice person. Quiet, well-educated, and very, very independent. Her father, who lives in New York, arranged for her to come. She lived, though, with her sister. Actually, her sister came here first, and arranged for her father to come and then her father arranged for her to come. You know she was never married, so it was easy.[20] She started knitting sweaters for my sister's business soon after she came. She did not want to live on her sister or her father. A very independent person. Relied on herself. What she made from knitting sweaters was enough for her to get by.

Q: Why did she come here?

A: Well, her father insisted. She was in China by herself. The whole family was abroad. She was young when the family left for Taiwan and somehow she was not brought along. Anyway, she could not find a job after she came to America, so she started knitting sweaters for my sister's company. And then we became friends. She later worked in a factory that made toys. She was not paid much, but they gave her good benefits. She worked five days a week. A more comfortable job. Her father found an apartment for her, for about $300 per month. It was interesting. She did not really demand too much, coming from China [where living conditions are very limited]. The apartment was one bedroom and one living room. She converted the living room into a bedroom and lived there herself and sublet the bedroom to a girl from Korea for $300. That way she did not have to pay rent. That way she could easily live on less than $600 a month, as long as she has money to buy food. And food does not cost that much. It is the rent. . . .

Well, I was just telling you that I learn different things from all three of these people. The four of us in New York, we were the best friends. Every weekend, we would get together, a meeting of the "Gang of Four," and the four of us—all from mainland China. We had a lot in common. We would meet and tell each other of our sorrows and our joys. We would cook and eat together. Wang Ya-Zhen lived by herself, so we would meet at her place. Chen Ai-Di was a Southerner, a Shanghainese, so she was a good cook. Sometimes each one of us bring some food and share. Didn't need very much money, but we were very, very happy together.

In the limited volumes of history written about Chinese immigrants and their experience in the United States, very little can be found about its female population. While a few success stories, such as those of news anchor Connie Chung and writers such as Maxine Hong Kingston and Amy Tan, are beginning to be heard, ordinary women such as Zhuang-Tse and her friends are seldom written about. Much less do people know about the sacrifices these women have to make. In their quest for their share of the American dream, many Chinese women like Zhuang-Tse have displayed indomitable courage and strength. With similar strength and fortitude, many immigrant women like Zhuang-Tse have pulled through, proudly pointing at their achievements, defined in their own terms. As Zhuang-Tse said, achievements and success are not measured in terms of fame and wealth. Success is defined by the achievements of what you wanted to achieve, no matter how insignificant it may seem.

Obviously, Zhuang-Tse's life is deeply influenced by the lives of the three female friends of hers. The stories, and the fact that she is telling their stories, have made Zhuang-Tse think about her life and about what she, as a woman and a Chinese, could accomplish in life. All of these women were professionals in China. Downward mobility accompanied their immigration experience. Their downward mobility may seem voluntary since those were their own decisions. Other choices, however, were not available to them. Stories of their experience had prepared Zhuang-Tse before she made the decision to immigrate to the U.S. Their examples have encouraged her to cope with the losses she encountered in the U.S. In times of difficulty they have inspired her to look into the future, and to look at the things that they, as women and Chinese, have accomplished in life in the United States.

Zhuang-Tse apparently identifies with the women in her stories. Apart from a common background and origin, their bond is found more in a common purpose in life and a shared experience of hardship as immigrant women. As mothers, wives, or simply women, each one of them has been struggling in her own way, trying to give meaning to her life. All of them share a common belief that "you don't live just for yourselves." Circumstances in the new environment forced them to take greater initiative in attempting to secure a better future for their children and family. Their courage to meet all challenges and their struggle to better themselves by bettering their family have redefined the role of Chinese women. These women choose to leave their homes, to give up their careers, and to create a new world for themselves and their families. A sisterhood and female companionship developed in the process, which provided them with emotional sustenance and physical assistance. But as individuals, each one of these women is a Woman Warrior, the legendary brave Chinese woman who joined the army in the disguise of a man to save her aged father from being drafted, an image that has become familiar to many Americans thanks to Maxine Hong Kingston's autobiographical novel *The Woman Warrior*. What Americans are not familiar with is the fact that many Chinese woman in America are Woman Warriors, and each one has a story to tell.[21]

Zhuang-Tse told me those stories on the day when she finally closed her food service. I took the opportunity to take a few photographs, photographs that I believed would be valuable in time. As it turned out, they record more than just what remained from this three-year-long business. These photographs, as I later found out, record the hope, the stories, and the ambivalence that were associated with the starting, the running, and the closing of this business. These photographs tell the stories of Zhuang-Tse Zhuang and her life in Atlanta and in the United States.

NOTES

1. Both the names of the subjects and the name of the restaurant have been changed at the request of the interviewed for privacy's sake.

2. Afong Moy was reportedly the first Chinese woman to visit America in 1834. The first two Chinese female immigrants arrived in 1848. One of them was Marie Seise, who came as a servant to an American family, and the other was Ah Choi, who came as a prostitute. See Judy Yung, *Chinese Women of America* (Seattle: University of Washington Press, 1986); Lucie Cheng Hirato, "Chinese Immigrant Women in Nineteenth Century California," in *Women of America: A History*, Carol Ruth Berkin and Mary Beth Norton, eds., (Boston: Houghton Mifflin, 1979); and Amy Ling, *Between Worlds: Women Writers of Chinese Ancestry* (New York: Pergamon Press, 1990).

3. Only recently has there been attention to collecting literature on and about Asian American women in general. As can be seen from the works cited, most writings on and about Asian American women have appeared since the 1980s. Other recent attempts have been made in collecting writings by Asian American women so that these women can tell stories of their own lives and from their own perspective. Two examples are: Asian Women United of California, ed., *Making Waves: An Anthology of Writings by and about Asian American Women* (Boston: Beacon Press, 1989); and Shirley Lim, Mayumi Tsutakawa, and Margarita Donnelly, eds., *The Forbidden Stitch: An Asian American Women's Anthology* (Corvallis, OR: Calyx Books, 1989).

4. Roberta Uno, ed., *Unbroken Thread: An Anthology of Plays by Asian American Women* (Amherst: University of Massachusetts Press, 1993), p. 3.

5. *Making Waves: An Anthology of Writings by and about Asian American Women*, p. 293.

6. Interview with Zhuang-Tse at her house in Lawrenceville, Georgia, May 31, 1992. The original interview was in Chinese. All translation done by the author. All quotations of Zhuang-Tse in the paper are based on translations from this interview, unless otherwise specified.

7. Zhuang-Tse's official title when she left China, which is equivalent to a managing engineer in the U.S.

8. Women who work in government-owned agencies in China are required to retire at age fifty-five, and men at age sixty.

9. At the time, the exchange rate between Renminbi Yuan and U.S. dollars was 4:1.

10. This part of the discussion is based on a phone conversation between the author and Zhuang-Tse, January 28, 1994.

11. Deborah Woo, "The Gap between Striving and Achieving: The Case of Asian American Women," in *Making Waves: An Anthology of Writings by and about Asian American Women*, p. 189.

12. Two of the most popular novels on the topic are Maxine Hong Kingston, *The Woman Warrior* (New York: Vintage Books, 1975); and Amy Tan, *The Joy Luck Club* (New York: Putnam's, 1989).

13. Mickey Pearlman, ed., *American Women Writing Fiction: Memory, Identity, Family, Space* (Lexington: University Press of Kentucky, 1989), p. 3.

14. Much of the flavor of her storytelling, however, is lost in the translation. Also, because of limited space, some editing had to be done, mostly details of Zhuang-Tse's own experience.

15. The "Gang of Four" were four notorious figures from the Chinese Cultural Revolution in the sixties and seventies who formed a clique and conspired to usurp power. Among the four were three men and one woman, who was the widow of China's late Chairman Mao Tse-tung.

16. This interview was conducted in 1992.

17. The revised immigration law for preference categories for the Eastern Hemisphere are: First Preference, Unmarried sons and daughters of U.S. citizens; Second Preference, Spouse and unmarried sons and daughters of aliens lawfully admitted for permanent residence; Third Preference, Members of the professions and scientists and artists of exceptional ability; Fourth Preference, Married sons and daughters of U.S. citizens; Fifth Preference, Brothers and sisters of U.S. citizens; Sixth Preference, Skilled and unskilled workers in occupations for which labor is in short supply; and Seventh Preference, Refugees. David M. Reimers, *Still the Golden Door: The Third World Comes to America* (New York: Columbia University Press, 1985).

18. A term most popular during the Chinese Cultural Revolution in the 1960s and 1970s. At that time, the term "*Youpai* (rightist)" was applied to anyone who embraced Western thoughts or ideas. Also used as "bourgeois rightist."

19. There are actually a total of seven preferences. See Note 17.

20. Parents with permanent residency status could apply only for their unmarried children for permanent residency.

21. For a discussion of the legendary Woman Warrior please see Maxine Hong Kingston's autobiographical novel *The Woman Warrior*.

More than a Mother
Some Tewa Women Reflect on Gia

3

Nancy Greenman

To address a person as "mother" is to pay the highest ritual respect.... while we change as Indian women, as Indian women we endure.

—Paula Gunn Allen, *The Sacred Hoop*

"The ... Tewa word 'gia' in its most frequent and simple usage is synonymous with "mother." ... It refers to a person who gives, loves, provides, protects, and assures balance and harmony ...."[1] Rina Swentzell and Tito Naranjo indicate that the designation is not limited to female nurturers, but also is applied to some males, as well as to the earth. Nurturing is central to Pueblo cultures, and the concept of gia, associated with that value, encompasses "... broad ideological concepts essential to Pueblo thinking and existence.... The traditional society embraced and reinforced the gia qualities inherent in all its members, male and female."[2]

Gia traditionally was used to refer to various levels of nurturer: (1) biological or family mother; (2) *Gia* as core person for an extended family; (3) *Gia* as community, religious, social and political leaders; (4) supernaturals and religious symbols; and (5) *Gia* as the earth, or ultimate nurturer.[3]

Perceptions of the concept of "woman" have been inextricably linked to the status "mother."[4] In fact, early feminist scholarship suggested that universal subordination of women was based on their universal role of motherhood, which kept them anchored to the domestic realm rather than the public domain. The public domain was seen as the male realm.[5] This framework suggested implications for the seats and distribution of power and authority cross-culturally, dichotomizing the female and male domains, and awarding custody of power and authority to the male domain in every case. However, recent feminist anthropological scholarship has more fully recognized the deleterious impact and disservice to analyses and understanding created by the often-unconscious imposition of Eurocentric and androcentric assumptions and theoretical frameworks on studies and interpretations of non-Western women.[6]

This essay focuses on some American Indian women's perceptions of what "woman" is, in relation to the notion of "mother" as embodied in the status of the Tewa concept, *gia*. A description of the study will be followed by brief discussion of some of the issues that have been introduced, manifested as themes that emerged from oral life history narratives. Illustrative portions of the narrative will make up the body of the essay.

NARRATIVE AND "GIVING VOICE"

Various forms of feminist scholarship have given increased attention to the use of narrative, especially life history and oral history, as a means of giving greater voice to women, thereby deconstructing Eurocentric and androcentric constructions of woman/womanhood.[7] Autobiography and oral life history have been found by some American Indian women to be effective for clarifying the centrality of women in American Indian cultures, as they have helped in self-definition in the context of tribal definition,[8] and personal authenticity through cultural authenticity.[9] Patricia Albers notes that traditional descriptions of American Indian women are suspended in time, framed in the ethnographic present: "Native women are pictured as unchanging—clinging to a traditional way of life that exists outside the vicissitudes of history."[10] Paula Gunn Allen views the identity search as much more immediate:

> Modern American Indian women, like their non-Indian sisters, are deeply engaged in the struggle to redefine themselves. In their struggle they must reconcile traditional definitions of women with industrial and post industrial non-Indian definitions.[11]

"To be named as a woman can be the precondition for some kinds of solidarity," notes Denise Riley, but she warns that, "Political rhetorics which orchestrate an identity of 'women' or 'mothers' may generate refusals from their ostensible targets."[12] Feminists of color have identified some of the assumptions about universalities and commonalities of womanhood and women's experience as ethnocentric, and even racist and neo-imperialist; however, the Eurocentric/androcentric worldview assumptions are so deeply embedded in Western cultural constructions that they continue to be applied.[13] Gwendolyn Etter-Lewis insists that " . . . *all* women must tell their own stories in their own words,"[14] and she identifies oral life history as an avenue through which to accomplish this and to ameliorate some of the barriers:

> Oral narrative offers a unique and provocative means of gathering information central to understanding women's lives and viewpoints. When applied to women of color, it assumes added significance as a powerful instrument for the rediscovery of womanhood so often overlooked and/or neglected in history and literature alike."[15]

In this tradition have emerged life histories of elders[16] and multi-generational stories, both scholarly and fiction.[17]

This essay draws from oral life history research[18] with three generations of women who are members of one family from Santa Concha,[19] a New Mexico Tewa-speaking Pueblo, as well as from eighteen years of interaction and observation with this extended family[20] (see Figure 3.1). The women in this group, who are described as exceptionally strong women by themselves, each other, and outside observers, all appear to be equally successful in both the non-Indian (or Anglo) and Indian[21] spheres of life; they have choices for their arenas of success, and move freely between the two realms. All have completed some degree of higher education, several with Ph.D.s, several with M.A.s, and all except the first of these three generations with a B.A. in hand or in progress. Almost all are involved with pottery-making to some degree, and some are world-famous potters and/or clay sculptors. Consistent with what appears to be an emerging pattern for contemporary Santa Concha women, the women interviewed have all spent a portion of their lives away from Santa Concha Pueblo, and now are involved in Pueblo life in varying degrees. Though in the past this would have signaled marginality from both emic and etic perspectives, current patterns indicate this may mirror a shifting norm.

Of the seventeen women in the three generations of the Migueles family, oral life histories were gathered for a sample of eight: (1) Ruby, or Gia Ahkonpovi represents the first, or elder generation; (2) Evelyn, Puye, Gertie, and Delores represent the second, or middle-aged[22] generation; and (3) Willow, Roberta, and Paula represent the third, or young adult generation.[23]

Each of the participants was given the opportunity to review any editing and final selection of narrative to be retained. After thematic analysis of the narratives, follow-up interviews and informal discussions were conducted to further explore and elicit emic insight. The themes and narratives selected for this particular essay were also shared with those of the participants who were interested, and the final manuscript was reviewed by those same participants. Elsewhere[24] I have addressed some of the issues that arose in developing this study and conducting the research, and in the politics of the research enterprise. Collection of the life histories appeared to be mutually enjoyable and insightful. Agreement was made to let the narratives speak for themselves as much as allowable by the publication process, with identification of some of the prominent metaphors and brief discussion of some of the emergent themes.

FILTERS AND FRAMEWORKS

Most of the prevalent themes are self-evident through the organization of the narratives; however, several distinct yet tightly linked themes will be the focus for elaboration here: identity/authenticity, nurturing, matrilinearity, power, change, and a "domestic" public dichotomy versus an inside-and-outside complementarity.

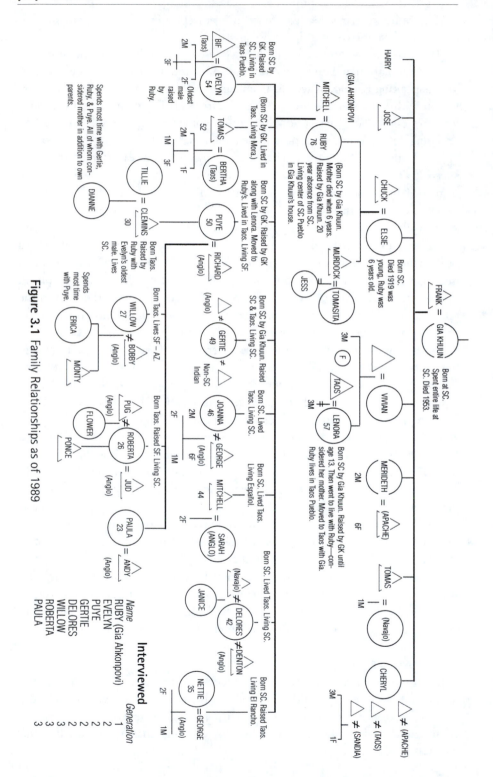

Figure 3.1 Family Relationships as of 1989

The issue of identity, or the cultural construction of self, and Western assumptions about personhood and autonomy and the nature of people in social interaction—or between the individual and society—invariably filter through the Western constructs of dichotomous opposition and imply sharp divisional lines between "domestic" (considered private) and "public" spheres of social life.[25] Furthermore, to be considered as persons, and even more as persons of value, do women have to be seen of import in domains usually considered male by Eurocentric/androcentric perspectives? As Moore indicates, "To assume that Western notions of the acting 'individual' or 'person' are appropriate to other contexts is to ignore the differing cultural mechanisms and expectations through which this process of evaluation proceeds."[26] If we all must tell our own stories, may we assume we have the right to define ourselves, and, in doing so, define the relationship between a personal self and a cultural self? Is, for example, "self" additive—an "ego" with attributes attached like ornaments on a Christmas tree—or is it substantive—a self that is a composite of cultural, familial, community, ethnic, global, and other identities? What type of personal self allows women to have and exercise power in their own right?

These questions raise the issue of emic versus etic definitions of power. Traditional frameworks for assessing these issues assume a hierarchical ordering of status and import regarding spheres of influence that, in addition to oppositional dichotomy, is typical of Western societies' paradigms or worldviews. Henrietta L. Moore suggests:

> The "domestic" versus "public" model has been, and remains a very powerful one in social anthropology because it provides a way of linking the cultural valuations given to the category "woman" to the organization of women's activities in society.[27]

Sue Ellen Jacobs points out that the model simply does not fit in Pueblo society, where traditionally there is an interactive web of status and power with a strong focus on communal success.[28] The moiety system evident in Pueblo society emphasizes complementarity rather than oppositional dichotomy.[29] Pueblo cultures were not unique in this arrangement. Patricia Albers notes that, "In many historic American Indian communities, there was not a pronounced separation between the strategic interests of women and men. Female-male relationships tended toward complimentarity."[30]

Alfonso Ortiz alludes to the same dilemma of etically imposed frameworks in reference to assignation of unilineal social organization rather than dual organization.[31] Early feminist scholarship entertained a strong debate as to the existence of matriarchy or gynocratic societies.[32] There is increasing evidence of, if not matrifocal, at least matrilocal, matrilineal societies, with maternal control of land and of household goods and resources, and strong female deities.[33] Swentzell believes that the Northern Pueblos were traditionally matrilineal, matrilocal and, perhaps, matriarchal, with negotiation in some realms, but that contact with the Eurocentric world gradually shifted that emphasis via ascribing power and status to the males.[34] Rayna Green notes that,

> . . . [F]requently matriarchal, matrifocal and matrilineal societies were neither acceptable nor comprehensible to members of the European patriarchies, who misunderstood Eastern tribes so profoundly that they sabotaged their own treaties regularly in making them with men who did not have the right to make such decisions.[35]

There is a growing body of literature addressing political economy that builds on earlier work focusing on the impact of colonization on the position of women in native societies.[36] Among other examples, Albers notes that in the Southwest, the Hopi (Tewa) women retained a strong position under colonization because they owned the land on which the crops were produced and controlled distribution of goods within and outside the household. Their social organization was matrilineal, and they used their economic autonomy to build institutionalized positions of power beyond their households.[37] Allen suggests; "Even in those tribes where something akin to male domination was present, women are perceived as powerful, socially, physically, and metaphysically."[38] For many, however, the impact of colonialism was to shift to patrifocality and patrilineal organization. Swentzell believes this was concretized with the Bureau of Indian Affairs (BIA) drafting of constitutions for the Pueblos.[39] In the 1930s, John Collier, anthropologist and head of the BIA, crafted the Indian Reorganization Acts which supported tribal men and ". . . virtually disenfranchised Indian women through dissolution of their traditional power systems . . ."[40] Further damage was done for a number of Southwestern such as Navajo and various Pueblos) and other native peoples with a shift of economy to wage labor, which brought a shift in status for both men and women: ". . . the new government initiatives encouraged males to become wage laborers and women and children to become dependents of working men or the state."[41] Thus, for many Pueblo societies, there now exist patrilineal rights and privilege that formerly would have been matrilineal.[42] This is obvious especially when a Pueblo member marries outside the Pueblo. Until very recently non-Pueblo wives of Pueblo members obtained rights, privileges, and benefits (such as free health care through the Indian Health Service) that non-Pueblo husbands of female Pueblo members did not enjoy. There is now a focus on enrollment along similar gender lines. Ortiz maintains, however, that all of the etically assigned designations are inaccurate. He describes the recruitment that takes place for moiety membership as indicative of an emically defined, negotiable, social organization.[43]

One can observe the integrative assignation of status and power in Santa Concha ideology and in traditionally defined roles such as that of *gia*, especially *gia* in the core community, and political and social spheres. As enacted in contemporary life, however, this quality has become somewhat obscured. Jacobs indicates that, at San Juan Pueblo, ". . . the public and private domains were more clearly interwoven than they appear to be today."[44] The Santa Concha women in this study attribute this contemporary, more rigid dichotomization largely to changes resulting from the influences of Western society. Embodying a mixture of traditional Western Victorian and contemporary perceptions of woman, the women in this Santa Concha study envision woman as maternal, gentle, and nurturing, *and* as vigorous and strong. These characteristics are not seen as dichotomous. Paula Gunn Allen indicates that likely to be present in women-centered social systems are:

> . . . nurturing, pacifist, and passive males (as defined by western minds) and self-defining, assertive, decisive women. In many tribes, the nurturing male constitutes the ideal adult model for boys while the decisive self-directing female is the ideal model to which girls aspire.[45]

Teresa LaFramboise and collegues note that ". . . for many Indian women, positions of authority and prominence are natural evolutions of their caretaking role."[46] Middle-aged and elderly women also gain power and authority over kin, claiming the right to extract labor from them and/or to exercise decision-making power over them.[47] One can observe this in *gia*. What has been etically defined as the subordinated "domestic" may be the center of the web from which power and authority weave the "public." Certainly the web involves complimentarity.

In this introduction and discussion I have repeatedly emphasized the need to suspend ethnocentric frameworks for interpreting Native American life history narratives in general, and perceptions of women in context. As the themes emerge from the following narratives, for understanding, they must be heard in the voice in which they are spoken.

PERCEPTIONS OF "WOMAN"

There is no question that these Santa Concha women's most typical descriptions of "woman" revolve around woman as nurturer, and include what have been identified as traditional, stereotypical, Western, female qualities: gentleness, femininity, warmth, concern, consideration, domesticity, nurturing, traditionally "not putting themselves up front," and, as Roberta describes, "a female fluid feeling thing." As noted, however, unlike the Eurocentric/androcentric cultural context, these descriptors hold a very positive valuation in the Pueblo, non-Western, cultural context.

Gertie sums up this view when she says of woman:

> Gentle. When I think of women, I think of femininity. I think of *inside* stuff, like gentleness. I think of warmth, I think of showing concern. I think of consideration

for others. I think of the home. I think of home as being a place where you can offer all of those things.

But strength is also a prime descriptor. Woman is "the backbone of a family," "quiet but with a lot of strength," "being strong without having to wear the feathers," "initiators of change—setting up the conditions for people to change." Women are also often assertive, but rarely, if ever, aggressive or confrontational. Evelyn has a M.A., is working in an administrative capacity for the BIA, and is a prize winning potter. She expresses it this way:

And I think the Indian women need to be more assertive than they have been in the past and to be recognized for their role in their homes and communities. But, even me, having been brought up in a different generation, I find it difficult. I find that my two daughters are able to assert themselves in the outside world much more aggressively than I do. I don't see myself as outgoing or aggressive.

However, her life history revealed a number of incidents in which she has been effectively and cleverly assertive, the results of which exerted power "in the outside world." Some of these incidents could even be viewed as subtle confrontation.

In these narratives there is also frequent reference to woman having a focus on the internal as opposed to a male external focus. Some of these women see the external focus as an obstacle to developing oneself internally. When asked to consider the question, "What is woman?" Willow responds:

A lot for me is in contrast to what male . . . you know . . . it's different than male . . . it's a lot of feeling. It's softer, yielding, more giving. The lines don't need to be as strict as males. *Those* labels, I think, are much harder.

Males tend to lean much more on labels . . . the external world is much more important . . . than I think for women. For women, the external world is different. It's coming from inside outward . . . to give out to the world. And I see in a lot of males that they need the outer world in order to take from within.

Many of these women are working, and, at times, struggling, with a personal balance and integration of the two, a personal complementarity. Gertie, for example, says:

I think you can do them side by side. I've often thought about the anima and animus inside of ourselves . . . and I've been very conscious about developing both of them. I haven't always known how to do it, but I've been very conscious of developing both of them. And I think that the female part of me . . . which would be the nurturing woman, and the male part of me . . . which would be the animus, no? . . . would be like the academic pursuits. And I think it's possible to have them side by side.

There is a tendency, in these women's perceptions, to see the "Pueblo world" as epitomizing the female qualities and the "Anglo world" as epitomizing the male qualities.

Willow, in struggling with the balance, relates:

And I keep wondering how ... for me personally ... I keep wanting to find a balance between that kind of *gia* ... because for me it represents a lot of strength and different qualities that personally I admire.... And a whole world view, also, that allowed it to exist ... that I see as very important. But, at the same time, living in this ... *of* this Anglo world ... very different with internal consciousness of self, with strong individualism ... which has its strengths also, that I would never give up.

And I see lot of strengths for women. And how do you bring the two to meet? I'm struggling myself with that. Where's the meeting? Where's my structure as a woman? For me, taking those two qualities with taking the strengths of both and using it.

Paula, referring to the Migueles women of the second generation addressed in this study, observes:

They are *strong* women ... and that is their gift ... and it is also their problem. They are fighting to be so strong to not just let anybody else be anything but what they want them to be. They're not gonna let the world be as it is.

Willow perceives this as a manifestation of the internal and external conflict:

Being a woman.... There's something in me that identifies with being softish on the outside, but strong on the inside.

See those Migueles women (referring to the second generation in this study), on the other hand are sometimes very strong on the outside and I look at *some* of them as very weak on the inside because, in a lot of them there was that goal of needing to go outside ... again ... get their sense of who they are from the outside world.

WOMAN AS GIA

The concept of *gia* becomes, as Gertie says, the "ultimate feminine." Gia Ahkonpovi (Ruby) herself talks of *gia* in these terms: "*Gia* takes the world in her hands ... and to me ... another thing ... she holds the cradle. At the same time you hold the world you hold the family and the cradle."

Roberta, in speaking of the strength and success of the second-generation women, says " ... it is because they come directly from Gia ... who came from an even more powerful Gia ... which means they have an incredible amount of power given to them as women."

All of the second-generation women in this study see their mother, Ruby, as their prime motivator and the foundation of their educational pursuits and ascribed success. As Evelyn says: "I have a strong allegiance to my mom, not only love allegiance . . . but I feel that she's the backbone. We are who we are because of our mom. That's what it boils down to. We couldn't have done it without her." All speak of the survival skills they learned growing up in her household, the values of hard work, resourcefulness and going beyond themselves, values instilled in them directly and because of their life experiences. As Gertie relates:

> I attribute a lot of who we are to my mother, and she must have picked it up from her Gia, Gia Khuun. But she taught all of us to be resourceful. And she didn't allow us to quit. She allowed . . . she made us think that we had to go and reach further . . . that we couldn't rest until we went beyond.
>
> . . . God . . . I can see so many applications in just that one thing, because . . . with our education, for example, you don't just stop at a college degree. You go *beyond* that to challenge your very, very being. When it comes to artwork, for example, you don't stop at doing just regular pottery. You stop and then look to see what other elements there are that you can look at and say, "Oh, maybe that will work." And it's that kind of . . . you know, I have to deal with experimentation along with resourcefulness.

Ruby consciously shaped her children's lives to ensure them access to and facility in various cultural contexts. She believes that education is an important avenue for preparation to deal with the changes occuring.

> In wondering why education is so strong in me and my children . . . my children all have education . . . even the foster children I raised. I think of the future . . . to make their own life . . . to be out in the world where they can understand what the leaders are talking about. Also, so no one would look down on them.

Gia is described variously by the women as; "bigger than life," "this *force*," "needing to be in control and controlling needing to dominate the situation," "liking or having to get her own way in either overt or subtle ways." Traditionally, "the nurturer," "caretaker," "giver," "the *source*," "the beginning of all the branches," "the tree trunk," "a knot in the wood—that point where it's strong," "a real coming-together spot," "a nucleus and things go around it," "the sun at the center of the universe," "the spider in the center of the web," "whole and intact," "sharp," "enlightened," "incredible," "very wise," "deserving of respect . . .".

As Gertie remarked,

> Gia Khuun was the Source, and with my mother Gia, for example, Ruby . . . my mother Gia . . . I mean there's no question that she's the source, and my father is the one that sits and watches the world go by while she makes it happen.

Gia is, according to Roberta, ". . . a woman very much in touch with everything around her and very loving. She has so much of herself together . . . people can come to her and learn from her . . . can receive something from just her presence."

Paula sees Gia as someone you can trust, "... a person who is there for other people and who knows how to take care of themselves." Gia consistently is described as "someone people gravitate towards."

Gia often is described as being in the "center," and, as each of these women talk about Gia, they begin to illustrate by drawing circles with their hands. Delores's description is especially graphic:

> This Gia person is kind of like a spider who sits real full and then as these webs that go this way and this way and this way and this way ... and this way and this way. And then she can tap and pull in her, one of her strings, you know, that tie up her kids and just ... chuuu ... pull them in through words, gestures, kindness, love, guilt, all of those kinds of things.
>
> When I think about my mother, I think about her in this place ... this physical place that's like the center ... of this wheel ... or the center of this thing. She's there at the center, and everything just goes around and around her and around her and around her in my head when I think of my mother. I put her right over there ... in the center of the world, you know ... in the center of the Pueblo.
>
> I see myself in that situation. I see myself just going one generation over. I've built this little world. I'm in the center of this world ... and I guard it ... very jealously in some ways, so I can see how my mother guards her little empire.

CHANGES AND CHANGING PERCEPTIONS

Just as Delores has built her own web—become a *gia* in her own sphere—so have the other second- and third-generation women. Ruby has a definite perception of herself as a core-person *gia*, and expects her children to respond accordingly to the core unit.[48] Changes in the past twenty or thirty years, however, have made that difficult at times:

1. The family members are dispersed both on the Pueblo and within New Mexico, though all are within a few hours' driving distance of Santa Concha. In the past, the extended families lived together in a cluster, so the exchange of support and responsibilities was a natural manifestation.
2. The influence of Western or Anglo societal values, especially independence, individuality, and the nuclear family, has become increasingly strong among the people of Santa Concha. This is especially true of the second and third generations of Migueles women, none of whom are married to Santa Concha men. Thus, the family structure is changing. As Evelyn describes this situation:

> I think my mother's extended family is more ... closely knit and now the extended families are not so dependent upon one another ... you can begin to see people way out on the peripheral as opposed to clustered together in another time period. But I think that's just the way society is going because ... I can think of very few families in Santa Concha ... or

> even at other Pueblos, who continue to be just . . . be very inbound . . .
> close-clustered. That there are people who are not adhering.

3. All of the women enjoy economic independence, some through their artwork
and pottery, others through upper-level employment outside the Pueblo, and
some through both. This removes the *need* for the extended family network
for *survival* purposes.

Because of the demands and responsibilities of the nuclear families, some of
the women resist the pull of the core *gia* and see some of the actions as manipulative.[49] This often has resulted in referring to the core *gia* role as the "*gia* concept, *gia* phenomenon, *gia* syndrome, and *gia* complex." In a sense, Ruby
Ahkonpovi set the stage for this influence to manifest itself. She has virtually
pushed her children through the door to the outside world. She relates that
when she was growing up, she felt the power of Gia Khuun very strongly. But,
she says:

> Somewhere along the line . . . I'll be honest, when I first got married I felt he
> looked down on me. He looked down on me a lot. So I just decided that when
> Evelyn in the early '40's, when she finished high school . . . I said to myself,
> "my girls or my children are not going to be like me. They are going to get
> their education so they can understand that *World* of the future and also
> understand what people are talking to them about." I didn't have that educa-
> tion that they did.

When Ruby was asked if, with all of the changes these days, it was difficult
being a *gia*, she responded: "Not really. Children always come back. One or
two will rebel, but they always come back." No matter how the women are
manifesting their own *gia* qualities, they always feel the power of Gia Ahkonpovi. Delores intimates:

> Well, probably the fact that I relate to myself as a mother first. That that was the
> first image of myself is very directly related to the *gia* image. The *gia* or mother
> image is just so strong. It's just so incredibly strong and just because some of the
> things that I've said . . . about my mother . . . don't always *sound* wonderful does-
> n't mean that that gave her any less importance, or makes her any less . . . of this
> godlike being that just completely overwhelms and encompasses all of us.

Many of the women attribute the changing attitudes toward *gia* to a change
in perception as well as a change in the times. While the power attributed to
that status is unquestioned, the means to exercise that power have changed.
Consequently, younger generations often question the manner in which *gia's*
power is used to achieve ends that they no longer consider valid.

Willow perceives the changes as both a shift in power and a conflict of cultural perspectives. She explains it as follows:

Looking at it in different contexts, judgments get placed on a certain thing . . . like the *gia* . . . and what happens around the gia. And in that very individualistic world it's viewed very much as negative. But in that Pueblo world, it is the most positive aspect in that community to have existed, because without it that Pueblo would completely fall apart. In the Anglo world . . . with it, the world . . . the Anglo world would fall apart. So there's that struggle.

Oh, without a doubt, in the past I don't think they were much different than Grandma, no. But it was felt differently, by the whole group in general. And it can't be felt the same way very easily anymore. If I try to be like Grandma it will be manipulative without a doubt. And that's not its strength.

And having to look at what is its strength is . . . are those nurturing . . . again we come back to . . . those nurturing, those being in a center spot somehow, yet without necessitating a limelight kind of center spot. Those qualities of seeing what each person has internally naturally . . . seeing each person's strengths. And letting them fall into their own place . . . into the workings of the whole. And doing that by trusting. By letting people . . . not forcing people into a situation that they don't belong.

And having it happen naturally . . . without placing yourself in a place of manipulation and saying, you come to me . . . you come to me . . . you come to me . . . that it happened naturally. And I think that's what happened in that older Pueblo view was it just happened naturally that way. And with this internal consciousness . . . saying, I'm going to be a *gia* . . . or something like that . . . that you step into that other realm that becomes manipulation.

Evelyn also explains the problem as one of discrepant perspectives:

And it's just how people view it because I find myself existed, because without it that Pueblo would completely fall apart. In the Anglo world . . . with it, the world . . . the Anglo world would fall apart. So, there's that struggle.

This culture realizes the strength of only that external . . . only the one who's wearing the feathers, and who's out there showing themselves. And very often disregards that one who's standing behind the kitchen door. What inner strength for me there is I see in those women not needing to be in that role of the feather wearer. It's good to have the choice to wear the feathers, but not out of need, or out of lack of an inner sense of strength.

In these days, women are allowed to take on different roles and to take on a conscious looking inward that wasn't really available to them before Anglo contact. And that's a real positive addition . . . the internal looking. It's gonna change that role of what the woman is and does.

In Grandma's situation, and with all my aunts and my mother, there were already two worlds coming together there . . . very strongly. And so in their point of view, yes, it's going to be very manipulated and orchestrated . . . viewing *gia* as very manipulative. But I think if you put it back a generation . . . it wasn't that because it was completely immersed in that other world. I don't believe it was even viewed that way, that it was felt that way that that was just the way it was, and the whole community operated in that way.

And now . . . yes, to have in this world a *gia* like Grandma . . . doing that too, and I see all of them doing it within their own little circles of families, you know, but when the shoe's on the other foot, or you're looking at it from another perspective, then it may seem like negative manipulation as opposed to what the initiator might consider it. For the good of the family, and yet, even if some members of the family seem to oppose it, it's good for the family.

WHAT OF THE FUTURE?

The role of *gia*, the role of women, and the family structure are all changing via both natural evolution and outside influences. What, then, will happen to the Migueles family when Ruby, the core-person *gia*, is no longer present to provide the pivotal point?

The role of core-person *gia* is both assumed and ascribed. Jacobs states that when a San Juan Pueblo Tewa woman becomes a grandmother, she "decides whether or not her familial and community roles will change at that time or later.[50] This may be compared to the assumption of the *gia* role, though one apparently does not have to be a biological grandmother to assume the role. The *gia* must choose to assume the role, or may choose in what realm or sphere to manifest her *gia* qualities. But the role is also ascribed. Not every biological *gia* has core *gia* qualities. As Delores indicates:

> *Gia* in the core sense is not synonymous with biological mother. I think in our family, it is, because we've inherited this strong sense of it from someone who was very, very strong. I can think of women who do not exhibit that kind of talent . . . and we're talking *Power*. I can think of Indian women who do not exhibit that kind of power.

Gertie expresses the transition to *gia*:

> I think there's one matriarchal figure just like in our family, when my great grandmother was living, she was the source. She was the beginning, it seems to me, of all of the branches. And you can have many mamas, but, then there's . . . this tree trunk, so to speak, that could be called *gia*. And even the name . . . is evidence of that. Because in our family situation, my great grandmother's name is Gia Khuun, which is grandmother corn, and then as she died, and then my mother became like the source, like the tree trunk, and then, for some reason, automatically—we were always calling her Mama—and then one day somebody just started calling her Gia, and now everybody calls her Gia.

The *gia* qualities discussed in this essay must be in place for the *gia* to be accepted, however much she may desire, choose or "feel the need for" the role. And the other members of the core unit must be willing to give their allegiance to the professed *gia*. In the Migueles family, there are several in the second generation who have those qualities in varying degrees. As yet, none of the women sees one core *gia* emerging to take Gia Ahkonpovi's place—and some see this situation as a natural progression, and even as a pattern that was traditionally manifested.

Evelyn intimates:

. . . because I see that once mom dies, I will see the family disintegrate. She's the binding force right now. Just like my grandmother was the binding force for her family . . . and after that they kind of all went off in their own direction. There's no central source that holds them all together. And I feel that our family also has that. We're a close family and we'll probably always be a close family, but not in that same sense as when Mom's there.

I think there are people that would like to think they could assume that role, but it's a difficult role. And there has to be a lot of trust in that one individual and unless that trust is there, it's never gonna happen . . . because that's the reason why it is as it is to begin with. Very definitely . . . but I, as I say, I don't think it's going to work, because each one has their own set of values, set of directions, their own ideas about their personal life, their personal being, family. There may be a semblance of it because we are a close family—that first and second and third generation of people will know one another but not in the same sense.

Gertie speculates:

I see people having characteristics of the *gia* role. I think, though, there's enough breakdown with this generation, that I'm not sure that we would . . . that there would emerge a *gia* like my mother, who would be the connecting point, or the connecting person to the extended family. When I think of the traditional *gia* person, I think of somebody who has the magnitude . . . or the magnetism to be able to . . . get people to gravitate toward her.

Puye, though attributed strong *gia* characteristics by many of the women, consciously chooses not to assume the *gia* role in the old core sense, but rather chooses to limit her realm to nuclear family and *chosen* extended family, including some non-Indian friends. She says she doesn't want the responsibility of a community or extended family core *gia*, as she feels a need for private time and space, which is why she chose to live away from the Pueblo.

Delores is very definite about the family evolving in a different way:

The connecting link will be simply that we are . . . family . . . and that we have grown up together and that we have that connection because sometimes we care about each other and sometimes we hate each other. And that's not so different. We have that, that connects us. But I don't think . . . I really can't see any one person emerging to take this place. I know that I personally could not give my allegiance to any, to anyone that I can think of . . . in my family or out of my family. There isn't anyone that strong. Because I'm just as strong as anybody else. I really can't see one person emerging as someone who could give us what we needed. I think instead that each family would become their own center. And that's OK, I mean, that's just simply the process. We're creating the next step. And I can see that ... I can see incredibly ... my daughter so strong with it already. She's a mini-*gia* already. And she doesn't know it or care right now, but she already is one. I can see it just heavy in her right now ... a caretaker ... a fixer. You know, a doer, a maker. Someone who puts things right. Someone who gives you what you need. Someone who makes sure things are OK.

Thus, *gia* qualities are emerging in the third-generation women. Roberta manifested those same qualities as early as her childhood. She was the initiator, the one to whom her sisters looked for companionship and guidance, and the one to whom both her younger and older sisters, as well as friends, came with their problems and confidences. She also was often a mediator between her mother and her older sister, Willow.

Roberta describes herself as strong, large, one who can help people through their emotional problems because she is "open and candid, and *dares* to be intense."

She sees herself as a "New Age *gia*." a "New Time Gia." Roberta describes Gia Ahkonpovi as different from her own role as she envisions it:

In my life she's the last *gia* around. *Gia* of long time ago ... *gia* of a different time. There's a lot of beauty there, but there's difficulty in the new time zone. My job is New Time *gia*. I can bridge the gap. I can be able to ... bring people back to their hearts. She [Gia Ahkonpovi] was just *gia* ... she just *was*. With me, I have to teach people how to go there again. A *gia*'s something felt and you can't have a *gia* unless people learn how to feel again. My mother's generation was the transition ... the stepping stone to the New Time.

Thus, speculation regarding the future changes for *gia* are broad and varied ... and open to all possibilities. The only thing that appears certain, at least to the Migueles women and to outside observers, is that the role of core-person *gia*, as Gia Ahkonpovi (Ruby) embodies it will be remembered as the *gia* of "Old Time."

As Delores, Evelyn, and others have indicated, however, the attributes and power of *gia* as related to the construct of 'woman' have not disappeared. They have dispersed, and with that dispersion, rather than weakening, they appear to have gained strength. *Gia* as "ultimate woman" is in all women.

NOTES

This chapter is based on a paper presented at the 1989 annual meeting of the American Anthropological Association, Council on Anthropology and Education (Session: *Women's Voices for Schools and Communities: The Dialogue Continues*), Washington, D.C., November 15–19, 1989.

1. Rina Swentzell and Tito Naranjo, "Nurturing: The Gia at Santa Clara Pueblo," *El Palacio* (1987), p. 36.
2. *Ibid.*

3. *Ibid.*
4. See Henrietta L. Moore, *Feminism and Anthropology* (Minneapolis: University of Minnesota Press, 1988) for an exploration of the implications of this relationship.
5. See, Dorothy Hammond and Alta Jablow, *Women in Cultures of the World* (Melno Park, CA: Cummings Publishing Co., 1976); Michelle Zimbalist Rosaldo and Louise Lamphere, ed., *Woman, Culture & Society* (Stanford: Stanford University Press, 1974), esp. chapters by Lamphere, Rosaldo and Sherry B. Ortner, which shape these arguments.
6. See, e.g., Patricia C. Albers, "From Illusion to Illumination: Anthropological Studies of American Indian Women," *Gender and Anthropology: Critical Reviews for Research and Teaching*, ed. Sandra Morgan (Washington, DC: American Anthropological Association, 1989), pp. 132–170; Paula Gunn Allen, *The Sacred Hoop: Recovering the Feminine in American Indian Traditions* (Boston: Beacon Press, 1986); Teresa D. LaFramboise, Anneliese M. Heyle and Emily J. Ozer, "Changing and Diverse Roles of Women in American Indian Cultures," *Sex Roles* 22 (1990), pp. 455–476; Sandra Morgan, "Gender and Anthropology: Introductory Essay," in Morgan, *Gender and Anthropology*, pp. 1–20; Moore, *Feminism and Anthropology*.
7. Sandra Morgan, "Gender and Anthropology: Introductory Essay," in *Gender and Anthropology*, p. 9.
8. Gretchen M. Bataille and Kathleen Mullen Sands, *American Indian Women: Telling Their Lives* (Lincoln, NE: University of Nebraska Press, 1984).
9. Marshall Berman, *The Politics of Authenticity* (New York: Atheneum, 1972), p. xv, presents the word "authenticity" as synonymous with identity, autonomy, individuality, self-development, self-realization, your own thing, all of which relate to "being onself," and places this squarely in political context. Political context, of course, is embedded in cultural context; identity, authenticity, autonomy (see Dorothy Lee's treatment of autonomy in *Valuing the Self and What We Can Learn From Other Cultures* (Prospect Heights, IL: Waveland Press, 1986)) and "self" are cultural constructions.
10. Albers, "From Illusion to Illumination," p. 132.
11. Paula Gunn Allen, *The Sacred Hoop: Recovering the Feminine in American Indian Traditions* (Boston: Beacon Press, 1986), p. 43.
12. Denise Riley, *"Am I That Name?": Feminism and the Category of 'Women' in History*, (Minneapolis: University of Minnesota Press, 1988), p. 99.
13. Morgan, "Gender and Anthropology: Introductory Essay," p. 9.
14. Gwendolyn Etter-Lewis, "Black Women's Life Stories: Reclaiming Self in Narrative Texts," pp. 43–58, *Women's Words: The Feminist Practice of Oral History*, eds. Sherna Berger Gluck and Daphne Patai (New York: Routledge, 1991), p. 44.
15. *Ibid.*, p. 43.
16. See, e.g., Julie Cruikshank's collaborative work, *Life Lived Like a Story: Life Stories of Three Yukon Native Elders* (Lincoln, NE: University of Nebraska Press, 1990), and The Delany sisters—Sarah and A. Elizabeth Delany with Amy Hill Hearth—*Having Our Say: The Delany Sisters' First 100 Years* (New York: Kodansha International, 1993).
17. See, e.g., Amy Tan, *The Joy Luck Club* (New York: Putnam Publishing Group, 1989), and Ruth McDonald Boyer and Narcissus Duffy Gayton, *Apache Moth-*

ers and Daughters: A Study of Four Generations of a Family (Norman, OK: University of Oklahoma Press, 1992).

18. Life history methodological expertise was gained from a number of sources, including: Margaret. B. Blackman, "Returning Home: Life Histories and the Native Community," paper presented in the symposium *The Afterlife of Life History* at the 89th Annual Meeting of the American Anthropological Association, New Orleans, LA, November 28–December 2, 1990; Franco Ferrarotti, "On the Autonomy of the Biographical Method," *Biography and Society: The Life History Approach in the Social Sciences*, ed. Daniel Bertaux (Beverly Hills, CA: Sage Publications, 1981), pp. 29–37; Sue Ellen Jacobs, Susan Armitage and Katherine Anderson, *A Handbook for Life History Research* (Seattle, WA: Women's Heritage Project, 1988); L.L. Langness and Gelya Frank, *Lives: An Anthropological Approach to Biography* (Navota, CA: Chandler and Sharp Publishers, Inc., 1981); William Schneider, "Writing Life Histories from the and Lawrence C. Watson and Maria-Barbara Watson-Franke, *Interpreting Life Histories: An Anthropological Inquiry* (New Brunswick, New Jersey: Rutgers University Press, 1985).

19. Santa Concha is a pseudonym.

20. See Figure 1 for a rendering of these women's positions in extended family relationships.

21. These women most often use the referent "Indian," rather than "Native American" or "American Indian," but use all interchangeably; therefore, in this chapter all of these referents will be used interchangeably with respect to the right of self-definition.

22. Though it is recognized that "middle-aged" is a cultural construction, for the purposes here it will refer to the generation that either have, or are old enough to have, adult offspring, but who are not considered aged or elderly. (see Judith K. Brown, "Cross-Cultural Perspectives on Middle-Aged Women," *Cultural Constructions of "Woman,"* ed. Pauline Kolenda (Salem, WI: Sheffield Publishing Company, 1988), p. 73.

23. All names, given and surname, are pseudonyms. Selection of the oral life history participants from the women of the extended family was made with regard to availability within the prescribed limited time for interviews. Interaction/observation included all family members. See Figure 1 for family relationships as of 1989.

24. See Nancy P. Greenman, "Mutual Manipulations in the Relationship-Research Dance," *International Journal of Moral and Social Studies*, 6, 3 (Autumn, 1991), pp. 257–268; and Nancy P. Greenman, Ellen B. Kimmel, Michele Foster and Navita James, "Conducting Social Science Research With Women of Color: A Panel of Women Researchers Share Their Experiences," *Economic and Social Issues In the New South: Perspectives on Race and Ethnicity, Proceedings from a National Research Conference*, ed. Marvin Moore (Tampa, FL: University of South Florida Printing Services, 1994).

25. Moore, *Feminism and Anthropology*, pp. 38–41.

26. *Ibid.*, p. 40.

27. *Ibid.*, p. 21.

28. Sue Ellen Jacobs, "Continuity and Change in Gender Roles at San Juan Pueblo," *North American Indian Gender Statuses and Roles*, eds. Laura Kleun and Lillian Ackerman, under review.

29. Allen, *The Sacred Hoop*, p. 19.

30. Albers, "From Illusion to Illumination," p. 144.

31. Alfonso Ortiz, ed., *New Perspectives on the Pueblos* (Albuquerque: University of New Mexico Press, 1972); and *The Tewa World* (Chicago: The University of Chicago Press, 1969).

32. For examples of the "con" side of the debate, see Rosaldo and Lamphere, *Women, Culture & Society*, especially the essay by Joan Bamberger, "The Myth of Matriarchy: Why Men Rule in Primitive Society," pp. 263–280. Paula Gunn Allen's *The Sacred Hoop* is one of the better known arguments for "pro" historical gynocracy.

33. Albers, "From Illusion to Illumination," and Allen, *The Sacred Hoop*.

34. Rina Swentzell, personal communication, Santa Fe, NM, 1989.

35. Rayna Green, *Native American Women* (Bloomington, IN: Indiana University Press, 1983), p. 2.

36. See Mona Etienne and Eleanor Leacock, eds. *Women and Colonization: Anthropological Perspectives* (New York: Praeger, 1980) for a look at the classical historical materialism arguments. The essay by Elisa Buenaventura-Posso and Susan E. Brown, "Forced Transition from Egalitarianism to Male Dominance: The Bari of Colombia," pp. 109–133 in that volume, appears particularly appropriate since with development plans instituting the "cacique" mirroring similar plans in the Southwestern United States.

    Albers, "From Illusion to Illumination," notes the impact of colonialism on various American Indian societal organizations.

37. Albers, "From Illusion to Illumination," p.142.

38. Allen, *The Sacred Hoop*, p. 48.

39. Swentzell, personal communication, 1989.

40. Green, *Native American Women*, pp. 5–6.

41. Albers, "From Illusion to Illumination," p. 146.

42. Traditional ethnographies of Tewa Pueblo communities, e.g., W.W. Hill, *An Ethnography of Santa Clara Pueblo New Mexico*, ed. and annotated by Charles H. Lange (Albuquerque: The University of New Mexico Press, 1982), p. 169, indicated a traditional strong patrilineal bias which characterized the culture, and, he said, "women were considered second-class citizens at Santa Clara Pueblo."

    For Santa Concha Pueblo, Gia Ahkonpovi insists that inhereitance has always been bilateral.

43. Ortiz, *The Tewa World*, and *New Perspectives on the Pueblos*.

44. Sue Ellen Jacobs, "Continuity and Change in Gender Roles at San Juan Pueblo," in *North American Indian Gender Statuses and Roles*, Laura Kleun and Lillian Ackerman, eds., under review.

45. Allen, *The Sacred Hoop*, p. 2.

46. Teresa D. LaFramboise, Anneliese M. Heyle and Emily J. Ozer, "Changing and Diverse Roles of Women in American Indian Cultures," *Sex Roles* 22 (1990), pp. 455–476.

47. Kolenda, *Cultural Construction of "Woman,"* pp. 76–80.

48. Swentzell and Naranjo, "Nurturing: The Gia at Santa Clara Pueblo," p. 39.

49. *Ibid.*

50. Sue Ellen Jacobs, "Being a Grandmother in the Tewa World," *American Indian Grandmothers*, ed. Marjorie Scheritzer, under review, p. 19.

Transformation

and

Change

"I Know Who I Am"
The Collaborative Life History of a Shoshone Indian Woman

4

Sally McBeth and Esther Burnett Horne

I believe there is value in sharing my philosophies and perspectives on the twentieth century, and I would not have agreed to have told you my whole life story unless I felt that it had some historical significance.... My life has spanned most of this century, and I have witnessed many of the issues, problems, and changes that affect our Indian people.

I know who I am. I am a descendent of Sacajawea;[1] my father who was White and my mother who was Shoshone taught me to be proud of both of my heritages. I am a product of the Bureau of Indian Affairs boarding school system,[2] and as a teacher in that system, I went on to instill in Indian children a sense of pride and dignity in who they are. I am a mother, a grandmother and a great grandmother to my own family, and to my large extended family and community as well.

—Esther Burnett Horne, *Naytahwaush*, Minnesota 1992

The theme of this essay is the collaborative nature of the fieldwork endeavor as evidenced in an in-process, experimental, collaborative, life history project. The subject of the life history is Esther Burnett Horne (born 1909), a mixed-blood Shoshone woman known as Essie. The person to whom the story is told is Sally McBeth (born 1949), an anthropologist by training. We decided to coauthor this essay, since from the very beginning the intent of our project was to produce a collaboratively edited manuscript. In the process we discovered new dimensions of our friendship as women, and learned about cultural and generational differences as well as about the relationship between Natives and anthropologists.

McBeth's interest in life histories is the result of a concern with the representation of Native American women in current ethnographic writing. The portrayal of Native women has persistently been one-dimensional, and their roles in American and Native American society have been neglected and trivialized in some (but not all) anthropological and historical literature. In addition, the way that anthropologists have represented the subjects of their studies has not always allowed the Native voice to be heard.

Current ethnographic writing is seeking new ways to adequately represent the authority of "informants" and to explore methodologies which more accurately legitimize the expertise of the members of the culture being investigated. This effort to share-out authority, or in other words, to acknowledge who the authorities and sources of our data really are, is part of a broader questioning of the motives and the objectivity of the anthropological endeavor. The need to shift the paradigm from one in which the aim was to salvage the last vestiges of a vanishing people, to one that records the lives of members of the culture as adaptive players and collaborators in the preservation of their own pasts and presents, is a critical one.

We face many dilemmas when attempting to generate an honest cultural representation of those we seek to understand, and collaboration with members of the culture offers a solution. The collaborative approach does not alleviate the power-laden relationships inherent in ethnographic writings, but it does acknowledge them. Horne's role in producing her life history reinforces the urgent need for Native Americans to play a stronger role in the research process.

Horne's interest in recording her life story stems from her desire to pass down what she has learned, as a student, teacher, and now elder, to the next generation. This knowledge includes: Essie's participation in the oral traditions of Sacajawea; the wisdom that she acquired as a teacher of Indian youth; her insights as a mixed-blood into both white and Indian cultures; and her feminist perspectives on the twentieth century. Also concerned with issues of representation, Horne is insistent that her voice be recorded and interpreted according to mutually acceptable and carefully scrutinized criteria.

This essay will be divided into four sections, each of which will focus on a relevant issue or component of the collaborative process. These include: (1) methodology (authored by McBeth); (2) selected excerpts from the life history (authored by Horne, with an introduction by McBeth); (3) a joint analysis and interpretation of the project in the form of a dialogue (authored by Horne and McBeth); and (4) conclusions (authored by McBeth).

METHODOLOGY

Life histories have long been regarded in the social sciences as legitimate approaches to understanding other cultures, for they emphasize the experiences of an individual and provide an insider's view of her or his life and culture. However, because life histories, as understood in the work of anthropologists, historians, and other social scientists, are usually translated, edited, interpreted, reorganized, and sometimes even rewritten by a collector, the result may violate the integrity of the storyteller's words and style, and hence diminish the intrinsic value of the document.

The life history project that Essie and I have been working on began (as do most) with a friendship. The source of the connection was a mutual interest in the effects that the boarding school experience had on American Indian youth in the twentieth century. My research interests in Bureau of Indian Affairs (BIA) boarding schools and Horne's firsthand experience as a pupil and teacher led to our initial meeting in 1981. I had recently completed research for my dissertation on Oklahoma Indians' perceptions of their boarding school experiences in western Oklahoma.[3] Shortly thereafter I moved to North Dakota and became interested in comparing the experiences of Northern Plains tribal members who had attended BIA or church-sponsored boarding schools with those of tribes from the Southern Plains of Oklahoma with whom I had worked.

In the process of interviewing and collecting data, Mrs. Horne's name came up again and again. Her students at the Wahpeton Indian School[4] in Wahpeton, North Dakota lauded her teaching as a highlight of their schooling experience. She was one of a group of Indian teachers who had dedicated their life to mitigating the negative effects of a boarding-school education on Indian youth and accentuating the positive aspects of that experience. I read Horne's pro-boarding-school testimony as recorded in the Hearing before the Senate Select Committee on Indian Affairs[5] with interest, then visited Horne at her winter home in the town of Wahpeton. Given her warmth and our mutual rapport, I found myself looking forward to my more and more frequent visits with this now-retired teacher and elder, herself a "product" of Haskell Institute, an Indian boarding school in Lawrence, Kansas.[6]

It was not until 1986, after I had moved to Vermont, that the idea of a collaborative life history project with Essie began to take shape. We began the project in 1987, and I have made numerous trips to her summer home on the White Earth Chippewa Reservation in Naytahwaush, Minnesota to continue work on the project.

In the beginning phases of the project (1987 to 1988) we recorded and transcribed Horne's life chronologically. Horne understands much of the Shoshone language, but is not bilingual; her first language is English, so translation was not an issue in the collection of her story. When clarifications were needed, I asked questions, but for the most part the ordering, the inclusion of relevant materials, and the recollections were Horne's. Of course, the surfacing of certain memories, triggered other recollections, which we relegated to the appropriate sections of the life history. There were many digressions in the process, as we commented on people and places that came to mind, discussed friends and family, and got to know each other better.

The immensity of the project that we had undertaken became apparent to both of us when, in the summer of 1989, we began to look more closely at the more than five hundred pages of taped transcriptions we had accumulated. I knew that transcripts of conversational data frequently appear to be chaotic and unordered relative to written texts,[7] but I was still surprised by the near-incomprehensibility of many portions of the written (transcribed) version of our conversations. The task of transforming the dialogue into a comprehensible written form became the focus of our work together (1989 to 1994). How, we asked, do we begin to translate this into a form that will be of interest to and understood by general readers? As we discussed the dilemma, we could not help but wonder why other "edited" or "as-told-to" life histories (with few exceptions) had never mentioned this difficulty. Could our conversations be so different from those of other "academics" and "Natives"? Were we less capable than other collaborators? We thought not, and became determined to not only coedit the transcribed tapes, but to document the process as well.

As we worked slowly, page-by-page, refining and condensing, we were daily made aware of the numerous decisions that we made as we translated the stories and conversations into written form. All of this work was done together, since Essie's health and busy schedule were not conducive to her single-handedly editing her life story.

Many nuances were certainly lost in the process, as we translated the way we talk into the way that we write. There were times when Essie would edit out what I thought were important examples of her style of speech. And there were times when we pulled out the thesaurus to search for a word that had exactly the meaning that both of us believed was important to getting the story right. Essie had a sense of how she wanted her story to sound. We worked together, and I assisted her in shortening lengthy or redundant phrases, but all final decisions were made by Essie. While I believe that much of her warmth, humor, and thoughtful reflections have been tempered by the writing process, her literary style has been retained throughout.

The cooperative work has also encouraged an examination of the process itself. The slow pace of the editing has permitted our intergenerational and intercultural friendship to develop. Our trust in each other has grown, as we more leisurely enjoy our work together, and come to understand the benefits of the collaborative nature of our endeavor. We believe that the partnership method creates an intimacy between the collaborators that enhances the end product.

EXCERPTS

The excerpts chosen for this section provide an example of how decisions are mutually made by the researcher and consultant; they also demonstrate how the "subject" is represented. In discussing which parts of her life to include in this short essay, Essie commented that the sections should not be too long, should be able to stand alone and be understood apart from the full context of the life history, and should reflect her sense of self. She believed that the oral traditions that she had heard while young about her great-great-grandmother, Sacajawea, would be both interesting and relevant to an understanding of who she is. She also wanted to include a section from her home life in Idaho before the death of her father, a section from her Haskell boarding-school days, and lastly a section describing her teaching experiences at the Wahpeton Indian School. In a phone conversation that we had as we discussed this essay, she said:

I think that we should include portions from each of these areas; all four are so vital to who I am today. The theme that ties these all together is the notion of instilling a sense of pride and dignity in being American Indian, an uncommon cause during the first half of this century. My parents instilled in we children a real sense of who we were. They did this by recounting stories of Sacajawea which tied us to our past, but also by developing in us a belief in our worth as individuals that would stay with us into the future.

Ella Deloria and Ruth Muskrat Bronson, two influential Indian teachers at Haskell, provided the same teaching. These two teachers tried to inculcate in us a sense of who we were. At Haskell, a wonderful tribal world opened up for me. There was so much student-to-student sharing, and we were so anxious to learn from each other. In spite of the best intentions of the school to destroy our Indianness, we took pride not only in knowing about our own tribe, but also in learning about the traditions of all of our friends. My horizons were broadened by that experience, even though a lot of our teaching and learning had to be done under the table, so to speak.

And then when I began teaching, I carried those same convictions into my own educational strategies. I shared with my students that same sense of pride in their Indianness, and taught them about their heritage. I actually wove this into the subject matter that I was teaching, including arithmetic, reading, science, and health. I taught them that it was not only important to have a healthy body, but that they also needed to develop a healthy mind and a healthy innermost. I told them that this is the Indian way. In this way I passed on the knowledge that had been instilled in me.

These four areas *have* emerged as central themes of Horne's life story. The oral traditions that surrounded the life of Sacajawea were recounted to her by her grandparents and other tribal elders, and Horne was singularly influenced by the tribal memories of her great-great-grandmother. She believes that she bears the legacy of an important "feminist" heritage. As such, her sense of personal and cultural worth is entwined with her ancestry, and many of her life experiences, including those as a student and teacher, are best understood as part of this legacy. These traditions and her sense of pride in who she is attest to the endurance of the tradition of Indian storytelling (and memory) as they are transformed into new literary forms. Native people empower themselves (and their communities) through oral tradition; Essie's life story exemplifies this concept.

Oral Traditions of Sacajawea (1909–present)

For as long as I can remember, my mother (Mildred Large) and father (Finn Burnett, Jr.) taught us about our relationship to Sacajawea.... They both told us stories about her travels and about the things that she had done. I can remember my mother showing us roots and berries that could be used for medicine, and then she would tell us that her great-grandmother had used these when she had traveled westward with a group of white men who had gone out to the Pacific Ocean, and that these roots had saved their lives. I recall her telling that her great-grandmother, Sacajawea, was a very fine swimmer and that she had saved important papers. I later realized that this incident happened during the Lewis and Clark Expedition, when their boat was overturned. . . .

My mother was also fond of relating that my great-great-grandmother had gone clear to the Pacific Ocean, and that she had seen a fish; she used to tell that she had seen a fish as big as a house. At that time (late 1800s) most of the Indian people (at the Wind River Reservation) were still living in their tipis at the fort. Sacajawea's adopted son and nephew Bazil, however, was given a log cabin next to the government agent's house. Our great-great-grandmother lived with him and his family in that house due to her high standing in the tribe. And as the people sat around the camp, she would tell them that when she was young that she had seen a fish as big as their house. But they would say, "*ishump*" which means "that's a lie." "No fish could be that big." But now we realize that that was a whale that she saw in the ocean. My father said that his dad had told him that Sacajawea saw "people" in the water and when she had tried to talk to them, they would just dive under. We think she must have been talking about seals! The many stories about her were told with humor and pride. She had been an important person on the reservation, and we were proud to claim her as a relative.

Sacajawea told my paternal grandfather, Grandpa Burnett, that she had been beaten by her husband Charbonneau, and that the redheaded man [Clark] had stopped him. I remember my mother telling me that Clark was very kind to Sacajawea and fond of her newborn son, Jean Baptiste, whom she carried with her on her back throughout the journey. I also remember hearing, I think probably from my mom's folks, that Sacajawea said that Charbonneau had wanted to sell her body to some of the men on the expedition, but that she had refused. Perhaps, we thought, he beat her because she was unwilling to disgrace herself. She would have had the tip of her nose cut off had she committed adultery in our tribe. Later, after the expedition, when Charbonneau took yet another wife, Sacajawea left him and began her migration back home to Wyoming. She wandered through many states, including Oklahoma, on her way home. . . .

Shoshone tradition has it that after many years of travel, Sacajawea returned to her people in what later (1890) became the state of Wyoming. Maggie Bazil, my maternal grandmother, was Bazil's daughter. We had connections to Sacajawea from both sides of our family. We were biologically related through our mother's side, but my father's side of the family had a long standing relationship with her too.

My grandfather, Finn Burnett, the frontiersman, who later became the agricultural agent or boss farmer for the Shoshones, worked with Sacajawea and knew her personally. . . . My great-great-grandmother and paternal grandfather were friends and coworkers, and had a great deal of respect for each other. Sacajawea was more or less a liaison between the Shoshone people and the military. You see, Fort Washakie was established as a military post to keep the Shoshones where the government wanted them to be: confined on the reservation. We had been a tribe of nomadic people, and the government did not want us roaming around.

Sacajawea spoke English and some French, as well as Shoshone and Hidatsa. She was also fluent in sign language, and so was able to help the Shoshones make their wants known to the government and Indian Agents, and vice versa. So that was her great service there. My dad tried to impress upon us that our great-great-grandmother, Sacajawea, was a helper of Chief Washakie.[8] He said that it was very unusual that a woman would be allowed to speak in council, as Sacajawea was allowed to do with and for her Shoshone people. He told us that Bazil and Baptiste were both subchiefs, and we understood that they were the chief's helpers, as was their mother, Sacajawea. Then he told us, with my mother sitting there and nodding her head too, that she was like a chiefwoman. He was trying to impress upon us the great leadership strength that she had. She was, we thought, one of the first women ever allowed to speak in council. Sacajawea not only helped Chief Washakie, but also helped my white grandfather in his teaching of the Indian people. Those individuals who do not believe that Sacajawea lived to be much older than twenty-five years old accused my grandfather of having read the Lewis and Clark journals, but he never read them. The things that he knew, and that so many of our people know about Sacajawea's life were those things that were passed down from her to us through oral tradition. We've always known who we were because the oral traditions of our tribe are truth personified. . . .

II Home Life (1909–1922)

One of the things that made public school in Idaho[9] less difficult for we four Indian children was that my mother and father worked very hard to instill in us the fact that we had a great deal to be proud of as Indians. They told us that what was American was, in essence, Native American. My mother told us a lot about the medicines that Indians in the Americas were responsible for introducing to the Europeans. So many things that seem popular now are actually old, and a part of the traditional teachings. As I think back on it now, I see that here was this white man, my father, married to a young Indian woman, teaching his part-Indian children and his Indian wife to be proud because they were Indians. Rather than trying to take the Indianness out of us, he always reminded us that our ancestors had given so much to the American way of life. My dad grew up with the Wind River Shoshones, and his peers were Indian. He spoke our language and learned about our culture.

III Haskell (1924–1929)

Two teachers at Haskell who had a profound impact on my life were Ella Deloria and Ruth Muskrat Bronson. They stood apart from the others as far as I'm concerned. Ella Deloria was Standing Rock Sioux and a graduate of Columbia, and I knew that she had worked with Franz Boas.[10] She taught girls physical education and drama. Ruth Muskrat Bronson was Cherokee and a graduate of Mount Holyoke; she taught English. They both had such a wonderful sense of humor. They taught non-Indian subject matter, but had a very strong respect for

Indian culture, and they were clever enough to integrate it into the curriculum. They taught their students to have a healthy respect for themselves as individuals and a pride in their heritage. They taught us about Indian values, and kept them alive in us. They were both well-educated Indian women, whose desire to help Indian youth led them to commit and dedicate their lives to this end.

IV Wahpeton (1930–1965)

On my first day of teaching duties, the principal accompanied me to my classroom. There were about three dozen fourth-grade students, evenly divided between boys and girls. When the students were settled, the principal said to me, "Mrs. Horne,[11] if there is any foolishness in this room, or if you have any trouble with any of these students, just send them to the office." He meant what he said. And I just as definitely said, "Yes, I will!" The size of the students amazed me.[12] I had been teaching first- and second-graders at the Eufaula Boarding School,[13] and these were fourth-graders many of whom were teenagers. In those days this was a common occurrence, because so many had started school late, and others lived too far from a school to attend on a regular basis. . . .

I talked to the kids after the principal left, and I said, "We're all Indians in this room. So let's make our classroom the best classroom at Wahpeton. We can do this if we help each other. If you will help me and if you will be responsible for your own behavior, we'll be successful."

Gene Tunney, a Turtle Mountain Chippewa, was one of the first students who challenged my discipline in the classroom. "Gene Tunney" was the nickname that everyone called this boy. He was big and he was a school boxer. Gene Tunney was the name of a famous prizefighter of that time, and this student was built like him and acted like him. There were rules and regulations about asking to leave the room, having your assignments done on time, and that kind of thing. He was making a point of not finishing his assignments, and when I got down on him for not handing his homework in, he said to me, "Mrs. Horne, what are you going to do about it?" And I replied, "Well, why are you asking me what I'm going to do about it; what are you going to do about it? . . ." Tunney looked at me for a long time, deciding how he would respond. He had to decide whether cooperating would rob him of his macho image. Somehow, and I don't know exactly why except that he took seriously my comment about our's being the only all-Indian classroom at Wahpeton, he decided to turn over a new leaf and become a responsible class member. Maybe he had never considered that there might be reason to be proud of an all-Indian classroom. Fortunately, not only did he become responsible for himself, but also made sure that no other boys gave me problems. Given his size, all he had to do was glare at a potential troublemaker, and they would settle down. I think that I had gained his respect by not backing down from his bullying style, and we both developed a mutual respect for each other.

DIALOGUE: ANALYSIS AND INTERPRETATION

The following discussion was recorded in June 1992 at Horne's home on the White Earth Chippewa Reservation in Naytahwaush, Minnesota. The questions were composed by both authors; the content was designed to provide the readers of this essay a joint analysis and interpretation of our collaborative methods.

MCBETH: I have called our project experimental, primarily because of its collaborative nature. The disadvantages of such an approach are that it is time-consuming and not always focused, what do you think the advantages of what we have done and are doing are? What are the disadvantages?

HORNE: I think the advantages are that I've had a chance to tell my own story without having things changed or words put in my mouth by the person doing the interviewing. And the trust that was built up in the beginning is important to our commitment to completing the project. If you'll remember, I took quite some time to think about sharing my life's story with you. But after knowing you for awhile and after having read your boarding-school manuscript, I began to build up some trust. Our rapport got stronger as we became better friends and got to know each other more thoroughly. I think too that the person being interviewed can and should assert themselves and not allow the interviewer to write down whatever they want. I haven't felt that there were very many disadvantages except that it is time-consuming, and it gets tiring at times. But our laughter at things that have come up in the interviews has relieved some of that tedium.

MCBETH: When I think of our project, as often as not I think of how much fun I've had doing it. We digress and share other parts of our lives. It has been a very intimate way of getting to know each other.

HORNE: Yes, I think of how much fun it has been too. I really do. Sometimes when you just crack up over something that I've said or the way I've said it, it makes me laugh too. Yesterday, when I told you that some of those old Shoshone men decided that what they needed to do to the author of that article we were talking about was, in their vernacular, to "hang that son of a bitch" we both got quite a laugh out of that. But that's what they said!

MCBETH: Yes, and remember when that young transcriber wrote that your mother worked in a deep hole, instead of a depot. That was the basis for some of our earliest belly laughter and ability to poke fun at our own seriousness. It led to both teasing and trust. As we work through the final editing of the manuscript, how do you feel as you hear your life's events read out loud?[14] What goes through your mind?

HORNE: Well, its been a very interesting experience to listen to my life unfold. I've had a very positive feeling about what I've shared and I thought, too, as I hear my life being read by you, that I've touched many lives in a positive manner. . . .

        All of this is so nostalgic; sometimes the memories bring happiness, and sometimes sadness. There is that full play of emotions that have come and gone over and over again as we've talked about my life. I've also thought about how very fortunate I've been in my life and how grateful I am that I've had so many different experiences; my horizons have been broadened by my travels in Europe and across the United States, and meeting so many different kinds of people. I think of how much stronger I have become through my contact with so many different cultures and nationalities. Sometimes it almost seems as though I am listening to someone else's life being read. And I have to bring myself up short every once in awhile and ask, "Is this really me?"

MCBETH: What *about* our audience? If we are fortunate enough to find a publisher for your life story, how will you feel about sharing this with the public?

HORNE: Being very objective, standing here and looking at me as not-me, I would be happy to share my life with a myriad of people. That is, after all, what teachers do. I believe that I have something to share with educators of American Indians. All through my life, the sharing of Indian values has been so important. There is, I think, a deep interest in and even a surprise at the depth and relevance of our Indian culture. And I'd like to think that, after I'm gone, the importance of maintaining these values will live on through this life history. Through my life, I've tried to live these values.

I've felt comfortable with our method but also real insistent on this being my story. And I feel that the way we've done it *is* my story, and not your words put into my mouth. In newspaper interviews I have done with the local press, frequently I pick up the article and think: "This is not what I said. These are not my words." You have been very careful about not rushing through this. We've been working on this for nearly six years, for short periods of course, but I feel very comfortable with our method and with your saying: "Are these your words?" "Is this how you want this to be worded?" One rarely has the chance to work like this.

MCBETH: Has your relationship to Sacajawea given you a stronger connection to your Native American heritage?

HORNE: It provided me with a connection, because my relationship to her preceded me nearly everywhere I went outside of my home community. In boarding school, and then when I worked at Eufaula, and then at Wahpeton, I didn't tell people that I was related to her, but they always seemed to know. Quite often I was introduced as Esther Burnett, a great-great-granddaughter of Sacajawea. I always wanted to be worthy of being her great-great-granddaughter. I wanted to learn as much about her life and about Native American culture as I could, so that I could defend her being with the expedition against some of our American Indian people who did not think that that she should have guided these non-

Indians across the United States, helping to open up the Northwest. Her reason for wanting to go was to get back with her own people; but when she did get back with them she felt a loyalty to those men, and to her husband, and to completing what she had agreed to do, which was to act as an interpreter.

MCBETH: Do you think that one of the themes of your life has been as a cultural broker?

HORNE: Yes. I have been called a "bridge" by a number of educators and others. A former student from Wahpeton wrote me last week and said, "You have bridged the gap." I've acted as a liaison. And I feel that that has been one of my very strongest roles. I try to teach my students that we are all people. Your tribe and your Indianness are very important, but in the end, it is your humanity that matters. We are, first, individuals. Secondly, we're Americans, and we are fortunate enough to have been the first Americans. And thirdly, we are Shoshone or Sioux or Norwegian, or whatever nationality or tribe that we are. I do have a fierce pride, but to have that you first have to be an individual. You have to have a confidence in yourself and a great deal of self-esteem. And if you class yourself first as an individual, then you're up there with everyone else. Being an individual first gives you the strength that you need to protect yourself and to feel dignity and worth in whatever nationality you happen to be. George Washington Carver said: "I will let no man belittle my soul by making me hate him." I have taken that as a part of my philosophy.

MCBETH: Sometimes I think that one of the greatest values of our project is the intimacy that results from the listening to and telling of stories. How do you react to this? Do you think there is value in the relationships formed as a result of the collaborative method? Do you think that this method could be used to successfully strengthen the relationship between anthropologists and Indians in the future?

HORNE: I'm sure that it could be. But I don't think that it should be. I think it depends on the Indian person. Because of my strength in not letting someone dominate me, it could be very rewarding. But as a whole: No. If there is a rapport and trust and knowledge of what will be done with the materials, then yes. But if there is not, then I would not recommend this process.

We have been aware of and have not lost sight of the goals of the project from the very beginning. Although I feel that you are one of my dearest friends, and I respect you and love you, still we must remember to respect each other in this work. You have not tried to take advantage of me and I have tried not to take advantage of you in this work. I feel that very strongly.

MCBETH: Do you think our friendship lessens the objectivity of the project?

HORNE: We have not let it. I would argue with any anthropologist who said that we could not maintain our objectivity because of our love for each other. Because both of us are too strong; we're too much the feminists to let that happen. Our friendship has enhanced the project; we've worked many hundreds of hours together, and I would not have shared my life with you had I not known and cared for you.

CONCLUSIONS

I clearly remember mentally recording a familiar exchange at the end of the taping session transcribed above. As was our habit, Essie and I made eye contact with each other in an "are we done?" expression. One or both of us would nod in the affirmative, and then Essie would gesture with her hand to "cut" the recorder off. For me, however, this particular taping session stood in sharp contrast to other more familiar and predictable ones. Essie's negative response to my question about whether collaboration could or should be used to strengthen the relationships between anthropologists and Native Americans surprised and troubled me, and I told her so. She laughed and said, "I thought I saw your mouth drop when I responded in that way." Her silence and the sound of the waves on South Twin Lake filled the room. Finally, she said with a smile, "Why is my answer so puzzling?" All I could muster was a feeble, "Well, I just didn't expect it, that's all." I was, indeed, nonplussed by her candid response. She chose to explain herself only briefly: "Sally, because it has worked for you and me does not mean that it is a solution to all of the dilemmas that anthropologists and American Indians need to work through. . . .

As I thought about her response and relistened to our taped dialogue, I began to understand a little of what she meant. My "scholarly" agenda in the context of this project was and is to experiment with innovative methodologies, and to examine the balance of power and issues of representation in ethnographic writing. My intellectual traditions emerge from the academy.

Horne's scholarly agenda is much more practical than mine. As a master teacher, tribal historian, elder, and philosopher, the sources of her intellectual traditions are grounded in the antiquity and culture of her people. Horne's purpose is to pass her knowledge and experience down to successive generations, to preserve the oral traditions that the elders shared with her, *and* to instruct in the process. While she certainly understands and is interested in the nature of our collaborative endeavor, it does not provide her with a rationale for the project.

Throughout our collaborative endeavor, we have considered the nature and meanings of personal narratives. Horne combines remembered experience with sage advice, as she constructs a narrative that reveals who she is. The meanings of her life emerge, as we talk and write about her experiences. She expresses who she is as an individual and as a member of a group, and assigns meaning to these experiences by telling her story. Essie's life is important and interesting not only for the events and insights that she shares, but also for the narrative motifs that are a part of her story. Essie and I have also searched for balance. We seek to find this balance in an oral history that broadens perspectives on American history and in our collective modes of interpretation and understanding.

The realities of our individual cultural experiences and intellectual traditions meet in friendship and in the intimacy that results from the listening to and telling of stories. These stories transcend our differences, and the trust created by our sharing provides the lens through which to view each other's worlds. We may share the motive of preserving Horne's story and oral traditions, but in the end we return to separate intellectual, cultural, and generational worlds. Our collaborative project has created an arena where our scholarly traditions converge. It may be a starting point in examining the interrelationships between anthropologists and Native Americans, but it is not the final solution.

NOTES

This collaborative life history project has been funded in part by grants from the Claire Garber Goodman Fund of Dartmouth College (1987, 1988), the University of Northern Colorado Research and Publications Board (1991, 1993), and the Minnesota Historical Society (1991). Portions of the historical research have been funded by The Newberry Library, D'Arcy McNickle Center for the History of the American Indian (1990, 1992). Permission to use segments of a previously published essay, "Myths of Objectivity and the Collaborative Process in Life History Research," in *When They Read What We Write* (1993), ed. Caroline Brettell, were granted by Bergin and Garvey, an imprint of Greenwood Publishing Group, Inc., Westport, CT.

1. Sacajawea (Sacagawea, Sakakawea, and so on) was the Shoshone interpreter of the Lewis and Clark Expedition (1804–1906). Around 1800, while her tribe was engaged in a hunting or war expedition, she was captured, most likely by the Hidatsa of the Knife River Village of Metaharta. She was about twelve to fourteen years old at the time of her capture. By 1804 she had been sold or gambled away, and had become the property and wife of Toussaint Charbonneau, a French-Canadian trader/trapper. In 1805, while wintering at Fort Mandan, which is located on the Missouri River in what is today North Dakota, Captains Meriwether Lewis and William Clark hired Charbonneau as an interpreter, requesting that he bring one of his Shoshone wives with him. He brought Sacajawea and their newborn son, Jean Baptiste. The goal of this "Corps of Discovery" was to locate a waterway across the continent to the Pacific Ocean. It is not likely that Sacajawea acted as "guide" (as many claim) but her services certainly contributed to the success of the expedition. It is possible that their success in discovering and mapping an overland route to the Pacific hinged on Sacajawea's presence as emissary, liaison, and interpreter.

   Sacajawea has become a controversial figure in American history. Most historians believe that she died on December 20, 1812, at Fort Manuel Lisa in South Dakota. She would have been about twenty-four or twenty-five years old. Horne and others have worked to encourage historians to consider Indian oral traditions and the writings of some scholars who believe that Sacajawea lived to be a venerated elder among her Wind River Shoshone people, and died in 1884. Conversely, some American Indians have depicted her as a traitor to her people for having acted as interpreter and "guide" to the Lewis and Clark Expedition, which opened the way for white expansion into the Northwest. Sacajawea has become an appealing figure in the history of the American West, and she continues to capture the romantic imagination of both the Indian and non-Indian American.

While most historians prefer the spelling/pronunciation "Sacagawea," I have retained the more familiar "Sacajawea" because this is the pronunciation most frequently employed by Horne for public discussion. "Sok-a-JAW-a" is, according to Horne, the Shoshone pronunciation, which translates: "someone who pushes the boat out from the land"; she uses this pronunciation frequently in private discourse.

2. One of the results of the assimilationist policy of the United States government was the creation of the boarding school, a unique educational facility for Native American children. These schools were created both by the Bureau of Indian Affairs (Department of the Interior) and by numerous religious denominations. The desired outcome of the boarding schools was to remold the Indians' system of values and to replace the core symbols of Indian culture with "the primer and the hoe."

The values, religions, and biases of a burgeoning American way of life were imposed on American Indians through the early education of Indian youth. The schools expected that Native American children would become part of mainstream America; children were removed from their homes and families, and were taught the basics of reading, writing, and arithmetic; they were also provided with some vocational training in their upper-division classes. This education ignored and/or actively suppressed the customs and symbols of Indian life; speaking Native languages or visibly adhering to a Native lifestyle were forbidden. Corporal punishment, strict military regimen, and kidnapping to assure attendance were common practices.

3. Sally McBeth, *Ethnic Identity and the Boarding School Experience of West-Central Oklahoma American Indians* (Washington, DC: University Press of America, 1983); "Indian Boarding Schools and Ethnic Identity: An Example from the Southern Plains Tribes of Oklahoma," *Plains Anthropologist* 28/100 (May 1983), pp. 119–28, "The Primer and the Hoe," *Natural History Magazine* 93/8 (July 1984), pp. 4–12.

4. The Wahpeton Indian School, located in Wahpeton, North Dakota, was founded in 1904. It is an off-reservation Bureau of Indian Affairs boarding school which is still in operation today. Like other BIA boarding schools which have remained open, the intentions and goals of Wahpeton have changed considerably since its inception; today they more closely reflect the needs of the students enrolled.

5. United States Congress, Senate Select Committee, Hearing Before the Select Committee on Indian Affairs; United States Senate; Ninety-Seventh Congress. *Second Session of the Bureau of Indian Affairs Proposal to Close Three Off-Reservation Boarding Schools*. February 24, 1982. (Washington, DC: U.S. Government Printing Office, 1982).

6. Haskell Institute was founded in 1884 and is located in Lawrence, Kansas. It was a typical off-reservation boarding school, the intent of which was to assimilate Indian children by removing them from their homes and communities. The old Haskell Institute today is Haskell Indian Junior College. While it is still under the

auspices of the Bureau of Indian Affairs, the goals of the school have come to reflect Native American concerns and needs.

After the death of her father in 1922, Essie's mother returned to the area near the Wind River Reservation with their six children. Financial and other factors forced their mother to send Esther, Bernice, and Gordon Burnett (the three oldest children) to Haskell in 1924. They were joined later by two of the younger children.

7. Hoyt Alverson and S. Rosenberg, "Discourse Analysis of Schizophrenic Speech: A Critique and Proposal," *Applied Psycholinguistics*, 11 (1990), pp. 167–84. Wallace Chafe, "Integration and Involvement in Speaking, Writing, and Oral Literature," *Spoken and Written Language: Exploring Orality and Literacy*, D. Tannen, ed. (Norwood, NJ: Ablex), pp. 171–84.

8. Chief Washakie was a leading Shoshone chief and a key negotiator between whites and Shoshones. He was present in 1863 when the Eastern Shoshone concluded a treaty of friendship (coupled with monetary compensation) with the United States. In 1868, the Wind River Valley was set apart for Washakie's people, and an agency was established there. Washakie's name has become synonymous with the Wind River Shoshone Reservation. Demitri Shimkin, "Eastern Shoshone," *Handbook of North American Indians, Vol. 11: Great Basin*, Warren D'Azevedo, ed. (Washington, DC: Smithsonian Institution Press), pp. 308–35.

9. Esther Burnett Horne's mother and father left the Wind River Reservation to get married. Neither her mother's Shoshone family nor her father's white family approved of the union, so they eloped and moved to Idaho.

10. Franz Boas (1858–1942) is often referred to as the "father" of American anthropology. A central figure in the emergence of American anthropology, he worked among the Eskimo (Inuit), the Northwest Coast Indians of the U.S. and Canada, and in other Indian communities.

11. Esther Burnett married her high school sweetheart, Robert Horne, a Hupa (Hoopa) Indian, in the summer of 1929. Bob left Haskell six months before Essie did, to accept a position working in the power plant at the Wahpeton Indian School. The superintendent at Haskell, Mr. C. M. Blair, helped Essie to find a teaching position at the Wahpeton Indian School so that she and Bob could be together. Robert Horne died in 1974.

12. Horne is about five feet tall. Her height, coupled with the size and age of her fourth-graders, explains this comment.

13. The Eufaula Boarding School was a Bureau of Indian Affairs boarding school located in Eufaula, Oklahoma; it was reserved primarily for Creek girls. Esther Burnett Horne's first teaching experience (1929–1930) took place at this school. She taught first and second grade.

14. During the summer of 1992, we spent several days reexamining the portions of the life history that we had already coedited. McBeth read the passages to Horne in order to expedite the process.

The Multiple and Transformatory Identities of Puerto Rican Women in the U.S.

Reconstructing the Discourse on National Identity

5

Celia Alvarez

Celia Alvarez

SITUATING MYSELF: A PUERTO RICAN WOMAN BORN IN NEW YORK

As a U.S.-born, second-generation, Puerto Rican woman, I would like to engage you in the processes of identity politics that I, and others like me, have had to negotiate as a result of our families having been catapulted to the United States in search of work during the mass migration of the 1950s.

The relationship between Puerto Rico and the U.S. and the migration of its people begin much earlier, however, with the Spanish American War. In 1898, the U.S. claimed Puerto Rico as booty from the war, and with the Foraker Act of 1917 gave its people U.S. citizenship. In 1948 Puerto Rico established itself as a Commonwealth and to this day is neither an autonomous nation nor a State of the Union. As U.S. citizens Puerto Ricans are able to be drafted into the U.S. army, and can reside, work, and vote in the U.S.

The migration of the fifties dislocated a critical mass of Puerto Ricans from the rural and urban working classes to the fields and factories of the U.S. A child of this migration, I am the first-born of a seamstress and a Korean War veteran. We lived in public housing or the projects, as we knew them, in downtown Brooklyn, New York. I was raised along the waterfront, in the vicinity of the Brooklyn Navy Yard with African Americans, Puerto Ricans, Dominicans, Italian and Irish immigrants, Chinese, and others in a predominantly poor and working-class neighborhood.

During the late forties and through the fifties and sixties, a critical mass of Puerto Ricans born and raised in New York City confronted the historical legacy of being Puerto Ricans located within the United States. Second- and third-generation Puerto Ricans were having to negotiate and define a situated identity which embraced their spatial, social, and cultural geographies in contestation with the historically hegemonic, homogenous—social, cultural, and linguistic—constructions of national and cultural identity which permeated both the island and the U.S.

We were Puerto Ricans in diaspora, catapulted from the island by socioeconomic and political transformations. Situated as immigrants, our rights as citizens to equal education, pay, and housing were violated, and this necessitated our historical struggle for civil rights and bilingual education in the U.S. We were racialized within the historically dichotomous black-white cultural construction of race in U.S. This left our families divided by phenotype, while our "American" identities were being constructed for us, as either black or white. No regard was made to our birth certificates, which defined us racially as "white," nor to the confluence of Africa, the Americas, and Europe in our bloodlines. Hispanicized by the erasure of our ethnicity, we were also characterized as alingual, that is, unable to speak either Spanish or English fluently. Denied our multiple linguistic and cultural positionings, as well as our unique integration, reformulations, and transformations of the cultural capital inherited from each (for example, the bilingualism emerging from the historical language contact of Spanish and English in our communities), we were orphaned by each of our respective motherlands, neither wanting to make claim to our birth. Puerto Ricans had the distinction then and today of living and surviving in conditions of persistent poverty. Economically and structurally marginalized, we were relegated to the service and manufacturing sectors of the labor force. Today these conditions persist with the majority of Puerto Rican households and families headed by women.

POSITIONING MYSELF

The question of language was foremost in my experience growing up in New York. I learned Spanish in my home, where I was surrounded by the language dominance of my mother and grandparents during my early childhood years. My mother was a cultural nationalist in her own right, who affirmed explicity and implicitly our Puerto Rican cultural identity in our home. My father experienced broader contact with "mainstream" U.S. society in the armed forces and as worker in the New York City hospitals after the war. Consequently it was my father who brought English into our home, and fortunately I had acquired it by the time I went to school.

I say fortunately, because bilingual education had not become a reality for many of us yet (during the early sixties), and basically we had to "sink or swim" in monolingual English classroom environments. Many of us unfortunately sank, and were unsuccessful in navigating the school system. I raise this issue to illuminate how, in the school context, I was continuously privileged by teachers for having a good command of the English language. They called attention to this ability, and used it to separate me from others in school.

I sustained and developed my Spanish language skills through my mediating role as a translator for my mother and numerous other families in the neighborhood, my use of the language in public settings such as the church, my contact with relatives, and through reading publications such as *El Diario La Prensa* (a New York based Spanish-language newspaper) throughout my childhood and adolescence.

During my high school years I became keenly aware of social and cultural langauge differences associated with the use of English. In an effort to desegregate the Catholic high schools in Brooklyn during the late sixties, I was sent to a school in Flatbush (the other side of Brooklyn) which was predominantly attended by Italian and Irish girls from the lower-middle class. I share this experience to highlight how, in addition to my bilingualism, my sensibilities toward standard and non-standard language practices emerged. It became clear to me that the way I talked defined who I was, and that while I could not define or name it yet, I was negotiating the norms of language use of several different English-speaking speech communities, associated with class, race, and schooling, at the same time.

This engagement with language was a central theme of my life and a way of positioning myself in the world. I observed the inequities to educational access which hinged on knowledge of the English language as well as the differences in academic preparation that I experienced from my friends in public schools. This motivated me to further my education and to seek the knowledge base necessary to address the educational and linguistic needs of my community. I was also seeking ways to reconcile my school identity with my community identity. My excellent academic preparation had to be reconciled with my second-generation, working-class, Puerto Rican, urban identity for me to pursue my studies in a more meaningful way.

With the support of my family and community to pursue a higher education, I left home for Hampshire College in Amherst, Massachusetts. I had been encouraged to apply to this new, progressive, liberal arts college in New England by a counselor in Aspira of New York, an educational advocacy organization founded by one of our women leaders, Antonia Pantoja, in the fifties. It was during this period of the early seventies that Puerto Rican studies departments flourished in the City University of New York, and the Centro de Estudios Puertorriqueños at, CUNY emerged as a key research and advocacy institution in our community. These were the fruits of our community's labor and struggle during the sixties in New York.

My research interests in language, culture, and identity and their relationship to educational policy were formulated during my undergraduate years. These interests brought me to the Centro de Estudios Puertorriqueños in 1974. I collaborated on numerous research projects in the Language Policy Task Force and Culture Task Force throughout my undergraduate and graduate career. I pursued graduate studies in Linguistics at the University of Pennsylvania and subsequently, in my postgraduate life, became a faculty member in Bilingual-Bicultural Education at Teachers College, Columbia University.

Gender became a central focus of my sociolinguistic research on oral narrative and concomitantly was embodied in my reality as a Puerto Rican woman navigating the halls of the American academy. While at the Centro de Estudios Puertorriqueños during the early eighties, I participated in conceptualizing and doing the first Centro research project on women's realities in the Puerto Rican migration (Benmayor et al. 1987); this was ten years after the Centro's inception as a major research center. Subsequently, I embraced the need to affirm Latinas and other women of color scholar/activists, and to create a new scholarship on women's realities in our communities using oral history as a point of entry.

Over the last ten years I have been engaged in collaborative, cross-cultural, women-of-color initiatives nationally and internationally. I have played a central role in the formation of the International Cross-Cultural Black Women's Institute. Since 1987 the Institute has engaged women of the North and South in a global dialogue. We have examined the intersections of our oppressions transnationally, and most notably addressed racism as a human rights issue to be addressed globally. Nationally, I have collaborated with women of color in the formation of The Majority People's Fund for the 21st Century, to support forward-looking, self-defined cultural and organizing initiatives by people of African, Asian and Pacific Islander, Latina/o, and Native descent which improve communities, and to work toward a future where the full humanity of people of color can be embraced. Most recently, on a national level, I have been involved in the formation of the Comparative Feminist Latina Research Working Group, which has brought together Puerto Rican, Chicana, Cuban, Dominican, and Central and South American scholars and creative writers to engage in dialogue and participate writing processes which will enable us to situate our work and relationships to community within and outside the academy. Engagement at all these cross-cultural, national, and international levels (intellectual, pedagogical, organizational, political) brought me to Women's Studies at Arizona State University.

My academic positions reflect the consolidation of my research interests in language, gender, and identity in the Puerto Rican community and my shifting positionality with respect to the focus of my work across my career span. My years at Teachers College enabled me to share the knowledge I had ascertained about linguistic and cultural processes with masters and doctoral student preparing to teach and work with bilingual/multicultural populations. In Women's Studies I am able to move beyond the structural limitations of my intellectual formation in sociolinguistics, to situate and elicit women's narratives within their cultural and historical context. Hence the shift of my work to the interdisciplinary field of oral history, with a focus on cross-cultural, national and international perspectives of women's realities globally.

NAMING OURSELVES: LANGUAGE AND IDENTITY POLITICS

The question of language has been central to discussions of identity among Puerto Ricans on the island and the U.S. In what language(s) (Spanish, English, bilingually alternating in both) can we affirm our cultural and national identity(ies) and be heard? How are our voices silenced by static, homogenous, one-to-one relationships established between a language, geography and identity (for instance, you speak English you are an American; if you speak Spanish you are a Puerto Rican)? What regard is there for the historical, cultural, and linguistic heterogenity of Puerto Ricans in discussions on language and cultural and/or national identity?

As a challenge to our sensibilities about language and identity in the U.S., I am going to present sections of this paper bilingually—both in Spanish and English. This is a rhetorical style and way of speaking which characterizes the bilingual experience of many Puerto Ricans born in the U.S. The study of this bilingualism, the role of gender and its relationship to language, culture, and identity in our community has been the focus of my research.

My entry points to this inquiry have been through my formal training in quantitative sociolinguistics and the ethnography of speaking; my experience with language policy and cultural issues in education; and the evolution of my work towards oral history, to examine oral narrative within the context of linguistic, cultural, and historical processes.

Unos de mis intereses principales de investigación ha sido hacer un esfuerzo de entender, captar, y cáracterizar la auto-definición de la comunidad puertorriqueña, de clase trabajadora, que reside en los E.E.U.U. y situar su experiencia dentro del marco más amplio de lo que definimos como la cultura y identidad puertorriqueña.

(A primary focus of inquiry in my work has been my efforts to understand and characterize how the working-class sector of the Puerto Rican community residing in the U.S. has defined itself and to situate their experience within the broader parameters of discussions on Puerto Rican cultural identity.)

Mi puerta de entrada y analisis ha sido el lenguaje—mi cuestionamiento el plantamiento histórico de la homogeneidad de la identidad puertorriqueña a base de una noción purista, estática, ahistórica y asocial de cultura que se niega reconocer y reclamar la heterogeneidad de experiencias de diferentes grupos sociales como auténticos y parte de la realidad cultural puertorriqueña.

(My entry point has been through language—my questioning of homogeneous conceptions of Puerto Rican cultural and national identity based on static, ahistorical, asocial purist notions of culture which neither acknowledge nor make claim to the heterogeneity of experiences associated with different social groups as authentic to the cultural definition of Puerto Ricans.)

Por el "encuentro" con los E.E.U.U., Puerto Rico se ha encontrado en una situación en el cual el idioma ha sido central en la lucha contra el bombardeo cultural y lingüístico norteamericano en la Isla. Mientras tanto el conocimiento

*del ingles ha esta do aliado tambien al ascenso economico. ¿Hasta que punto
están las posibilidades de conseguir empleo en la isla vinculado a una edu-
cación privada, en inglés?*

(Because of its "colonial encounter" with the U.S., Puerto Rico has found
itself in a situation where the politics of language has been central to its struggle for national identity in resistance to the imposition of North American culture and the English language on the island. Meanwhile it is the knowledge of
English which correlates with social mobility. Therefore, to what extent are the
possibilities for employment and mobility on the island related to access to a
private education, in English?)

*La afirmación de una identidad cultural puertorriqueña está aliada a una
homogeneidad lingüistica que deja afuera de sus esferas la experiencia de aque-
llos que por su posición de clase, no tuvieron la posibilidad de mantener el
español en los E.E.U.U. o de desarollar ambos idiomas o de aprender a leer y
escribir el español en Puerto Rico.*

(The affirmation of a Puerto Rican cultural identity which is based on
notions of linguistic homogenity associated with the elite of a society, leaves
outside of its domain the experiences of those who because of their class position are unable to maintain and develop their Spanish language abilities (that is,
learn how to read and write) or to develop their bilingual abilities (oral and literate norms in both Spanish and English) either on the island or in the U.S.)

*¿Qué ha pasado? Dentro de este esquema, ¿dónde se ha quedado la comu-
nidad Boricua en Nueva York? ¿Cómo se autodefine esa comunidad como
puertorriquena? ¿Qué rol juega el idioma en esa definición? ¿Qué rol juega la
mujer en la reprodución y transformación cultural?*

(What's happened? Within this cultural frame where has the Puerto Rican
community in New York been situated? How has that community defined itself
as Puerto Rican? What role has language played in that definition? What role
do women play in the reproduction and transformation of culture?)

CLASS AS A MEDIATING FORCE IN LINGUISTIC ATTITUDES AND PRACTICES

Circulatory migration flows to and from the island have contributed within the
Puerto Rican community to the close and continuous contact between Spanish
and English (Language Policy Task Force, Centro de Estudios Puertorriqueños,
1980; Zentella 1981). In New York City this resulted in the development of a
bilingual Puerto Rican community in East Harlem, the oldest continuous Puerto Rican settlement in the U.S. (Language Policy Task Force, 1980).

In a study of language attitudes (LPTF 1980, 1980, 1988a) of Puerto Ricans
who lived on a block in East Harlem and the Puerto Rican teachers who came
to work in the public schools of that community, the Language Policy Task
Force (of which I was a member) uncovered differences between speakers' attitudes and reported and observed practices. The teachers on the block claimed
that to be Puerto Rican one had to speak Spanish. However, in their own every-

day language practice the teachers were predominantly English-speaking. This was not unusual, given the predominance of English-language use among educators in the New York public school system, including among coordinators and teachers in bilingual education programs. The residents of the block, however, maintained that to be Puerto Rican you could speak either Spanish or English, or both.

The differences in attitudes reflect a class differentiation among the speakers. The teachers are perpetuating in the schools prescriptivist, middle-class ideals which promote homogenous language use and ascribe one language (in this case, Spanish or English) to a cultural and national identity; that is, a Puerto Rican is associated with Spanish-language use, while being English-speaking is associated with being an American. The contradictions between behavior and idealized norms become evident in actual linguistic and cultural practice.

Many of the teachers were educated in English and are now teaching in an English-dominant educational environment. It is only in a very limited way, through bilingual education (the majority of programs are transitional in nature, with a minority engaged in dual-language development), that the New York City public school system fosters language development and the use of Spanish. The teachers' institutional positioning within the schools differentiates them from the economic and institutional marginality of many of the residents of the block. This positioning becomes reflected in the differences in local community attitudes and behavior toward language which are characterized by an awareness and acceptance of the fluidity of the relationship between language and identity (that is, to be Puerto Rican you can speak either English or Spanish, or both).

CLASS DIFFERENTIATION OF BILINGUAL NORMS: CODE-SWITCHING

Another important research project of the Language Policy Task Force (and the focus of my dissertation, Alvarez 1988b) included the numerous studies on code-switching, the alternation or switching between Spanish and English among Puerto Rican bilingual speakers. Defining characteristics of this bilingual speech community (Gumperz and Hymes 1972; Hymes 1974) have been the lack of functional differentiation in the use of Spanish and English among in-group members in informal settings, and the prominence of language mixing as a mode of communication (Varo 1971; Granda 1972; LPTF 1980; Pedraza and Attinasi 1980).

The phenomenon of code-switching has been described by some researchers as a deficient linguistic mode of communication, characteristic of uneducated and uncultured sectors of Puerto Rican society incapable of speaking Spanish adequately (Varo 1971; Granda 1972). Although characterized as an impoverished Spanish which is being replaced or heavily influenced by English (Meyn 1983), sociolinguistic studies of code-switching in this speech community have shown that in order to switch appropriately, speakers must be knowledgeable of the grammatical systems of *both* Spanish and English (Poplack 1979; 1978; LPTF 1980).

Poplack and Pousada make a distinction between code-switching, that is, the alternation from one language to another within and across sentence boundaries, and borrowings which were the result of the phonological, morphological, or syntactic integration of Spanish into English as a result of language contact (Poplack and Pousada 1981). The latter is the phenomenon we all know as "Spanglish."

Both these linguistic processes have occurred historically in other language contact situations. This is evident, for example, in the integration of loan words from French into English. But for Puerto Ricans this language contact phenomenon between Spanish and English has been problematized. In the case of Puerto Rican bilinguals, we have ascribed negative social value to its use, reflective of the social class positioning of its speakers.

The "corruption" or influence of English on Puerto Rican Spanish (the variety of Spanish spoken on the island), and implicitly the Americanization of a Puerto Rican national identity, have been attributed in large measure to Puerto Rican bilinguals residing in the U.S. The social class positioning of a majority of these speakers, who are working class or marginally employed, as evidenced by the persistent poverty rates of Puerto Ricans in the United States (Miranda 1991), is used as a basis from which to reinforce such stereotypes. The full range and complexity of language contact processes which have resulted on the island and in El Barrio, across class lines and over time, have yet to be fully explored and delineated. Transnational cultural and linguistic influences have crossed geographical and social spaces, permeating class boundaries in distinctive ways.

GENDER AND LINGUISTIC INNOVATION: THE ROLE OF WOMEN

El code-switching o intercambio de idiomas puede suceder a varios niveles de complejidad sintáctica; al nivel de palabra o frase, por ejemplo. Distinguimos dentro del uso de code-switching aquel relacionado con el habla de una persona que está aprendiendo un idioma con aquél que es una forma de hablar entre bilingues. Además ambos grupos se distinguen de aquellas personas que aprendieron ambos idiomas por separado, y relacionados con distinctos grupos y contextos culturales. En todo caso, elegir hablar el español o el inglés o ambos en un intercambio de idiomas con otra persona depende de con quién uno esté hablando. Todo esto implica su conocimiento de las reglas gramaticales y normas culturales relacionada con cada código.

(Code-switching or the alternation of codes can occur at numerous levels of syntactic complexity; the individual word or phrase, for example. The code-switching practices of individuals learning a second language are distinct in their complexity from those of bilinguals for whom the alternation of two languages is a way of speaking. In addition, the alternating language practices of these two groups are different from those individuals who learned both languages separately and who differentiate each language with distinct groups and/or social domains. In any case, the choice to speak Spanish or English or both depends significantly to whom one is speaking and the speakers' shared knowledge of the rules of grammar and norms of use associated with each.)

En las investigaciones sociolingüísticas del LPTF 1980, Shana Poplack y Alicia Pousada, establecieron que en el code-switching de los puertorriqueños viviendo en Nueva York, había una relación sintáctica entre el español y el inglés en los puntos de intercambio. Por fin, pudieron resolver lingüìisticamente que este fénomeno no era "una barbaridad" como se había pensado en el habla y pensamientos de los puertorriqueños bilingues de Nueva York, sino que el code-switching requería un conocimiento gramático-social particular para poderse hacer; es decir, un conocimiento más allá que el de hablar el inglés o el español y usarlo entre monolingües. Los que hablan el español y el inglés no necesariamente pueden alternar idiomas apropriadamente; esto requiere conocimiento de las normas culturales y lingüísticas de la comunidad bilingüe.

(In the sociolinguistic investigations of the Language Policy Task Force 1980, Shana Poplack and Alicia Pousada established that the code-switching of Puerto Ricans in New York was rule–governed and occurred at the points where syntactically there were overlaps between the grammar of Spanish and English. They were finally able to resolve through linguistic analysis that this phenomenon was not barbaric and unsystematic, as the speech and logic thinking patterns of Puerto Rican bilinguals in New York had been characterized, but rather that to code-switch required specific knowledge of the grammatical and social norms of the use of both languages simultaneously that was differentiated from the knowledge necessary to speak either language as a monolingual speaker. Knowledge of how to code-switch or alternate codes was not implicit merely because one could speak either or both; this required knowledge of the grammatical and social norms of use appropriate to a bilingual speech community.)

Uno de los resultados de estos estudios sociolingüísticos fue descubrir el rol de la mujer en esta forma de hablar. El code-switching, como una forma innovadora de hablar de la comunidad, se daba más entre las mujeres. Esto fue un resultado interesante porque en el mundo, las mujeres juegan un rol lingüístico contradictorio: es decir, somos la que mantenemos las normas sociales lingüísticas y en ese sentido conservadoras, mientras que a la misma vez somos las innovadoras, dándole impulso a cambios lingüísticos dentro nuestras comunidades.

(One of the outcomes of these sociolinguistic studies was to discover the role of women in relation to the code-switching practices of the community. As a linguistic innovation of the community residing in the U.S., code-switching was found to occur most often among women. This was an interesting outcome because sociolinguistic studies have characterized women's language practices as contradictory: on the one hand, women maintain the accepted linguistic standard norms of a society, thereby being conservative in their language behavior, while at the same time women are innovators of linguistic change, giving impulse to new linguistic practices in their communities.)

En sus investigaciones, el LPTF estudió el uso de idiomas relacionados con género, edad, y etapa de vida de las personas.

(In its research the LPTF 1980 studied the relationship of language to gender, age, and development of the life stage of individuals.)

En un caso (Pedraza and Attinasi 1980) see examinó el uso de idiomas durante diferente etapas de la vida de una muchacha del Barrio. Se encontró que en su adolesencia el inglés predominaba de acuerdo a las influencias de sus amistades o "peer group." Pero cuando se hizo madre, resucitó su conocimiento del espanol. Como madre, hablaba mucho más el español. Claro, esto tenía mucho que ver con quién ella se estaba relacionando en cada etapa, adolescentes o otras madres con hijos del bloque, en el segundo. Sus necesidades lingüísticas y culturales cambiaron con el tiempo. A base del repertorio de conocimiento lingüístico y cultural que ella tenía pudo adaptarse a nuevas condiciones. Confirmó que estos procesos no eran estáticos y que podían cambiarse durante la vida de una persona. Lo que sí afirma es que aunque ella se comunicaba en inglés con sus amistades como joven, pudo rescatar y desarollar de nuevo su conocimiento del español como adulta y madre.

(In one case study (Pedraza and Attinasi 1980) the language use and practices of one young woman was examined across different life stages. They discovered that English was predominant during her adolescence, given the influence of English-speaking friends and peer groups during that period of her life. But when she became a mother, her knowledge of Spanish was resusitated again. As a mother in El Barrio she spoke much more Spanish. Of course these practices reflected who she was associated with during each stage of her life, adolescents or other adult mothers with children on the block. Her linguistic and cultural needs changed with time. Given the range of her linguistic and cultural repertoire, she was able to adapt to new conditions. This study confirmed that these processes were not static and that they could change and evolve throughout the life span of an individual. Her dramatic shift from English in adolescence to Spanish in motherhood exemplified the fluidity of these practices over time.)

TURNING THE ASSIMILATIONIST MODEL ON ITS HEAD: BILINGUALISM, EDUCATIONAL ATTAINMENT, AND SOCIAL MOBILITY AMONG PUERTO RICAN WOMEN

What, then, was my contribution to this research? Within the context of the research done for my doctoral dissertation in linguistics at the University of Pennsylvania, I examined the use of code-switching within the oral narratives of personal experience of members of this same speech community in East Harlem. According to Poplack (1978, 1979) the significance of code-switching in this speech community was that it marked in-group membership among speakers in this community; that is, their identity as members of the Puerto

Rican community in New York. Given that sociolinguistic research documented the ways speakers use phonological, morphological, and syntactic forms to communicate social and linguistic meaning, I set out to explore how speakers in this community used code-switching to communicate meaning in the telling of stories. I chose to examine code-switching beyond the sentential level (Poplack's research had focused on the sentential level), and to examine its use within oral narrative texts.

To be able to ascertain in what ways code-switching conveyed linguistic and social meaning beyond an emblematic function of group identity, it was necessary for me to situate its use beyond the sentential level of analysis. I was able to shift the focus of analysis by contextualizing the occurrences of code-switching within the structure of oral narrative. I examined its use and distribution across the structure of the narrative using Labov's 1972 taxonomy for the structure of oral narratives of personal experience. I examined the occurrences of code-switching in the Spanish and English narratives told by twenty-eight Puerto Rican bilingual adult men and women in the context of formal (interview) and informal (group interaction) speech.

The outcomes of my research were significant with respect to gender. The women who had lived most of their lives in New York City related stories in both Spanish and English while their bilingual male counterparts did so only in English. The women were the ones who had a more extensive repertoire of bilingual abilities; *es decir, manejaban mejor, aunque ambos grupos eran bilingües, la producción de la narrativa en español y en inglés, y ademas, usaban mucho más el code-switching en ambos.* (That is to say, that although both men and women had bilingual abilities, the women had a broader range of usages exemplified by their more extensive use of code-switching and their ability to narrate stories in both languages.)

Con respecto al uso del code-switching, se esperaba que en su mayoría el alternar de idiomas fuera del español hacía el inglés como unos de los procesos intermediarios de la adquisición del inglés y hacía la asimilación cultural. Pero los resultados indicaron que la mayoría del code-switching era del inglés hacía el éspañol. Estamos hablando de una población que ya hablaba inglés y reside en un país donde no hay necesidad de usar el español. Entonces, lo que yo planteo en mi estudio es que el uso de code-switching en esta comunidad (With respect to the use of code-switching, it was anticipated that the majority of language switching would be from Spanish to English, characterizing an intermediary stage in the acquisition of English and cultural assimilation into U.S. society. But the results indicated that the majority of code-switching was just the opposite, that is from English to Spanish. Remember this was a population that already spoke English, the language of the society, and was not newly acquiring it, and therefore had no necessity to resort to Spanish for purely linguistic reasons. Therefore, what I maintain in my research is that the use of code-switching (in this community) is a form of Spanish-language maintenance within an English dominant society which could be interpreted as a form of cultural resistence. That is, while the Puerto Rican community in East Harlem values the speaking of Spanish, the issue becomes how much you use it, and to what extent at the lexical, syntactic and/or level of the speech act.

I found that within the structure of the narrative, code-switching co-occurred with evaluative as opposed to narrative clauses; as such, it was an evaluative device conveying linguistic and social meaning beyond emblematic in-group identity. In the English narratives, the occurrence of code-switching was highest at the beginning of the narrative, or in the orientation; while it occurred the most in the end or resolution of the Spanish narratives. While the code-switching functioned as an evaluative device overall, its distribution across the structure of the narrative (abstract, orientation, narrative clauses, evaluative clauses, resolution, and coda) varied according to the language of the narrative.

While both Spanish and English language use are associated with being Puerto Rican by the members of this block (recall the results of the earlier attitudes study), the use of both languages, that is, bilingual language use, is the norm—as evidenced by the code-switching found in both the Spanish and English narratives. These bilingual norms are to be differentiated from the norms acquired by monolingual speakers of either language.

Additionally, while the overt prestige norm of the society is the acquisition of English—to have social and economic access in the U.S.—the use of Spanish is a covert prestige norm of the community. This covert prestige norm is evident in the higher incidence of code-switching from English to Spanish rather than from Spanish to English, which one would expect in the process of linguistic and cultural assimilation to U.S. society.

In the context of the narratives themselves, the higher occurrence of code-switching towards Spanish in the beginning of the English narratives affirms this covert prestige norm; while the higher incidence of code-switching towards English at the end of the Spanish narratives affirms the bilingual (versus monolingual) prestige norms associated with this speech community.

As noted in the research of Ana Celia Zentella (1981), the range of Spanish language use in the Puerto Rican community in New York varies significantly. There is a continuum which ranges from bilingual to monolingual Spanish or English speakers. One significant finding among second-generation Puerto Ricans born or raised most (60 percent) of their lives in New York City was the tendency for the women to have developed their language abilities in both languages and to code-switch more, while the men's language use shifted predominantly towards English. Spanish predominated among both women and men born and raised in Puerto Rico.

Despite the social myths associated with the acquisition of English and educational and economic attainment, I found that the highest rate of employment occurred among the Spanish-speaking males with less than a high school diploma. In comparison I found that the second-generation women who had the greatest range of bilingual ability also had the highest level of educational attainment—they had graduated from high school, and one or two had some college education—but they were also the most marginal in the paid labor force: all were single heads of household with children, and unemployed.

Recent studies on poverty in the Puerto Rican community discuss our continued structural economic marginality in the U.S. As Miranda (1991, 33) notes:

> Half of all Puerto Rican children live in female headed families. The labor force participation rate of Puerto Rican women is substantially lower than that of other Latina, white or Black women. About 44 percent of Puerto Rican women participated in the labor force in 1990 compared with 55 percent of all Latina women, 58 percent of white, 60 percent of Black women." (*Latino Child Poverty in the United States*, Letticia C. Miranda, Children's Defense Fund, Washington, DC, 1991)

My sociolinguistic findings raised questions for further study in understanding the social and structural conditions of Puerto Rican women in the U.S.: What is going on here? What are the decision-making processes underlying women's participation or non-participation in the labor market? Have Puerto Rican women been excluded from the labor market for structural/institutional reasons—that is, institutional racism or relocation of industries, for instance, the garment industry from New York City? Can this exclusion be due to the value attributed to the labor of women in the reproduction of the family and the prioritizing of childrearing as a form of work? (Rina Benmayor, Rosa Torruellas and Ana Juarbe, 1992). To understand the cultural, economic, and structural processes at work in our unique marginality within the U.S. economic system, it will be important for us to pursue the answers to these questions.

STORIES TO LIVE BY: A TURNING POINT

My interest in examining oral narratives went beyond the structural linguistic level which I addressed in my sociolinguistic research. I wanted to examine stories of personal experience in context: as entry points to understanding cultural values, norms, human agency, and significance in the lives of Puertorriqueñas. During the early eighties I had an opportunity to explore these issues within the context of the Centro de Estudios Puertorriqueños interdisciplinary oral history project on the Puerto Rican migration to the U.S.

This project was one of most significant experiences for me in the context it provided for the integration of my lives. The project enabled me to situate myself historically within the Puerto Rican migration, and to understand why I had come to be born and raised on the Brooklyn waterfront, the importance of that community in earlier settlements during the twenties and thirties, and the political significance of that community in the formation of the Puerto Rican community in New York. I interviewed women who had settled in Brooklyn

(*Los Pioneros*) during the twenties and thirties, as well as those who worked in the garment industries in the forties and fifties to forge a life for themselves and their families. The public events associated with the project engaged participants of the project with a wider community audience, and personally, enabled me to create a context to affirm my own mother's contribution to the migration process and to recognize her labor in the garment industry. We published the life histories of our mothers' and grandmothers' migration, including their work and socialization experiences on the island and in New York. "Stories to Live By: Continuity and Change in Three Generations of Puerto Rican Women" (Centro, Hunter College, CUNY 1987) was an intergenerational study by some of us who had lived in the United States and were now looking at ourselves in relation to our mothers, grandmothers, and other women of the thirties, forties and fifties.

My participation in the Centro oral history project was a turning point for me in my own personal and professional development. It enabled me to integrate all of my multiple selves. I could stand back in the third person and use all my analytical frameworks to develop an analysis, but I could also stand in the first person in juxtaposition to the experiences of different women with whom we had been working to position my life story within the continuous thread of social and cultural history in the making within my community.

CLAIMING A SPACE: TELLING OUR STORIES, OUR WAY

I think that, in terms of issues of method, oral history is one approach in which we can negotiate our subjectivity and intrasubjectivity within our communities. It enabled me to negotiate and situate commonalities and differences across generations, as well as to explore from a comparative perspective the U.S. and island experiences. The oral history process can enable us to explore the relationship between ourselves, as subject and object of inquiry—from first to third positionings—within the context of our work. We can examine the continuity and change in our cultural formation and the *trayectoria* (trajectory) we bring with us and see ourselves across historical moments and social spaces.

When examining issues of culture and identity, we have to look at the heterogeneity in our communities that relates not only to issues of class and gender, but also to race, and to bring that into the discourse of identity. I think we have to talk about cultural rights in the ways that we have been talking about human rights and reproductive rights. That is, we have the right to claim a language which includes our multiple forms of linguistic and cultural expression; and we have a right to claim our worldview and the ways we organize our lives, irrespective of where we are geographically located. We have a right to reclaim the experiences that have been left out—the legacy of continuity and change—of those historically excluded from the discourse of naming the world. We must continue to challenge the hegemonic notion of linguistic and cultural homogeneity as the basis of a national or cultural identity.

WORKS CITED

Centro de Estudios Puertorriqueños, Hunter College, City University of New York:

Alvarez, C. (1993). "El hilo que nos une—The Thread that Binds Us: Becoming a Puerto Rican Woman." In Virginia Cyrus, ed., *Experiencing Race, Class and Gender in the United States*. Mountain View, CA: Mayfield Publishing Company.

―――― (1991). "Code-Switching in Narrative Performance: Social, Structural and Pragmatic Function in the Puerto Rican Speech Community of East Harlem." In Carol Klee and Luis A. Ramon-Garcia, eds., *Sociolinguistics of the Spanish-Speaking World: Iberia, Latin American, United States*. Tempe, AZ: Bilingual Press/Editorial Bilingue.

―――― (1990). "El hilo que nos une: Becoming a Puerto Rican Woman," revised version. In Paul Thompson and Raphael Samuels, eds. *Myths We Live By*. London: Routledge.

―――― (1989). "Code-Switching in Narrative Performance: A Puerto Rican Speech Community in New York." In Ophelia Garcia and Richard Orteguy, eds. *English Across Cultures, Cultures Across English: A Reader in Cross-Cultural Communication*. Berlin: Mouton.

―――― (1988a). "An Interpretive Analysis of Narrative in Social Interaction." Centro de Estudios Puertorriqueños Language Policy Task Force, *Speech and Ways of Speaking in a Bilingual Puerto Rican Community*. NY: Hunter College of the City University of New York.

―――― (1988b). *The Social Significance of Code-Switching in Narrative Performance*. Ph.D dissertation, University of Pennsylvania, Philadelphia.

―――― (1988c). "El hilo que nos une—The Thread that Binds Us: Becoming a Puerto Rican Woman," revised version. *The Oral History Review*, Vol. 16, No. 2, pp. 1–46.

―――― (1987). "El hilo que nos une—The Thread that Binds Us: Becoming a Puerto Rican Woman." Centro de Estudios Puertorriqueños, Oral History Task Force, *Stories to Live By: Continuity and Change in Three Generations of Puerto Rican Women*. NY: Hunter College of the City University of New York.

Granda, German de (1972). *Transculturacion e interferencia linguistica en el Puerto Rico Contemporaneo (1898-1968)*. Rio Piedras, Puerto Rico: Editorial Edil, Inc.

Gumperz, John J. and Dell Hymes (1972). *Directions in Sociolinguistics: The Ethnography of Communication*. New York: Holt, Rinehart and Winston.

Hymes, Dell (1974). *Foundations of Sociolinguistics: An Ethnographic Approach*. Philadelphia: University of Pennsylvania.

Labov, W. (1972). *Sociolinguistic Patterns*. Philadelphia: University of Pennsylvania.

Meyn, M. (1983). *Lenguaje e identidad cultural, un acercamiento teorico al caso de Puerto Rico*. Rio Piedras, PR: Editorial Edil, Inc.

Miranda, Letticia C. (1991) *Latino Child Poverty in the United States*. Washington, DC: Children's Defense Fund.

Poplack, S. (1979). "Sometimes I'll Start a Sentence in Spanish y Termino en Español. Centro de Estudios Puertorriqueños, Language Policy Task Force. New York: City University of New York.

Poplack, S. (1978). "Syntactic Structures and the Social Function of Code-Switching." Centro de Estudios Puertorriqueños, Language Policy Task Force. New York: City University of New York.

Poplack, S. and Alicia Pousada (1981). "A Comparative Study of Gender Assignment to Borrowed Nouns." Centro de Estudios Puertorriqueños, Language Policy Task Force. New York: City University of New York.

Varo, C. (1971). *Consideraciones antropologicas y politicas en torno a la ensenanza del "Spanglish" en Nueva York*. Rio Piedras, PR: Ediciones Libreria Internacional.

Zentella, Ana Celia (1981). "Language variety among Puerto Ricans." In Charles A. Ferguson and Shirley Brice Heath, eds., *Language in the USA*. New York: Cambridge University Press.

Culture and the Arts Task Force

Benmayor, R., R.M. Torruellas, and A.L. Juarbe (1992). *Responses to Poverty among Puerto Rican Women: Identity, Community and Cultural Citizenship*. working paper.

Oral History Task Force

——— (1988). *Aprender a luchar, luchar es aprender*. Literacy reader. Spanish only. (with Language Policy Task Force)

Benmayor, R., A. L. Juarbe, C. Alvarez, and B. Vazquez Erazo (1987). *Stories to Live By: Continuity and Change in Three Generations of Puerto Rican Women*. Working paper.

——— (1986). *Extended Roots: From Hawaii to New York, migraciones Puertorriqueñas a los Estados Unidos*.

Language Policy Task Force

Attinasi, J., P. Pedraza Jr., S. Poplack and A. Pousada (1988a). *Intergenerational Perspectives on Bilingualism: From Community to Classroom*, 2nd. edition.

Alvarez, C., A. Bennett, M. Greenlee, P. Pedraza, Jr., and A. Pousada (1988b). *Speech and Ways of Speaking in a Bilingual Puerto Rican Community*.

LPTF (1980). "Social Dimensions of Carzvage Use in East Harlem."

Pedraza, Jr., P. (1987). *An Ethnographic Analysis of Language Use in the Puerto Rican Community of East Harlem*. Working paper No. 12.

Pedraza, Jr., P and John Attinasi (1980). *Rethinking Diglossia*. Working Paper No. 9.

Documentaries

Nosotras trabajamos en la costura: Puerto Rican Women in the Garment Industry. Fifteen-minute slide show, available in English or Spanish.

Nostras trabajamos en la costura. Thirty-minute radio documentary about Puerto Rican women in the garment industry, available in English or Spanish.

"I Have a Frog in My Stomach"
Mythology and Truth in Life History

6

Janneli F. Miller

Lucia told me that there had once been a frog in her stomach. She also told me of a black dog with flames shooting out of its eyes. She dreamed of this dog, and the next day it came to her as she walked through the woods near her home. She said that she had been born with powers, and could see through the hood of a car into the engine, or through people's skulls to see their brains working.

In this chapter I present a part of the transcription generated during life history interviews with this Mayan woman. I touch upon some issues that it brings up in relation to the construction of self, including the notions of turnings and the mythologizing of the self. Finally, I address what I consider the most interesting issues to arise as a result of Lucia's story, these being truth, belief, and reality. I explore the nature of these concepts as they relate to this case, to me personally, and to anthropology in general. My assertion is that anthropologists doing life histories must have what is known in Buddhist philosophy as "beginner's mind." This entails a self-awareness and openness about the nature of reality, an entry into what Victor Turner has called the subjunctive mood.[1]

The interviews were undertaken in the spring of 1991 in a small city in the southwestern U.S. The subject, Lucia Soc, was an acquaintance who had previously expressed a desire to have her life story recorded. She was a motivated "informant" who wished to preserve memories of her childhood in Guatemala. She felt that her story could be instructive as an illustration of the experiences and adjustments Central Americans have to make upon moving to America. Though she is not a political refugee, her story offers insight into the plight of such refugees, or even migrant workers, by bringing to life the poverty, oppression, and despair that often compels these individuals to leave their homeland. The stories she tells of life on the streets in Guatemala City as a child, and in her village, may be considered typical of a Central American underclass, the Mayan Indians. However, I do not intend to make a case for Lucia as being representative of contemporary Mayan women. What is presented here is simply one woman's story—a story which challenges Western assumptions about the possibilities of lived experience.

I do not go into the specifics of the daily lives, customs, religious beliefs, or political atrocities suffered by the Mayan Indians of Guatemala because this has already been thoroughly and articulately expressed in the life histories of Rigoberta Menchu, Ignacio Bizarro Upjan, and Shas Ko'w', who are all Guatemalan Mayan Indians.[2] Cultural themes and activities described in these works are consistent with the material provided by my informant. The reader who wishes more information regarding the political, economic, and sociocultural aspects of Guatemalan life is referred to these as background and context to the present essay. Here I use a focus that is perhaps more introspective and subjective, bearing upon the questions of authenticity and personal representations and understandings of reality.

Lucia Soc is a forty-one-year-old Guatemalan woman of Mayan descent, born to a Mam mother and Cakchiquel father. This mixing of tribal identities was frowned upon by relatives from both sides, and subsequently Lucia was ostracized from her Mayan heritage—unable to claim Mam, Cakchiquel, or Ladino affiliation. Lucia's mother was young and single, and when Lucia was forty days old, Lucia was given to her grandmother who lived in a small village outside Guatemala City. Here Lucia was received with hostility, her aunts treated her cruelly, and there was no one to look out for her or to care for her.

She describes her childhood as being a series of hardships, one after another, in which she portrays herself as an outcast, *la bastarda*. She had difficulties with schoolmates and teachers, in her village with neighbors, and with her family. She describes herself as a "survivor" and also at this time as *macho*—a fighter. She stubbornly defended herself, and sought revenge on anyone who caused her harm or humiliation. Because of this trait, which she attributes to the fact that she held on fiercely to her Indian identity, she earned a reputation as a trouble-maker. This early period was one of constant struggle—with her family members who did not want her, with the school children who taunted and teased her, with school officials who blamed her for inciting violence, and with herself as she sought to discover a niché in an unfriendly world.

Yet, in spite of constant daily misfortunes, she managed to cultivate a strong sense of self-reliance and pride in her status. She claimed her Indian heritage and used it as a way to forge an identity. She learned the Mam dialect, and spent hours listening to her paternal grandmother's stories of Indian village life. She took pride in her Mayan ancestry, a pride which is still evident today.

Currently Lucia lives in a small city in the Southwest. She married an American she met in her twenties while he was working in Guatemala City. She has two teenage children, both born in the United States, and lives what could be said to be an "average" American lifestyle: her husband works a nine-to-five white-collar job, her children attend public schools, and she lives in a split-level house in a suburban neighborhood. She keeps current on the political news of her home country, and often wears traditional Guatemalan clothing as a sign of her support and solidarity with her homeland. She has been back to Guatemala twice since arriving in the United States eighteen years ago, and stays in touch with members of her family who are still there. However, she is under great political risk during her visits to Guatemala, which is a constant source of strain for her. Although she knows how to be an American, having successfully assimilated into modern society, she is still the victim of frequent discrimination because of her Indian appearance and language ability. She has been refused several jobs teaching English to native speakers because of her cultural identity as a Guatemalan Indian woman. Hence she remains even more committed to the eradication of social injustice and violence. The experiences and lessons of her childhood recalled here remain a strong part of her identity today.

Approximately six hours of interview were taped. Lucia is lively and talks freely. She directed the subject matter of the interviews, as well as the timing and ordering of issues. I asked few questions, usually only to clarify something, or to get her to elaborate on a subject already mentioned. She began the life history with her early childhood, concentrating on this time period because she felt it was important. Although she speaks English clearly, her story is interspersed with Spanish words and phrases, because, as she explained, at times it is difficult to translate. This code-switching is a part of her normal speech patterns—I have never heard her speak without lapsing into Spanish.[3]

What follows is an excerpt from the transcribed interviews. I chose this piece specifically to represent her life story because it embodies some of the major issues and concerns having to do with the construction of a self as well as the social negotiation of reality. Bracketed text contains my comments and questions, Spanish words are italicized, and translations are provided in the appendix so as not to interfere with the original flow of the narrative. This session began with an account of her relationship with a boy, Ramón, who was her first and only "true love." Lucia will speak to you now.

LUCIA'S STORY

And then about three months right after the earthquake he was hit by a car on the freeway, and that's how he ended, you know. And that was the sad part of my life, because I really loved that kid. But during the time, that we were going out, his mother put a spell on me, and so I started having *ataques*. It's just like sometimes I was standing up and suddenly I just fainted, and I didn't know anything, and I just, my mind went blank. And so my grandmothers took me to this, *un brujo*, you know, *para ver que pasó* and then they find out that I have a, a frog in my stomach and I didn't believe it. I thought that was a joke (laughs). I swear to God, I thought it was a joke. And so we, the whole family put their money together and they took me to Aguazacapan which is the very, the town is full of *medos brujos*. [Aguacapan?] No, Aguazacapan, it is *por, por la costa, por la costa, y por Santa Lucia Cotzimalguapa, y todas a yendo* [*Tengo un* map] OK, *vamos a buscar la mapa*, yeah, *y es un pueblecito muy chiquitito pero es muy peligroso y muy*—It is dangerous for the witchcraft that's going on in there. I went and then I saw this, uh, midget, he was a short man. I mean, shorter than my grandmother. She was four feet tall but this guy was about three feet tall. He had a beard all the way to his feet. It was a white beard, you know, and he was dressed up in white, and when I saw him I start trembling, you know. And the he says "That girl has a, a frog in her stomach." He just said that looking at me! (laughs) And then I said, wait a minute that's, this, this is, how he can do that? You know, he's not God, only God can do those things.

Well, but then he giving me drinks, and drinks. I stayed there for a week with my mother. We sleep in *un petate* in one of his places, and I was supposed to *llorar*, you know, and flowers. My mother was washing me in a cross style, and then you know doing some prayers in Mayan dialect, and incense, no incense, *como se, copal y todo eso* you know. And then one day he says "Today," he says, "you going to the bathroom and don't let her to see what's coming out of her, her belly, OK? Today is the day where she have to just deliver whatever she has in it, but you just grab everything and put 'em in a bag because I need to bury this and we have to do some studies out of this." And I thought that was, the whole time, I swear to God, I was laughing. I thought it was ridiculous.

Boy o boy, then that day I need to go to the bathroom. It was like having a baby you know. Now that I have babies I know this feeling. It was, you know, it's just like, oh my back (uses hands to gesture). It was straining, and suddenly I have this, it was like a big *sapo*, you know *sapo*? You know, a frog, it was a little baby frog. This is one of those, what do you call, toads. A huge one came out of my body, you know. And I didn't see it, my mother grab it and and put it, it was sick. Like having a baby. It was like having a baby, and my mother got it you know, and put it and took it to this person, and this person buried and pray and everything.

You know, next day, when we come back, we find out that the father of Ramón died that day, that day, his father died. You know, so whatever it, that's why I be, always I have been so afraid of their witchcraft, even if I know a lot of things because of my family having practice this, because these things are effective. They are true. What this woman did, she want to kill me. He (the *brujo*) did all of these things then, and the father died. You know, that, and they said, oh boy, that ruined my childhood, you know my teenager years, because everybody knew in the neighborhood, you know. Everybody knew. They thought that I was a witch. And the people used to say "Don't look at her eyes, she's gonna *encant* you" and all these things, so they blamed the whole thing to me.

Oh I'm shaking just to think about it because I remember, you know I was a girl, I mean, how could I? But I was laughing the whole time, and then these things happen, you know?

[Do you think that has something to do, the fact, like with Ramón's *loqui*—going crazy, you know?]

Locura? yeah I think so too. Because I think the reason her moth—his mother want me to have those symptoms, and instead of me having them it went to Ramón and the father. And it's amazing, the two people that she loved the most, they're the ones that got hurt. Well you know this lady still is alive, she still is alive, and she still comes to my neighborhood, and everybody knows that she did what she did, and she has been regretted all her life, you know. And it's just like, you know *el cuento de La Llorona?* Well it is the same thing. She cries. Her husband and her sons are dead, and she still blames me because she says I got into his way, you know. I was in *su camino.* And then her life, after being so important in social status and being so wealthy, and being so—you know—I mean, her husband died, and then the only daughter got like three or five or six kids, no husband, neither time they have husband, and then the other three kids that were in the military school and I think they got killed by the guerillas. So this woman is alone now, you know, she is wandering around there in a very bad situation.

And I, sometimes I feel like I should go and help her, do something because I feel like, I don't know, I feel responsible for her misery. But really I didn't do anything. I swear to God, and God, God knows that I was a child. I was a girl, it's like if somebody witching your daughter, you know? Innocent girl! My only fault was in loving her son. And he was the only love of my life, you know.

And, that was the scariest part of my life. I remember going to those meetings after I came back to, you know, and then after I saw this—[They let you see it?] No I didn't see it but my mother saw it and my mother doesn't lie you know, and she didn't have no reasons to lie. After that we went to another *brujo,* and I have to go like nine days, it's like a, with the same prayers, the same baths, and we used a lot of, a lot of herbs, very strange herbs you know, and I drink a lot of stuff, and I was, I was in isolation, for about three weeks. They didn't, the *brujos* thought that they should not see me because if somebody sees me, you know, they will get hurt, all the bad things that I had it was gonna go into them. So I was, you know. It was very strange. And they, they dressed me up in white the whole time, and they had to cut a lot of my hair, because they thought that my hair was doing damage and I had to lose that hair and I have to be shaved. I was purified, that's what it was. You know, purification? And I remember one of the *brujos* used to say "Lucia, you gonna be one of the most beautiful person. I know that and you can have a good future." But I thought that when he was saying "You're gonna be beautiful," I thought maybe, I come up with the blue eyes (laughs). And I was gonna grow up beautiful, and then I got the same size.

But it was like my soul become beautiful, because I never hurt, I never have been hurt anybody, and always I have been dedicate myself for social justice, very heavily. And I felt like that has something to do with me because I was working for social justice, because I thought nobody has the right to step on top of anybody just because our misery of our country. And then I realized that we, our country was so wealthy, natural resources of course, and that it was in the hands of the wrong people and I felt like I have to be, since I didn't have very much to lose, I lost the love of my life, and my brothers were getting older, and my mother didn't need me anymore, and I was already at twenty-one, which is an older woman there, nobody would marry me after that, after. I mean the whole neighborhood, the three little *colonias* knew about what happened to me you know, and what happened to Ramón, and so, you know, a lot of people, even in these days, they still think that I have very witch power.

It's kind of interesting, because I swear to God, to me, I, it's still even these days I don't believe it, but every time I think about it I shake in my skin. Because I remember going, you know, giving birth to a toad, you know, it's incredible, *mira como estoy yo tambien* (looking at goose bumps on arms). But this *etapa de mi vida es una etapa muy dolorosa*, you know, *que me convertió en la persona que soy. ¿Comprende? Me moldó y me ha, y siempre con esa, con, por esa experienca yo nunca piensa en la soldeno o la maldad a nadie, y no, por eso tal vez soy muy* "gullible" *muy naive con respecto a las amistades y con respecto a la gente. [Antes de que, y despues?] No—ahora, no antes, antes era muy busa, yo, antes* nobody step on top of me, despues it is like I, something happen to me then.

It's like this *hermano* used to call it, you can be very beautiful but he was talking spiritually, you know, he thought that I was gonna be very important, that I came to this world to, to do something very important in this world, and that people like this lady who's trying to hurt me, was not gonna be strong enough to hurt me and he was right, because during all of these years, you know, this is twenty years, or more than twenty–thirty years after this happen, and since then, I have been close to death, very very close, you know, I have been at the door, but I guess it's not my time, when it's my time, I will know right away, you know, I will know right away.

THE CONSTRUCTION OF A SELF

In the article "Ontologies of the Self: On the Mythological Rearranging of One's Life-History," Agnes Hankiss asserts that individuals structure their adult self-image in relation to their conceptualization of childhood. She outlines four strategies, one of which, the "antithetical," can be seen to apply to Lucia's story. According to the model, in the antithetical strategy:

the basis for the ontology of the self rests on consciousness of the self having been developed without prior antecedents, by sheer hard work as it were, even in spite of the original situation existing in childhood. As far as the subject is concerned, he has personally achieved everything positive or successful that has ever taken place in his present life despite adverse initial conditions by outwitting, as it were, those conditions and their logical conditions.[4]

Lucia meets these criteria, since she describes her childhood as being bad but currently has a positive self-image. The positive self-image she now has is due to having overcome the difficulties of her childhood. In spite of being fatherless, accused of witchcraft and ostracized, she now lives a comfortable life, and adheres to principles of justice and "goodness." In reference to her difficult childhood, Lucia says: "But this stage of my life is a very painful stage that changed me into the person that I am." The above story, indeed, could be what Hankiss terms a "mythological rearranging" of life history. To quote Hankiss again:

> At this level of his ontology of the self mythological episodes portray the rejected child as constantly repressed but nevertheless always brilliant, always the finest.[5]

While this may be appropriate to Lucia's story, it brings up the notion of what constitutes a "mythology." Is it fair to say that Lucia's memory of this life period is a mythological reconstruction of events, or can what she says be taken as having really happened the way she describes? Without external confirmation, how can we know that her story is authentic, and really happened as she says it did? How do we know whether or not the story is a myth, or a text? I return to these questions shortly.

TURNINGS

Turnings are important moments in a life, "critical junctures" in which an individual takes on a new set of roles, enters into new relations with new people, and acquires a new self-concept.[6] According to Lucia, her current positive self-image is due to the account given above, which she herself describes as the major turning point in her life. She was unjustly accused and suffered because of the false accusation. Yet the end result is that the experience changed her into a better person. Whereas before this experience she was tough, and initiated vengeful acts to get back at those who ridiculed her, afterwards she sought only to do good. She made a commitment to never do evil, and began her political work for social justice, work which she still continues today. In her own words "... before I was very low, a thief, I, before nobody step on top of me, after, it is like I, something happen to me then." This stage of her life *"me convertió en la persona que soy. ¿Comprende? Me moldó."*

The story recounted by Lucia is classic in that it has an innocent child struggling to get by alone in a hostile world. She is treated unfairly time and again, and finally, the culmination is when she falls in love with a rich boy, who in turn falls in love with her. They are thwarted by his mother, who by intentionally seeking to do harm to Lucia actually makes her own life worse. Because Lucia is an innocent victim, she is saved by her family and the *brujos*, who remove the evil from her. This purification then shapes the rest of Lucia's life, as she knows firsthand what it means to be unjustly accused and ostracized. She subsequently dedicates her life to doing good, because she does not believe that innocent victims, like herself, should have to suffer the kinds of things she had to.

Lucia's faith in the *brujos* and belief in their powers are made more credible by the fact that she denies any prior alliance with witchcraft. She says time and again that she was only an innocent girl, and that she thought the whole thing was a "joke." It is only because she experienced this herself that she is able to swear to its truth. She emphasizes this point, as evidenced in the following excerpts:

> It's kind of interesting, because I swear to God, to me, I, it's still even these days I don't believe it, but every time I think about it I shake in my skin. Because I remember going, you know, giving birth to a toad, you know, it's incredible.
>
> But really I didn't do anything. I swear to God, and God, God knows that I was a child. I was a girl.
>
> But I was laughing the whole time, and then these things happen, you know?
>
> And I thought that was, the whole time, I swear to God, I was laughing. I thought it was ridiculous.
>
> . . . and then they find out that I have a, a frog in my stomach and I didn't believe it. I thought that was a joke (laughs) [laughs]. I swear to God, I thought it was a joke.
>
> And then he says "That girl has a, a frog in her stomach." He just said that looking at me! (laughs) And then I said, wait a minute, that's, this, this is, how he can do that? You know, he's not God, only God can do those things.

It is clear that in Lucia's mind she believed in God, and was an innocent victim. At first, and even today, the whole episode seemed incredible to her. However, she had a powerful experience, and as a result, has changed her mode of being in the world. She confesses that, although as a child she did do harm to others purposely for the sake of revenge, in this specific instance with Ramón she was truly innocent. Thus, several effects stem from the experience. In a sense, she is punished for her previous wrongdoing and made to suffer, while at the same she is accused unfairly and made to suffer unjustly. The end result is that she is purified and made stronger. She comes to see the futility of her previous reactions to injustices, and commits now to a life of doing good to others.

The experience is a turning point in that she takes on a new role, begins to associate with different people, and takes on a new self-concept. Instead of being *la bastarda*, she is now someone with a purpose and meaning in life: "I came to this world to, to do something very important in this world." Her uniqueness has been transformed. She is still different, but now she is different because she is special and has a mission in life, which is to alleviate social injustice. Her personal history, the harsh childhood, now serves as a motive to improve circumstances for others, so that they will not have to suffer as she did.

REALITY, MYTH, TRUTH, AND BELIEF

I have mentioned that Lucia's story is made more credible, in her own mind, and to others as well, by the fact that she claims no prior knowledge of or association with witchcraft and supernatural powers. She professes innocence, and mentions repeatedly that she thought this talk of frogs in her stomach and spells was "ridiculous" and "a joke." She says over and over again "I swear to God," and demonstrates a belief in God by saying such things as "God knows that I was a child" and ". . . only God can do those things." In her mind, these sorts of things were not real.

Yet she comes to believe in the reality of the frog in her stomach, the spell placed on her by Ramón's mother, and the subsequent purification. She asserts that these things are real as she tells them, and her story is again made credible by the certainty with which she describes the events, and the emphasis she places on the eradication of her doubts.

> It was like having a baby, and my mother got it you know, and put it and took it to this person, and this person buried and pray and everything. You know, next day, when we come back, we find out that the father of Ramón died that day, that day, his father died. You know, so whatever it, that's why I be, always I have been so afraid of their witchcraft, even if I know a lot of things because of my family having practice this, because these things are effective. They are true. What this woman did, she want to kill me.
>
> No I didn't see it [the toad] but my mother saw it and my mother doesn't lie you know, and she didn't have no reasons to lie.
>
> So, you know, a lot of people, even in these days, they still think that I have very witch power. It's kind of interesting, because I swear to God, to me, I, it's still even these days I don't believe it, but every time I think about it I shake in my skin. Because I remember going, you know, giving birth to a toad, you know, it's incredible, *mira como estoy yo tambien* (looking at goose bumps on arms).
>
> I thought it was ridiculous. Boy o boy, then that day I need to go to the bathroom. It was like having a baby you know. Now that I have babies I know this feeling. It was, you know, it's just like, oh my back (uses hands to gesture). It was straining, . . .

Her story is confirmed by the linking of past memory to present experience and by the sheer physical nature of the experience. She had goose bumps as she spoke. She knows the feeling because it was like giving birth. Ramón's father died at the same time she expelled the toad. The story is also confirmed by the supporting evidence of her associations. Her mother doesn't lie. The *brujo* said she would become beautiful and now she believes she is, in spirit, by having dedicated herself to alleviating the suffering of others. Everybody in her village knows the story and believes her to have powers. Ramón's mother went on to live a miserable life in payment for her attempt at bewitching Lucia.

The truth of Lucia's account cannot be assessed on the basis of external verification—I have spoken only to Lucia about these events. However, Lucia believed her story, and I believe she was telling the truth. I consider this to be the most curious of issues raised by Lucia's account. What are the relationships among and between the concepts of truth, belief and, by association, myth and reality? Lucia's thoughts are strongly associated with her self-concept as a Mayan woman. Yet her conceptions differ markedly from what Americans consider to be possible and "real."

At this point I introduce a quote from one of Gregory Bateson's lectures which involves an experiment he performed with his audience.

> First I would like you to join me in a little experiment. Let me ask you for a show of hands. How many of you will agree that you *see* me? I see a number of hands—so I guess insanity loves company. Of course, you don't "really" see me. What you "see" is a bunch of pieces of information about me, which you synthesize into a picture image of me. You make that image. It's that simple. The proposition "I see you" or "You see me" is a proposition which contains within it what I am calling "epistemology." It contains within it assumptions about how we get information, what sort of stuff information is, and so forth. When you say you "see me" and put your hand up in an innocent way, you are, in fact, agreeing to certain propositions about the nature of the universe in which we live and how we know about it.[7]

These agreements are culturally construed. The notion of reality involves shared assumptions about the nature of the world and how it operates. Most anthropologists would agree with this, as it is a recognized "fact" that people in different cultures ascribe different meanings and interpretations to similar events. It is also acknowledged that what is accepted as "normal" behavior for members of one culture can be construed as deviant behavior for members of a different cultural group. Kinship status, marital allegiances, spiritual beliefs, and even food sources provide ample evidence of the cultural construction of social realities. Following this logic, I assert that what is perceived as "reality" in one cultural milieu may be labeled "myth" by individuals with a different cultural background.

Myth and reality, as well as truth and belief, cannot be said to be absolutes. If I were to say that it is impossible for a woman to have a toad within her, and to expel that frog by using herbal potions, I would be relying upon a biological determinism that is an American cultural construct based upon a belief in the scientific paradigm. If I could not see beyond my own paradigm into the realm of possibility, I would be denying not only Lucia's reality, but also the world of her relatives, her neighbors—her entire culture.

By asserting that her story is untrue, or a personal mythology fabricated by her to construct an integrated self-concept, I am imposing a Western framework upon her world, and insisting that my view is true while hers is impossible. If we will not accept her story as truth, then we deny her entire existence and, in fact, we belittle her and her culture by asserting that what she experiences as real is impossible, and merely a "belief." John Farella spoke to the dangers associated with a reliance on the concept of "belief" as explanation in his discussion on Navajo philosophy:

> Beginning with a fact rather than a belief-based premise in evaluating philosophy forces us to examine different levels of meaning in an attempt to make sense out of what is being said. Treating something as belief can result in a rather passive acceptance and recording of anything that is reported. Examining something as fact requires an active participation in understanding and discovering meaning. To reiterate a previous point: it treats knowledge as interactional rather than artifactual.[8]

In our Western society, with its reliance on the scientific paradigm (repeatable observable occurrences) for the validation of reality, the assumption we share is that a woman cannot give birth to a toad, people cannot put spells on each other, and the related facts of Lucia's story are explained as "coincidence" because they cannot be observed repeatedly nor verified externally or objectively. Lucia's cultural idiom allowed the expression of the above story as history, a text, as reality. However, Westerners have difficulty accepting the same story because they operate from a different cultural idiom, and thus must label it "myth" or "belief." The problem for anthropologists committed to uncovering "truth" is to accept contradictions, seemingly impossible situations (having a frog in one's stomach), and other apparent discontinuities in such a manner as to warrant continued engaged exploration and relationship.

When I read the above transcription to a group of graduate students, within minutes of having heard it three out of six listeners determined the story to be that of an abortion. According to these Anglo listeners (all women), the story was impossible. In order to understand it they had to put it into a framework which made sense to them. Thus the toad almost instantaneously became a fetus in their minds. The story of a woman expelling a toad was mythological, but an abortion story was personal history. The fact that Lucia said she had not yet had sex at that time, had had abortions later and so knew what they were, did not consider herself to be pregnant at the time, and did not think she was aborting did not matter to these listeners. They imposed their worldview upon the story, therefore implicitly denying Lucia any claim and authority to her own life experience.

In a sense, they were saying that Lucia did not know any better, and that *they* had the "correct" interpretation of the story. When I countered that to disbelieve Lucia's story was to deny her a voice, they responded that to believe the story as it is was to fail to use "critical thinking." This only proves my point however, as the notion of "critical thinking" is itself a reliance on scientific process, which is a shared assumption of Western epistemology. The listeners were so embedded in their belief system that they could not tolerate any other perspective of "truth" or "reality" save their own. They were constructing arti-factual knowledge rather than interactional understanding.

However, when telling Lucia's story to an American Indian woman, I encountered a different reaction. The woman found the story to be credible, and knew firsthand of a similar situation in which one of her young relatives had to have a lizard removed from his body. The lizard was placed in the young boy as a result of a bewitching, and a shaman was engaged to expel it. This lis-tener did not need to translate Lucia's story into a different one in order to understand it, because there were enough shared assumptions between cultures to provide understanding without denying the truth or reality of the story. In this listener's mind, the toad story was personal history, not a mythology.

In light of the evidence that personal histories are interpreted differently by members who do not share the same cultural constructs, an interesting ques-tion becomes whether or not it even matters if something is "true" or not. In his volume, *Tradition as Truth and Communication*, Boyer contends that truth is a matter of adherence to beliefs. He maintains that there is a continuum between "truth" and "falsehood," and what counts is the degree of adherence to the beliefs and the cultural salience of the adherence:

> More precisely, judging a statement "true" can result in a variety of atti-tudes, from a slightly doubtful adherence to complete, rock-bottom com-mitment. This cannot be described in a theory which recognises only two states, belief and unbelief, corresponding to truth and falsity.[9]

In the transcription above, Lucia's belief in witchcraft is appropriate within her (Guatemalan) cultural context. Obviously, she is committed to her story. Yet per-haps it can be said that, as a result of her assimilation into American culture, and because she was relating the story to an American, she had to expand upon the apparent incredibility of the story, while still asserting her belief in its reality. In a sense, she had to emphasize what was culturally incongruous from an American perspective in order to make it appear believable from her own point of view.

Upon closer examination of the story, it appears to be culturally salient in many ways. Her story is true because: (1) she was an innocent child; (2) she did not believe in witchcraft; (3) her mother said it was true; (4) she experienced it; (5) other people she trusted believed it to be true; (6) it changed her; (7) the pre-dictions came "true," that is, she became a good person, different, special; (8) it affirmed her notion of being different from others, which still holds. Finally, (9) she remains firmly committed to the story as personal experience, not as myth or fabrication. The story is congruent with her present sense of self, her cultural context, and remains "true" because of the effect it had and has upon her current status as an individual.

In his essay, "Apparently Irrational Beliefs," Dan Sperber dismisses the idea of cultural relativism, and offers a systematic way to interpret stories that appear incredible:

I have suggested that we should make two psychological distinctions between propositional and semi-propositional representations, and between factual and representational beliefs. Then all we need in order to dispel the appearance of irrationality of cultural beliefs is to establish that they are representational beliefs of semi-propositional content. Indeed, when all the members of your cultural group seem to hold a certain representational belief of semi-propositional content, this constitutes sufficiently rational ground for you to hold it too.[10]

Within her cultural context, Lucia's story is rational. It becomes irrational or "untrue" in the translation to a Western framework.

But does it matter whether or not Lucia's story is true, according to some sense of Western cultural reality? And if so, why? The story offers insight into one woman and her sense of what is real. Because it was different from my own personal experience (with toads, magic, *or* abortion), and because my understanding was that she was not lying, it challenged me to question my conceptualization of reality, belief, truth, and myth. What is personal history, what is cultural reality, and what is mythology? My resulting discovery was that reality is a shared construct, a social negotiation between individuals.[11]

I do not believe that there can be an absolute reality, a provable distinction between truth and falsehood, belief and unbelief, or myth and text. And yet, to hold the cultural relativist position, and dismiss differing perceptions of the world as "entirely different" and separate would also be mistaken. Sperber alludes to this when he concludes:

In prerelativist anthropology, Westerners thought of themselves as superior to all other people. Relativism replaced this despicable hierarchical gap by a kind of cognitive apartheid. If we cannot be superior in the same world, let each people live in its own world.[12]

To say that we live in separate worlds and that there can be no understanding of other belief systems is another imposition of the Western worldview. By asserting this separation, we are claiming that only our shared assumptions are right for us and that there can be no bridging or renegotiation of cultural values. This is a stagnant worldview, and one that will serve to impede our ability to adapt to our changing world.[13]

Reality is a fluid phenomenon which is constantly being recreated and renegotiated by individuals around the world.[14] It changes each time a European gives an African a Timex watch, or a Mexican or Guatemalan crosses the American border. It is recreated in classroom or employment situations where Asian, Anglo, Native American, African, and Mexican men and women share discussions, offices, and deadlines.

Life histories are one way in which these shared realities can be negotiated. If I tell you my life history, and you tell me yours, then together we will have created a sense of "truth" which is real, albeit dependent upon our individual selves. To quote from Watson's paper on "Understanding a Life History as a Subjective Document":

> When all is said and done, the only purpose to which the life history lends itself *directly*, that is, where it is not used as a basis for inferences tied heavily to external constructs, theories, or measures, is as a commentary of the individual's very personal view of his own experience as he understands it.[15]

If we claim that the life stories people offer us from other cultural contexts are myths, beliefs, or untrue, we invalidate the person's (and culture's) humanity, rationality, and integrity. The same is true when dealing with differences in perspective due to class, gender, or socioeconomic status. As anthropologists, as educators, as individuals, we must not presume to have an edge on the nature of reality. The life stories told us can provide insight into other worlds which we ourselves have not experienced. If we respect the narrator and the story, then perhaps together we can invent a reality which includes both perspectives and fosters understanding. Again, Watson's comments apply:

> . . . understanding means grasping the operating characteristics of the context in which the life history as a production is played out. This, it must be added, is possible only when a true dialogue is established whose dialectics break through the different contexts in which the dialogue is initiated, eventuating in a merging in which understanding occurs.[16]

The sort of respect needed to understand "apparently irrational beliefs" demands a firm commitment to the discovery of meaning and also an attitude which allows for what Turner has called the "subjunctive" mood:

> The subjunctive designates a verb form or set of forms used in English to express a contingent or hypothetical action. A contingent action is one that may occur but that is not likely or intended. Subjunctivity is possibility. It refers to what may or might be. It is also concerned with supposition, conjecture, and assumption, with the domain of "as-if" rather than "as-is."[17]

This "as-if" attitude involves an openness which requires ruthless self-examination and the courage to trust our informants. It also necessitates a willingness to acknowledge confusion, ambiguity, and ignorance. Only when we admit that we do not know, will we find out.

BEGINNER'S MIND

I do not know why Lucia chose to tell *me* these stories. However, I do know that in order to be responsible to her, and to the story, I had to overcome my assumptions about what constitutes reality in order to allow room for her sense of what is real. In the process of so doing, I was obliged to confront my own attachments to reality and view them as simply another cultural construct, not necessarily any better or worse than Lucia's system.

My conclusion—that truth, reality, or even the physical world are not absolutes—challenged my orientation to life, which was predictably based upon western scientific materialism. Although the reorientation was disconcerting, it allowed for discovery. Listening to Lucia's life history became a method for unraveling the mythology of postmodern fragmentation. As we move into the world community of the twenty-first century, this understanding is increasingly necessary. Renato Rosaldo notes that:

> rapidly increasing global interdependence has made it more and more clear that neither "we" nor "they" are as neatly bounded and homogeneous as once seemed to be the case.[18]

Exchanging life histories offers insight into the daily contingencies of our worldwide cultural interdependencies. It is also a means for bridging boundaries and negotiating borderlands.[19] However, the attempt to collect life histories must be genuine, and not merely another imposition of a Western worldview. As listeners, we must be aware of our own personal and cultural predilections and values. We must not enter the life history relationship as "experts," but rather, in the subjunctive mood, as "beginners":

> If your mind is empty, it is always ready for anything; it is open to everything. In the beginner's mind there are many possibilities; in the expert's mind there are few.[20]

Can a woman give birth to a toad? I don't know—it seems implausible to me. But I believe Lucia, and the idea that such a story could be true enriches my sense of the world.

APPENDIX

Note: translations are in the order they appear in the chapter.

la bastarda	bitch
ataques	seizures
un brujo	a witch (male or female) medos brujos—real witches
para ver que paso	in order to see what happened
por, por la costa, por la costa, y por Santa Lucia Cotzimalguapa, y todas a yendo [tengo un map] OK, vamos a buscar la mapa, yeah, y es un pueblecito muy chiquitito pero es muy peligroso y muy	by the coast and by Santa Lucia Cotzimalguapa, and all of us were going there, [I have a map] OK we will look at the map yeah, and it is a very small little village but it is very dangerous and very-

un petate	straw sleeping mat
llorar	to cry
como se, copal, [copal] y todo eso	how is it, copal, [copal] and all this
sapo	toad
encant	enchant
locura	madness
el cuento de La Llorona	the story of La Llorona
su camino	his road
como se dice? el sapo	how do you say it? the toad
colonias	small villages
mira como estoy yo tambien	look how I am also

etapa de mi vida es una etapa muy dolorosa, you know, *que me convertió en la persona que soy. ¿Comprende? Me moldó y me ha, y siempre con esa, con, por esa experience yo nunca piensa en la soldeno o la maldad a nadie, y no, por eso tal vez soy muy "gullible" muy "naïve" con respecto a las amistades y con respecto a la gente*

stage of my life is a very painful stage, you know, that changed me into the person that I am. Understand? It shaped me and I have been, and always with this, with, because of this experience I never think of doing evil to anyone, and not, because of this however I am very gullible, very naive with respect to friendships and with respect to the people

Antes de que, y despues?

Before this, and after?

No- ahora, no antes, antes era muy busa, yo, antes

No- now, not before, before I was very low, thief, I, before

despues	after
hermano	brother

NOTES

1. Victor Turner, *On the Edge of the Bush: Anthropology as Experience*, Edith Turner, ed. (Tucson: University of Arizona Press, 1985), p. 264.

2. See Elisabeth Burgos-Debray, ed., *I. Rigoberta Menchu: An Indian Woman in Guatemala*, Ann Wright, trans. (London: Verso, 1984); Benjamin N. and Lore M. Colby, *The Daykeeper: The Life and Discourse of an Ixil Diviner* (Cambridge, MA: Harvard University Press, 1985); and James D. Sexton, ed., *Son of Tecun Uman: A Maya Indian Tells His Life Story* (Tucson: University of Arizona Press, 1981); *Campesino: The Diary of a Guatemalan Indian* (Tucson: University of Arizona Press, 1985).

3. I speak Spanish, and frequently our conversations would be in both languages. Perhaps she might not have lapsed into Spanish so often if she were recounting her story to someone who did not know the language.

4. Agnes Hankiss, "Ontologies of the Self: On the Mythological Rearranging of One's Life History," in Daniel Bertaux, ed., *Biography and Society: The Life History Approach in the Social Sciences* (Beverley Hills, CA: Sage Publications, 1981), p. 205.

5. Ibid., p. 206.

6. David G. Mandelbaum, "The Study of the Life History: Ghandi," *Current Anthropology* 14 (1973), pp. 177–206.

7. Gregory Bateson, "Pathologies of Epistemology," in *Steps to an Ecology of Mind* (New York: Ballantine, 1972), p. 478.

8. John Farella, *The Main Stalk: A Synthesis of Navajo Philosophy* (Tucson: University of Arizona Press, 1984), p. 9.

9. Pascal Boyer, *Tradition as Truth and Communication: A Cognitive Description of Traditional Discourse* (Cambridge: Cambridge University Press, 1990), p. 118.

10. Dan Sperber, *On Anthropological Knowledge: Three Essays* (Cambridge: Cambridge University Press, 1982), p. 60.

11. See Peter L. Berger and Thomas Luckman, *The Social Construction of Reality: A Treatise in the Sociology of Knowledge* (New York: Doubleday, 1966).

12. Sperber, *On Anthropological Knowledge*, p. 62.

13. Gregory Bateson put forth an interesting and related argument on adaptation and addiction in his explanation of stochastic processes. See Gregory Bateson, "Adaptation and Addiction," in *Mind and Nature: A Necessary Unity* (New York: Bantam, 1979), pp. 191–93.

14. The reader is referred to the work of John and Jean Comaroff in order to distinguish the situated negotiation of culture and history from the apolitical version of negotiated reality provided by Berger and Luckman. See John and Jean Comaroff, *Ethnography and the Historical Imagination* (Boulder, CO: Westview Press, 1992). It is this more recent perspective, termed "neomodern" by the Comaroffs, that I am alluding to here.

15. Lawrence C. Watson, "Understanding a Life History as a Subjective Document: Hermeneutical and Phenomenological Perspectives," *Ethos* 4:1 (1976), p. 97.

16. Ibid., p. 128.

17. Turner, *On the Edge of the Bush*, p. 265.

18. Renato Rosaldo, *Culture and Truth: The Remaking of Social Analysis* (Boston: Beacon Press, 1989), p. 217.

19. For insight into the concept of "borderlands" see Gloria Anzaldúa, *Borderlands/La Frontera: The New Mestiza* (San Francisco: Aunt Lute Books, 1987).

20. Shunryu Suzuki, *Zen Mind, Beginner's Mind* (New York: Weatherhill, 1970), p. 21.

Language,

History,

and

Culture

"Tryin' to Make Ends Meet"
African American Women's Work on Brooks Farm, 1920–1970

7

Valerie Grim

RACE, CLASS, GENDER, AND WOMEN'S WORK: A CONCEPTUAL FRAMEWORK

Prior to the Civil Rights Movement of the 1960s, race, class, gender, and work functioned in unique ways to protect white supremacy and the Southern way of life. With the restoration of Southern political, conservative, and democratic power during the late 1870s, black men and women were excluded from participation in the dominant society's politico-jural sphere, and were denied access to authority. Furthermore, according to Diane Lewis, special measures were implemented to reaffirm black male inferiority. Since slavery coexisted with male dominance in the broader society, African American men, as men, constituted a potential threat to the established order of white superiority. As a result, laws were formulated that specifically denied black men normal adult prerogatives. Racial intimidation acts—such as lynching and the rape and sexual exploitation of black women—further intensified African Americans' powerlessness.[1]

Because whites believed themselves to be superior and blacks inferior, race and skin color were used to establish a system of segregation where blacks were expected not only to respect their presumed social "betters," but also to accept their place and way of life in the American society. In this system of Jim Crowism, blacks' movement and interactions were limited. They could not engage in social intercourse with whites which would have allowed them to attend the same recreational and educational facilities as their social counterparts. They could not vote or engage in political activities. Neither could they expect equal distribution of jobs, wages, and union representation once they obtained employment. Segregation, established and protected by a system of racism, created such a discrepancy between the standard of living among African Americans and that of whites that blacks were always struggling to survive and to gain respect for their race outside the African American community.[2]

To help advance and protect black people, African American women, because they had established a historical tradition of operating in the public sphere—working outside the home, for example—manipulated racism. Although they were given the lowest-paying factory, service, and domestic jobs, African American women's participation in the labor force helped to reduce the economic strain black families felt due to racism. With their pennies, nickels, dimes, and few dollars, African American women helped to construct black communities that specialized in racial uplift through the establishment of businesses, institutions, and organizations that served blacks' needs. Although racist attitudes and conventional norms suggested that developments in the African American community were inferior to those that evolved in white areas, they nevertheless created ways for black women to make contributions to their families and communities despite racial and class segregation and domination.[3]

The struggle blacks encountered to gain respect and equal opportunities was not only induced by race. Class formations and systems also helped. Lacking political, social, professional, educational, cultural, and economic prestige, African Americans were assigned to the lowest class status. Even with the best of education, as W. E. B. Du Bois noted, blacks were still perceived as a lower form of human life. Their skin color assigned them to inferior social positions where they were beneath the poorest, uneducated, and most uncultured whites. Taken together, both race and class created a caste for African Americans which they are presently trying to destroy. In the American society, class helped to sustain racism and segregation, while racial prejudice and discrimination continued to protect the interest of the white elite. Through racial identification, the elite was supported by poor whites, who joined in the effort to protect white supremacy. This system on the one hand oppressed them because of their poverty and class, but on the other hand made them feel valued because of the color of their skin and their position over blacks.[4]

Despite the social, political, and economic injustices class and race created on the part of blacks, both served, to some extent, as a motivator providing black women with the incentive they needed not to be totally victimized by race and class oppression. Instead, black women worked within racial and class confines to improve the standard of living for themselves, as women and blacks, as well as for the whole of the African American community. "We didn't care," Carrie Gordon said,

> 'bout how or what white folk really thought 'cause the only thing that mattered was what we thought of ourself and how what we felt was goin' to push us forward in ways that was gone keep us from starvin' and bein' totally mistreated.[5]

Gender is a socially constructed experience, not a biological imperative, that has historically been used to oppress women. In discriminating against women because of sex—biological identity as male or female—and in defining them primarily, and sometimes only, as nurturers and providers who cooked, cleaned and cared for their children and husbands, society has not had to show respect for the contributions women made to their family, community, and the American society, because their efforts were not translated into economical/monetary terms. The lack of respect and appreciation that women have experienced is due, in part, to the sexual division of labor and the way in which it has been internalized by society. Economists view the sexual division of labor as central to the gender differentiation of men and women. By assigning the sexes different and complementary tasks, the sexual division of labor creates different and complementary genders.[6] For example, in Brooks Farm, women—because of their supportive roles and because of their biological ability to bear children—typically performed household roles, including child care and rearing as well as cooking and cleaning, while men usually concentrated on inter-familial activities which allowed them to be considered the heads of the households and the bread-winners of the families. However, in farm communities—as the Brooks Farm experience will show—women, by also performing atraditional work roles, reduced the amount of power men held due to the sexual division of labor. The division became insignificant as Brooks Farm women, in addition to performing household chores and responsibilities, also planted, chopped, and picked cotton, marketed the crops, hauled crops to the gin and elevator, and gathered firewood and water for household use. What this adoption of nontraditional work roles suggests was that, while some women experienced gender oppression through the acceptance and performance of traditional work roles, others may or may not have, especially since race and class differentiated their experiences.

Due to race and class domination, black women have occupied a structural position subordinate to white women in society. They have had less access to deference, power, and authority. Historically, Western women, for example, accepted deference in their often highly valued roles as helpmates, objects of sexual desire, or the driving force behind successful men. In contrast, black women, who have played important economic roles in societies, have lacked deference. African American women, because black men were excluded from the job market, have been forced to share with black men marginal participation in the public work world of the dominant society through low-paying jobs. Because their economic role assured them power over the limited resources available to a racially excluded group, black women, on the basis of power over crucial resources, held a relatively high position within a dominated society.[7]

This contrasts with the deference accorded white women in the same society. For unlike white women, black women have lacked deference in the dominant society principally because of the stigma of race. Within the dominated society, their source of power has become one basis of denial of deference. As a result, the highly valued roles played by white women—the driving force behind every successful man and the objects of sexual desire—were frequently denied black women because black men were excluded from the workplace, while African American women were denied all possibilities of attaining a white standard of beauty. Yet against these odds, African American women's resistance and courage have been essential to their people's struggle for survival, freedom, and self-determination. For centuries, black women have stood at the intersection of race, class, and gender oppression, but they were rarely cowed by the burden of these injustices. Instead, they created a legacy of hard work and fierce dedication to themselves, their families, and their community, as well as a militant struggle against oppression and domination which they fought through active participation in the workplace and in their society.[8] As Brook Farm women's experiences will show, African American women, even on farms in the countryside of the rural, segregated South, found ways to circumvent race, class, and gender oppression to feel empowered.

BROOKS FARM: HISTORICAL PERSPECTIVE

During the 1920s, in the Yazoo, Mississippi delta, a wealthy white Virginian, Palmer Herbert Brooks, established an African American community, Brooks Farm, in the small, rural town of Drew, Mississippi. Brooks Farm initially existed as a plantation until the 1940s, when P. H. Brooks sold the land to families in Brooks Farm, thereby helping these former plantation workers—day laborers, sharecroppers, tenants, and renters—achieve their goals of self-management, self-sufficiency, preservation, and landownership. In this achievement, families in Brooks Farm became the only community of people in the Yazoo Mississippi delta, during the first half of the twentieth century, whose landownership evolved from the initiation of a white planter. During the 1940s and 1950s, the community attained its largest population. It grew from sixty families during the 1920s to ninety by the 1930s to 125 during the 1940s, and 175 by 1960.[9]

From the onset, women were involved with Brooks Farm's development; desiring more than individual independence and large families, they, along with men and children, sought to establish a self-sufficient community. These African Americans founded their own economic, social, religious, and cultural institutions. To develop an economic foundation based on landownership and crop production, men and women in Brooks Farm purchased land from P. H. Brooks. To complement their agricultural economy, they erected molasses and saw mills, gins, boarding houses, cafes, juke joints, and grocery stores. To supplement their incomes, some families created home businesses where they sold surplus vegetables, eggs, meats, and fruits. Women also established in-house sewing, laundry, and hairdressing businesses.[10] "We did all we could to make a livin' from the land and have it make a livin' for us," Birdell Vassel explained, and 'cause there was women out here who own they own land, farm, stores and business, they naturally saw themself in a different light and was good examples for other women to follow, so they could understand how to operate in a society that like to make the man the head and black folk the bottom.[11]

Understanding the relationship between self-reliance and personal and community improvement, women in Brooks Farm helped to establish churches and schools to address the community's religious, cultural, and educational needs. To develop moral, spiritual, and intellectual training simultaneously, women in Brooks Farm helped to erect nine churches and four schools. With nickels and dimes generated from chicken dinners, bake sales, rallies, pledges, and donations, Brooks Farm families, in conjunction with other black families in neighboring communities and towns, founded Merry Grove Missionary Baptist Church, East Mount Olive Baptist Church, New Hope Methodist Church, and Palestine Church of God and Christ during the 1920s; Smith Methodist Church, Christian Union Baptist Church, and New Light Baptist were established during the 1930s; Stranger Home Baptist Church was built during the 1940s; and Morning Star Baptist Church was established during the 1950s. Established also at central locations throughout the community were the Brooks High School and Rosenwald Elementary, built during the 1920s, and Rosenwald High School and Spruill Elementary, constructed during the 1930s, to enhance social development within the community.[12] "I can remember my mother, grandmother, and they women friends," Willie McWilliams explained,

searchin' for places they thought churches and schools should be built because it was the women who was gone spend most of the time takin' care of the church and school, and 'cause of this fact, they felt they had a right to want them built within workin' and walkin' distance from the house and the fields.[13]

Recognizing the need to offer more than advice and direction in the physical construction of the community, Brooks Farm women also assisted with other infrastructural developments. They helped to clear virgin land of trees, shrubs, and brushes. These African American farm women dug roads and hauled lumber to mills and to places where houses, schools, and churches were to be constructed. Furthermore, these twentieth-century southern rural black women made suggestions as to where and how houses should be built so large families could be somewhat comfortable, and they used their money to help purchase gravel for roads, vehicles for transporting children to schools, and low-input implements to begin farming. In their spare time, usually on Saturday nights and Sundays, women in Brooks Farm raised the majority of the money needed to furnish and decorate the community's religious and educational institutions and to carry out their social relief programs.[14]

During the formative years, women's work and progress in Brooks Farm were aided by the politics of separation. In the small, rural town of Drew, Mississippi, where Brooks Farm was located, blacks and whites, like both races throughout the rural South, lived separate lives, except for the instances where their occupations intersected. Members of both races interacted on the plantations and in the homes of whites, where blacks worked primarily as maids, cooks, gardeners, butlers, chauffeurs, butchers, and laundresses. The distrust that blacks and whites had of each other forced each group of people to attend segregated churches and schools, and to live in segregated housing, with whites on one side of the railroad tracks and blacks on the other. Each group also attended separate recreational and amusement facilities. White-only parks, restaurants, hotels, and theaters were created, while blacks took their meals and overnight stays in black-owned cafes and boarding houses in the countryside. The politics of separation and discrimination in Drew, Mississippi, and throughout the rural South provided the opportunity for African American rural and farm women in Brooks Farm not only to make economic contribution to the family, farm, and community, but to feel empowered as a result of their efforts, despite the racial, class, and gender oppression of black women throughout America.

BROOKS FARM WOMEN'S CONTRIBUTIONS TO THE FAMILY

Women in Brooks Farm performed many of the traditional roles that the majority of farm women inherited from the family and community. They managed the household, cleaning, cooking, and providing for their spouses and children. They also worked in the fields, and when time permitted, they took care of the sick and elderly, and organized community functions. But it was their work as nurturers and providers that was most important to family stability and community survival.

This was evident in the amount of time given to child care. To ensure that Brooks Farm survived and that family life remained stable, women implemented programs that taught children how to become progressive adults. First, they developed moral and spiritual character. In this training, women taught values that emphasized belief in God, cooperation, respect, obedience, and sacrifice. This value system was necessary, since Brooks Farm was a community that depended on collaborative efforts to survive. The essence of the moral and spiritual training taught children, according to Fannie Turner, "that they should treat each other and other people how they want to be treated, talk to people the way they want folk to talk to them, and just do unto other the way they would have folk do unto them."[15]

The role Brooks Farm women played in community child-rearing was consistent with black women's nurturing responsibilities throughout America. In African American communities, fluid and changing boundaries, according to Patricia Hill Collins, often distinguished biological mothers from other women who cared for children. Biological mothers are expected to care for their children. But African and African American communities have also recognized that assigning one person with the responsibility of mothering a child was not the best strategy to adopt. Consequently, othermothers—women who assist blood mothers by sharing mothering responsibilities—traditionally have been central to the institution of black motherhood. The ability of Brooks Farm women, like other African American women, to define, value, and shape black motherhood as an institution does not only show comparable diversity, but also illustrates the severity of oppression they faced and how they resisted it. More-over, Brooks Farm women viewed their child-rearing work as both contributing to their children's survival and instilling values that encouraged their children to reject "their presumed place" as blacks and to strive for an improved life.[16]

Women's training, in addition, involved teaching children how to work. Boys and girls learned their work roles from their mothers who, in many instances, disregarded the sexual division of labor, and taught every child how to cook, clean, wash, sew, can food, and work in the fields. "I taught all eight of my children," Willie McWilliams explained, "to do all kind of work in the field and the house, so that when they got older they wouldn't have to depend on nobody to live, eat, sleep or cook for them."[17] "This was important," Freddie Wiley added,

> because we live in a society that didn't think much of black folk and didn't think our need was all that important, so we thought of ways to make ourself, and our children, and our community be important by doin' things to make every aspect of it better despite the racism and low class status we was given.[18]

Perhaps women in Brooks Farm gave tremendous attention to their children out of concern for their welfare. During the early twentieth century, black men and boys were frequently accused of rape and were lynched repeatedly for such allegation, while African American women and girls faced constant sexual exploitation from white men. Through a system of community control where women and men kept eyes on each other's children from one house to the next and especially when they traveled outside of the community, women in Brooks Farm helped to save their daughters from the grip of white men's lust and their sons from affairs with white women who often cried rape when their sexual interludes with African American men were uncovered.

The importance of African American farm women's role in the family can be seen in the amount of respect they commanded as the family organizer. This was evident in the amount of time women spent coordinating household and work schedules to complete the work day. For example, having to work eight to ten hours a day in the fields, most women rose around 5:00 A.M. Breakfast was served no later than 6:00 A.M. Dinner was ready at 12:00 A.M., and by 7:00 P.M., supper was completed.

Scheduling became even more important when women, in addition to preparing meals, had to determine how to incorporate washing, ironing, waxing, mopping, sewing, quilting, and dusting into their weekly routine. Black farm women, like those in the Brooks Farm community, usually washed, ironed, mopped, and waxed on Saturdays. On Friday nights, water was hauled and washing began early Saturday morning. When African American farm women had to sew or quilt, they ironed and mopped during the week so clothes and bed linens could be made on Saturdays. During the canning season, farm women preserved food on Sunday evenings and during their noon dinner hour. In farm communities, a day's work began with the women, and they determined how much work the family would complete, not only by establishing an efficient cooking and eating schedule, but by their attitudes and their sense of importance to the family and farm.[19] Performing these roles and involving themselves in the work, both as laborer and organizer, black farm women compensated for the gender oppression women, in general, felt.[20]

BROOKS FARM WOMEN'S ECONOMIC CONTRIBUTIONS TO THE FAMILY AND FARM

As economic contributors, black farm women assisted their families in two important ways. Through their work, they saved the family unnecessary expenses, and by establishing makeshift businesses, they added to the family's income.

Working both to earn and to save money, women in Brooks Farm became very involved with farm production. They planted, cultivated, and harvested crops. Some plowed the fields, chopped and picked cotton, packed the cotton trailers, carried the cotton crop to the gin and the grain crop to the elevator, and made frequent trips to town "to pick up some machine parts, seeds, feeds or whatever we need," Mae Liza Williams recalled.[21] As partners in the farm business, women often "kept the books" or records of each transaction, and they supervised the children in the fields. Calculating the value of women's field work on the basis of potential cost had the family employed laborers, statistics show that a black farm woman's daily work in the field saved the family $1.15 per day during the 1930s and $3.32 per day by 1960. Stated differently, women's farm work during the busiest months of farming, June to September, saved $23.73 per month during the 1930s and $139.00 per month by the 1960s.[22]

The female farm workers in Brooks Farm were members of landowning, sharecropping, tenant, and day-laboring families. Unlike many African American farm women during the late nineteenth and early twentieth centuries who lived in old slave quarters and who were put to work in labor gangs at low wages and who often resisted this post-slavery economic system by slowing down the pace of work and by withdrawing themselves and their children from labor force, women in Brooks Farm continued to work hard to make ends meet because they believed they were working for themselves.

In the absence of state commodity and welfare programs during the early twentieth century, Brooks Farm women contributed economically by producing the majority of the family's food. Garden and livestock production provided meals for farm families throughout the year. Women grew vegetables, planted fruit trees and vines, and produced poultry. "We didn't have to spend money on food," Birdell Vassel explained, "'cause we women was out in the garden plantin' all kind of vegetable for the family to eat."[23] Because of their importance to family and community survival, these food production roles Brooks Farm women played, although gender-specific, transcended both gender and racial oppression women in the American society generally felt, because the performance of these roles constantly reinforced not only the importance of women's work, but the necessity of their contributions to community survival.

Published reports from Agricultural Experiment Stations, Cooperative Extension Services, and the United States Department of Agriculture showed that black farm women's work on the farm, between 1920 and 1970, saved approximately fifty percent of their families' total income. Using the 1940 decade as an example, research showed the contribution women made to their families' food budgets. Forty-two percent of the families had values of food produced of $100.00 and under; twenty-one percent of the families had values of $300.00; and thirty-seven percent had values of $101 to $300. The importance of these numbers is better understood when one considers the fact that most black farm families' yearly income in the rural South during the 1940s never rose above $500. For the majority of black farm families in Southern rural communities, whose income, by 1946, ranged from $250 to $400, the value of women's food production ranged from a third to a half of the family's income.[24]

Trying to ensure the survival of the family and farm, black farm women, in addition, created ways to add to the family's earnings. Farm duties aside, nearly all Brooks Farm women sold eggs, milk, cheese, butter, and vegetable produce. They also sold livestock, made clothes and sold them, took in laundry and boarders, and dressed hair for a price. An income was also earned from delivering babies, and operating and managing one-room stores from their homes. In addition to working on the farms which they owned, rented, or sharecropped, Brooks Farm women also worked as seasonal laborers for white farmers to earn extra money for their families.[25]

Off-farm employment during the late 1950s and early 1960s helped Brooks Farm women make additional economic contributions to their families. Although jobs were limited, some women found employment in factories as seamsters and machine operators. Others worked in schools as cooks, janitors, and teacher's aides. Still others obtained work from grocers as butchers, stackers, and janitors. Yet others secured work in the traditional service fields. They worked as maids, nannies, cooks, and chauffeurs for middle-class white families. Ocean Myes explained:

Although we knowed we was given these kind of jobs 'cause folk thought that this was all black women could do, our spirit was not broken 'cause we would always see the value of our work in our home and community when the children and our husband and friend would say, did you make enough to help out with things at home and we would say yes we did. . . . Our husbands would meet us at the door tellin' us how proud they was of us goin' out in that tough world—where nobody really care 'bout black folk—just so we could help make ends meet.[26]

Although Brooks Farm women held jobs that had been defined for them by America's class and racial systems, the empowerment they felt as a result of their contribution transcended the oppression black women typically experienced as blacks and women because they, unlike the majority of white women during this time, before the 1960s, operated in the public sphere and held jobs that were not always gender specific. Due to the seasonal and marginal nature of black men's work, black farm women's economic contribution to the family was crucial, especially when environmental factors such as floods, droughts, and insects prevented the family from harvesting a bountiful and profitable crop. During disastrous years, the money farm women made helped to pay property taxes and bills associated with food items not produced on the farm—flour, sugar, and rice, for example—and furniture such as beds, chairs, dressers, and tables.[27] Even with the tremendous demands on their money, women still found ways to use it to help the community and to fund social activities—dances, picnics, festivals, church, and school programs—in Brooks Farm.

BROOKS FARM WOMEN'S CONTRIBUTIONS TO THE COMMUNITY

Women in Brooks Farm engaged in a variety of activities that enhanced community relations. This was evident in the amount of assistance they provided during bereavement, illness, and childbirth. In each of these circumstances, women moved from one house to another, assisting those in need. For example, during childbirth they assisted the midwife in delivering the baby by providing warm water, clean towels, and their energy to help the mother through the delivery. Following delivery, they helped with the care of the infant child and with the women's household responsibilities. As supporters, women cooked, cleaned, and washed clothes.[28]

To show the sick and elderly that they were still valued members of the Brooks Farm Community, women provided them with similar assistance. Rotating the responsibilities, women stayed at the homes of those people who were too ill or old to provide for themselves on a constant basis. Like the mothers of infant children, the sick and elderly also had their houses cleaned, meals prepared, and errands run. At times, their gardens were worked, food canned, and water and firewood hauled. On weekends, Brooks Farm women organized themselves into groups of prayer warriors, and traveled throughout the community visiting the sick and elderly, praying for their spirit and health.[29]

Especially during periods of bereavement, women's prayers and assistance provided comfort to community members. Women assisted in funeral arrangements, child care, and housework. Recalling the help he received from women after his wife Ruby died, George Turner explained:

> I received a lot of support when my wife Ruby pass. The care of the people in this community pull me through. I didn't want for nothin' 'cause whatever I need I could tell some of them women and some of them would cook, wash and clean up for me. When Ruby died, the women done all they could to make things pleasant 'til I could do for myself.[30]

Through these community functions, women in Brooks Farm established relations throughout the community that helped Brooks Farm function as a family of people who relied on each other to survive.

As nurturers and supporters of the community, black farm women continued to perform roles that made the Brooks Farm Community stronger as a body of people. In their role as community organizers, they used their money, energy, and time to strengthen community relations by organizing activities that encouraged participation from every member of the Brooks Farm society. Like many black women throughout America, women in Brooks Farm arranged dances, picnics, parties, and community dinners, usually held at churches, so residential and nonresidential families could socialize. Meetings of this sort provided the opportunity for intimate conversations about children and family, as well as the chance for individuals to see persons whom long working hours had kept them from visiting for periods of time.[31] These kinds of activities showed that Brooks Farm women desired to establish relations with each other and other women who played major roles in developing rural communities.

Much of Brooks Farm women's work in the community and within their families resembled the work of members of the National Association of Colored Women. Within this club movement during the late nineteenth and early twentieth century, African American women in cities dedicated themselves to educating and aiding poor African American women and girls as well as to politically mobilizing black women of all classes.[32]

The success of Brooks Farm Women's work solidified their influence in this segregated rural community. Eva Glenn explained:

> When we saw how much the children and grown people was enjoyin' themself, we knowed we was doin' a good thing, 'cause it was clear to us, on every occasion, that the community could not survive without we women.... We was not only told by our husband and children what a good job we was doin' to make things better for ourself and folk in the community, but we was also told by the white women—who a lot of us iron, wash, cook and clean for—that we color women was sure a credit to our race 'cause we didn't sit back and let the men run the house, the business, the church, and everything in the community like they sat back and let the white man do.[33]

"We had," Josie Fountain added:

a life in Brooks Farm that was respected by everyone and we had a life outside
our community that other folk acknowledge as valuable work to our people
'cause our contribution was at the core of the survival of our family.[34] Through
their various work roles, these African American farm women in Brooks Farm,
like many black women throughout America, defied deference and achieved in its
stead self-respect and personal empowerment. Denied access to the public podi-
um, women in Brooks Farm did not spend time theorizing about alternative con-
ceptualizations of community, instead, they, through daily actions, created
alternative communities that empowered them.

The lack of a clearly defined sexual division of labor was one of the reasons
why black farm women's work was recognized as a significant contribution to
the family, farm and community. Black farm communities were located in the
backwoods of established towns. In these communities, black rural and farm
people lived in closed societies with limited contact with whites, except when
conducting business. Much of their work and daily living took place within the
community, and everybody worked so the family and community could survive. Although men and women performed different roles, responsibilities over-
lapped where both sexes, especially the women, performed the same roles.
Because farming was their life, Brooks Farm women worked more frequently in
the fields than men did in the home. While women worked daily in the fields,
men occasionally gardened, cared for the chickens, hauled wash water, and
sold vegetables, eggs and butter. They sometimes looked after the children
when the women were away working or selling their goods.

Consequently, the responsibilities black farm women accepted created
respect for their work, while the lack of a well-defined division of work roles
placed women in Brooks Farm on equal footing with men in the community,
even though they, like black women throughout the United States, continued to
be victims of racism and classism within the broader society.[35] However, this
attitude in Brooks Farm is not meant to suggest that men in this and other
black farming communities did not believe in patriarchy, because they did.
They, however, recognized that being "head of the house," according to Earnest
McWilliams,

didn't give we men the right to treat the women, our wife, any kind of way, not
allowin' them to do what they could to help and not givin' them the respect they
deserve for all the work they did in the house, on the farm and out in the community.[36]

Two significant circumstances explain Brooks Farm women's position in the
family and community. Women were involved with the building of Brooks
Farm from its initial stages. Like past generations of black women, they helped

erect institutions, worked in the fields and community, and established community support networks through kin and non-kin groups. Because of black farm women's involvement with community development at every level, it was more difficult for black farm men to completely subordinate black farm women, since they had established themselves not only as laborers and nurturers, but as providers for the family, farm, and community. By making the community stronger, women in Brooks Farm became empowered, and because of their invaluable work and contribution, the community of Brooks Farm served as a source of support when they encountered race, gender, and class oppression within the dominant society.

NOTES

For the purpose of this study, more than fifty persons were interviewed between 1987 and 1992. Twenty-two men and twenty-eight women agreed to answer questions on the history and life of Brooks Farm. Their ages ranged from thirty-nine to one hundred and five. These were individuals who still lived in Brooks Farm and surrounding communities. Others were persons who lived more than fifty miles away, but who had worked and lived in the community. Each of the interviewees answered the same questions on religion, education, work roles, especially the roles of women and men in the context of community development, social life, economic development, sharecropping, tenant farming, day laboring, rural businesses, family life, the roles of the church and school, landownership, gender, class, caste, and race relations. Questions pertaining to perception and attitude regarding work roles and individuals' contributions to the family, farm, and community, as well as their participation in the labor force, were also asked. Each interview was taped. In an effort to get a representative sample of life and work in Brooks Farm, persons were chosen randomly.

1. For a general understanding of the black experience and expression in America, see John Hope Franklin and Alfred Moss, *From Slavery to Freedom*, 7th edition (New York: Alfred K. Knopf, 1993). For additional analysis of race, class, gender, sex, and caste and their impact on the black community, especially African American women, see Diane K. Lewis, "A Response to Inequality, Black Racism, and Sexism," in Micheline R. Malson et al., eds., *Black Women in America* (Chicago: University of Chicago Press, 1988), p. 41; Teresa L. Amott and Julies A. Matthaei, *Race, Gender, and Work: A Multicultural Economic History of Women in the United States* (Boston: Southend Press, 1991); Margaret L. Anderson and Patricia Hill Collins, *Race, Class, and Gender* (Belmont, CA: Wadsworth Publishing Company, 1995); and Patricia Hill Collins, *Black Feminist Thought: Knowledge, Consciousness, and the Politics of Empowerment* (New York: Routledge Press, 1990).

2. For a discussion, see T. L. Amott and Julies A. Matthaei, *Race, Gender, and Work: A Multicultural Economic History of Women in the U.S.*; M. L. Anderson and P. H. Collins, *Race, Class, and Gender*; and P.H. Collins, *Black Feminist Thought: Knowledge, Consciousness, and the Politics of Empowerment*.

3. For a discussion, see William L. Andrews, *Sisters of the Spirit: Three Black Women's Autobiographies of the Nineteenth Century* (Bloomington: Indiana University Press, 1986); Paula Giddings, *When and Where I Enter: The Impact*

of Black Women on Race and Sex in America (New York: Bantam Books, 1984); Bert James and Ruth Bogin, eds., *Black Women in Nineteenth-Century American Life: Their Words, Their thoughts, Their feelings* (University Park: Pennsylvania State University Press, 1976); Gloria T. Hull, Patricia Bell Scott, and Barbara Smith, *All the Women Are White, All the Blacks Are Men, But Some of Us Are Brave* (New York: The Feminist Press, 1982); Micheline R. Malson, Elisabeth Mudimbe-Boyi, Jean F. O'Barr, and Mary Wyer, *Black Women in America* (Chicago: University of Chicago Press, 1988); and Dorothy Sterling, *We Are Your Sisters: Black Women in the Nineteenth Century* (New York: W.W. Norton and Company, 1984).

4. For a discussion see W. E. B. Du Bois, *The Souls of Black Folk* (Atlanta: Atlanta University Press, 1903).

5. Carrie Gordon, interview with author, Cleveland, Mississippi, August, 23, 1988.

6. For a discussion, see Teresa L. Amott and Julie A. Matthaei, *Race, Gender, and Work*; Margaret L. Anderson and Patricia Hill Collins, *Race, Class, and Gender*; Patricia Hill Collins, *Black Feminist Thought*; and Micheline R. Malson et al., *Black Women in America*.

7. Ibid.

8. Ibid.

9. Merry Grove and East Mount Olive Baptist Churches, Records, 1920–present, Drew, Mississippi. See also School Records, 1930–1970, Leflore County, Leflore County Board of Education, Greenwood, Mississippi; School Records, 1930–1970, Sunflower County, Sunflower County Board of Education, Indianola, Mississippi.

10. Eva Glenn, interview with author, Drew, Mississippi, April 29, 1987.

11. Birdell Vassel, interview with author, Minter City, Mississippi, April 30, 1987. For discussion and comparison to other farm women, see Janet Bokemeier, Carolyn Sachs, and Verna Keith, "Labor Force Participation of Metropolitan, Nonmetropolitan, and Farm Women: Comparative Study," *Rural Sociology* 4 48, (1984), pp. 515–39; Sara Brooks and Thordis Simonsen, "You May Plow Here," *Southern Exposure* 8, 3 (1980), pp. 50–61; Robert O. Blood Jr., "The Division of Labor in City and Farm Families," *Journal of Marriage and the Family* 20 (1958), pp. 170–74; Cornelia Flora and Sue Johnson, "Discarding the Distaff: New Roles for Rural Women," in Thomas Ford, ed., *Rural USA: Persistence and Change* (Ames, IA: Iowa State University Press, 1978); and Sally Hacker, "Farming Out of the Home: Women in Agribusiness," *Science for the People* 10, 2 (1978), pp. 15–28.

12. School Records, 1920–1960, Leflore County, Leflore County Board of Education, Greenwood, Mississippi; School Records, 1920–1960, Sunflower County, Sunflower Board of Education, Indianola, Mississippi; Church Records, Merry Grove and East Mount Baptist Churches, 1930s–present, Drew, Mississippi.

13. Willie E. McWilliams, interview with author, Drew, Mississippi, June 10, 1989.

14. Beatrice Collins, interview with the author, Drew, Mississippi, April 29, 1987. Also, Mason Cooper, interview with author, Drew, Mississippi, June 3, 1989; C. B. Myes, interview with author, Drew, Mississippi, June 19, 1989; and Steve Hearon, interview with author, Drew, Mississippi, June 11, 1989.

15. Fannie Turner, interview with author, Drew, Mississippi, July 12, 1989. For a discussion and comparison, see Howard W. Beers, "A Portrait of the Farm Family in Central New York State," *American Sociological Review* 2, 5 (1937), pp. 591–600; L. Bescher–Donnelly and L. W. Smith, "The Changing Roles and Status of Rural Women," in Raymond T. Coward and William M. Smith, Jr.,

eds., *The Family in Rural Society* (Boulder, CO: Westview Press, 1981); and Robert O. Blood, Jr., "The Division of Labor in City and Farm Families," *Journal of Marriage and the Family* 20 (1958), pp. 170–74.

16. Patricia H. Collins, *Black Feminist Thought*, pp. 118–25.

17. Willie E. McWilliams, interview with the author, Drew, Mississippi, June 10, 1989.

18. Freddie Wiley, interview with the author, Ruleville, Mississippi, June 16, 1989.

19. For a comparison, see Joan M. Jensen, *Promise to the Land: Essays on Rural Women* (Albuquerque: University of New Mexico Press, 1991); Carolyn Sachs, *The Invisible Farmers: Women in Agricultural Production* (Totowa, NJ: Rowman and Allanheld, 1983); Lillian Schlissel, "Mothers and Daughters on the Western Frontier," *Frontiers* 3, 2, (1978), pp. 29–33; and David E. Schob, *Hired Hands and Plowboys: Farm Labor in the Midwest, 1815–1860* (Urbana: University of Illinois Press, 1975).

20. For a discussion, see Margaret L. Anderson, *Race, Class, and Gender: An Anthology*; Patricia Hill Collins, *Black Feminist Thought: Knowledge, Consciousness, and the Politics of Empowerment*; and Teresa L. Amott and Julie A. Matthaei, *Race, Gender, and Work: A Multicultural Economic History of Women in the United States*.

21. Mae Liza Williams, interview with author, Drew, Mississippi, May, 1987.

22. United States Census of Agriculture, 1930–1970. See also Jacqueline Jones, *Labor of Love, Labor of Sorrow: Black Women, Work, and the Family from Slavery to the Present*; and National Advisory Committee on Farm Labor, *Report on Farm Labor: Public Hearings . . . Washington, DC, February 5–6, 1959.* (New York: National Advisory Committee on Farm Labor), 1959.

23. Birdell Vassel, interview with author, Minter City, Mississippi, April 30, 1987.

24. United States Agricultural Experiment Station Records, 1920–1970 (see the cost of food and food production in the Southern states); United States Cooperative Extension Service Reports, 1920–1970 (see the cost of food and food production in the Southern states); and United States Department of Agriculture, Annual Reports, 1920–1970.

25. For a discussion, see Minnie Miller Brown, "Black Women in American Agriculture," *Agricultural History* 50, 1 (1976), pp. 202–12; Ruth Allen, *The Labor of Women in the Production of Cotton* (Austin: University of Texas Press, 1931); Bengt Ankarloo, "Agriculture and Women's Work: Directions of Change in the West, 1700–1900," *Journal of Family History* 4, 2, pp. 111–21; Milton C. Coughenour and Louis Swanson, "Work Statuses and Occupations of Men and Women in Farm Families and the Structure of Farms," *Rural Sociology* 48 1, (1977), pp. 23–43; and James A. Sweet, "The Employment of Rural Farm Wives," *Rural Sociology* 37, 4 (1972), pp. 553–77.

26. Ocean Myes, interview with author, Drew, Mississippi, June 16, 1989.

27. Hattie Philip, interview with the author, Drew, Mississippi, April 28, 1987. For a comparison and contrast, see Dorothy M. Brown, *American Women in the 1920s: Setting a Course* (Boston: Twayne Publishers, 1987); Susan M. Hartmann, *American Women in the 1940s: The Home Front and Beyond* (Boston: Twayne Publishers, 1982); Eugenia Kaledin, *American Women in the 1950s: Mothers and More* (Boston: Twayne Publishers, 1984); and Susan Ware, *American Women in the 1930s: Holding Their Own* (Boston: Twayne Publishers, 1982).

28. Francis Walker, interview with author, Drew, Mississippi, May 2, 1987.

29.   Irene Scott, interview with author, Drew, Mississippi, April 28, 1987. Also, Beatrice Collins, interview with author, Drew, Mississippi, April 29, 1987.

30.   George Turner, interview with author, Drew, Mississippi, June 10, 1989. Also, Ella and Jodie Hearon, interview with author, Memphis, Tennessee, July 3, 1989; and Edna and Edward Scott, interview with author, Drew, Mississippi, July 7, 1989.

31.   Margaret Ball, interview with author, Drew, Mississippi, April 27, 1987. For an additional discussion of black women's work and the impact of it on social developments in their communities, see Robert L. Daniel, *American Women in the Twentieth Century: The Festival of Life* (New York: Harcourt, Brace, and Jovanovich, 1987); Linda Kerber and Jane DeHart-Mathews, *Women's America: Refocusing the Past* (New York: Oxford University Press, 1987); and Glenda Riley, *A Place to Grow* (Arling Heights, IL: Harlan Davidson, Inc., 1992).

32.   For a discussion, see Paula Giddings, *When and Where I Enter: The Impact of Black Women on Race and Sex in America*.

33.   Eva Glenn, interview with author, Drew, Mississippi, April 29, 1987.

34.   Josie Fountain, interview with author, Drew, Mississippi, April 30, 1987. For a discussion on the politics of empowerment from a black woman's perspective, see Patricia Hill Collins, *Black Feminist Thought*.

35.   For a discussion, see William L. Andrews, *Sisters of the Spirit: Three Black Women's Autobiographies of the Nineteenth Century*; Paula Giddings, *When and Where I Enter: The Impact of Black Women on Race and Sex in America*; Gerda Lerner, *Black Women in America*; Bert James Loewenberg and Ruth Bogin, *Black Women in Nineteenth Century American Life: Their Words, Their Thoughts, Their Feelings*; Micheline R. Malson et al., *Black Women in America*; Gloria T. Tull et al., *All the Women Are White, All the Blacks Are Men, But Some of Us Are Brave*; and Dorothy Sterling, *We Are Your Sisters: Black Women in the Nineteenth Century*.

36.   Earnest McWilliams, interview with author, Drew, Mississippi, June 10, 1989.

"Comrade Sisters"
Two Women of the Black Panther Party

8

Madalynn C. Rucker and JoNina M. Abron

INTRODUCTION

Throughout their history in the United States, African American women have experienced and reacted to racial and sexual oppression. However, little has been written about black women's involvement in revolutionary political movements in America.[1]

One such movement in which black women were active was the Black Panther Party (BPP), one of the most militant Black Power organizations to emerge during the decade of 1965 to 1975. Founded in 1966, the BPP advocated armed resistance against U.S. racial and economic exploitation. Black Panther men and women were committed to altering the relationship of African Americans as a group to the U.S. political systems.[2] Being a Black Panther, according to former party chairperson Elaine Brown, meant:

> committing your life. . . . It meant that we had to surrender up something of ourselves, our own lives, because we believed that the struggle we were involved in, which we thought of as socialist revolution, would take our lives. . . . It meant really seeing yourself as part of a whole, and part of an entire process, and that you were a soldier in the army . . . a vanguard army. . . .[3]

From the party's inception, "comrade sisters"[4] played a vital role in the BPP. Panther women served free, hot breakfasts to inner-city children, ran the party's free medical clinics, and organized political rallies. They were leading officials and rank-and-file members in the organization. Many women were leaders of BPP chapters, particularly in cities where extensive confrontation with law enforcement officials caused large numbers of male Panthers to be incarcerated, go "underground," or be killed. BPP women did their share of jail time, too.[5]

The excerpts from the following interviews provide a glimpse of what life was like for two "comrade sisters" in the rank and file of the Black Panther Party. Gloria Abernethy, a "natural introvert," was seventeen when she joined the party in 1968 in her hometown of Sacramento, California.[6] Tondalela Woolfolk, a self-described rebel, was eighteen when she joined the party in 1969 in New York City's Harlem.[7]

In conducting the interviews, we sought to bring life to the extraordinary phenomenon of the Black Panther Party from two women's perspectives. Their stories provide a mere introduction to a large body of evidence documenting women's roles in the Black Panther Party.

We hope that this study will serve at least two useful purposes. First, if the life situations and personal attitudes of women who joined the Black Panther Party can be better understood, something may be learned, overall, about the vulnerabilities and influences that inspire this type of political participation.

Second, if those aspects of the BPP experience which contributed to members leaving the organization can be understood, it may be possible to suggest the weaknesses and threats which should be avoided in similar present and future movements and organizations. Additionally, the identification of influential strengths and attributes of the organization which may be duplicated would certainly be a worthwhile contribution.

METHODOLOGY

Ex-Panthers are often reluctant to publicly discuss their past BPP affiliation, particularly with people who were not party members. The opportunity to engage Gloria Abernethy and Tondalela Woolfolk in an intensive interviewing process was benefited by our shared status as former Black Panther Party members. Hence, in each interview, an open and comfortable flow of communication was easily achieved.

Additionally, as former BPP members, we are knowledgeable about many of the people, places, and incidents discussed by Abernethy and Woolfolk. While the study is an interpretation based on the personal perceptions and experiences of the interviewees, in many instances we found it necessary to fill in gaps with data to provide a clearer picture of the historical circumstances referenced in comments in the interviews. These insights were added only to provide depth and clarity. The significant findings are drawn together from the actual perceptions of the interviewees.

We carefully avoid any overclaiming of significance in our analysis. We began our research with the basic assumption that members of the BPP were not a homogeneous community of revolutionary activists. There were broad differences of social and economic class, political beliefs, and expectations. Former BPP members also differ in how they perceive the experiences they had in the party. Some of these differences are based on demographics, specific individual experiences, standing (rank) in the party, proximity to leadership, and other significant variables.

Our focus on the basic questions of *why they joined, why they left*, and *what effects their experiences had on their political beliefs* allows us to identify some interesting similarities, between Abernethy and Woolfolk, despite the differences in backgrounds, length of tenure in the party, and personal experiences.

The interviews reveal the very different perceptions and experiences of two rank-and-file BPP women on opposite coasts of the country. Although Abernethy's family was not without its share of problems, it was a fairly stable, middle-class, two-parent household. Woolfolk, the second oldest of eight siblings, helped to raise her younger brothers and sisters in a Chicago housing project after her parents separated. Abernethy's tenure in the BPP was five years; Woolfolk's was one year.[8]

The focused interview was used in this study. This qualitative method provided a means of targeting specific aspects of Abernethy's and Woolfolk's lives which led to their decisions to join the Black Panther Party—and thereby hopefully provided more in-depth accounts of their personal experiences. (The interview questions may be found in the Appendix.)

The integration of structured and unstructured questions was used in the interviews. In the main, however, the interviews were structured as loosely as possible, using probes to clarify some points. Abernethy and Woolfolk were asked to reminisce about their experiences and their feelings toward the experiences, and to report their personal evaluations in as much richness of detail as possible. We were interested in the BPP as seen through the eyes of Abernethy and Woolfolk as former party members, not as a report of the objective facts.

In order to put the interviews in a historical perspective, we will begin with a brief overview of the turbulent early years of the Black Panther Party and the role of women during those years.

THE BLACK PANTHER PARTY: THE EARLY YEARS, 1966–1969

The cry of "Black Power!" reintroduced by militant activists in the Student Nonviolent Coordinating Committee (SNCC) during a civil rights march in Mississippi in June, 1966,[9] was heard by Huey P. Newton and Bobby Seale in Oakland, California. There, in October, 1966, the two young black men founded the Black Panther Party for Self-Defense. The party's initial Ten Point Platform and Program demanded "land, bread, housing, education, justice and peace" for black people.[10]

Newton, twenty-four, and Seale, twenty-nine, then college students, formed BPP partly as a response to police brutality—a problem faced by many urban blacks in mid-1960s America. The BPP platform demanded "an immediate end to POLICE BRUTALITY and MURDER of black people." Invoking the constitutional right to bear arms, the BPP advocated organizing armed self-defense groups "... dedicated to defending our black community from racist police oppression and brutality."[11]

To combat what they considered police occupation of Oakland's black community, Newton, Seale and other BPP members conducted "community patrols" of the police. As outraged police looked on, Black Panthers, armed with shotguns, observed police arrests and harassment of citizens, and advised those arrested or harassed of their legal rights.[12]

The police patrols brought retaliation from the California power structure, then headed by Governor Ronald Reagan. Legislation aimed at disarming the BPP was proposed to change the existing law by making it illegal for an unlicensed person to carry a loaded gun, concealed or unconcealed, in a public place.[13]

Six women were among thirty members of an armed BPP contingent, led by Bobby Seale, who marched into the California Legislature in Sacramento on May 2, 1967, to protest the legislation. The incident gained the fledgling BPP its first national notoriety. The legislation was later passed.[14]

Less than four months after the BPP marched on Sacramento, in August, 1967, the FBI, in response to growing black militancy in America's cities, launched a covert action program to destroy the Black Liberation Movement. The initial purpose of the Counterintelligence Program (COINTELPRO) against "Black Nationalist Hate Groups" was to:

> ... expose, disrupt, misdirect, discredit, or otherwise neutralize the activities of black nationalist, hate-type organizations and groupings, their leadership, spokesmen, membership and supporters....[15]

The BPP, although not on the FBI's first list of "Black Nationalist Hate Groups," nevertheless soon experienced the fallout from the covert campaign. On October 28, 1967, Huey P. Newton was arrested and charged with murder and attempted murder, following a shoot-out which left a white Oakland policeman dead and another one seriously wounded. Newton was also seriously injured in the confrontation. A picture of the BPP leader, lying handcuffed to a hospital gurney, appeared on national TV and in newspapers. The BPP, charging that the two police officers had tried to murder Newton, launched a "Free Huey" campaign to get him out of jail. As a result, hundreds of urban black youth across America joined the BPP.[16]

Kathleen Neal Cleaver, then BPP communications secretary and one of the first women to join the party, played a leading role in the campaign to win Newton's release from prison. Recalling the first "Free Huey" rally in 1968 in Oakland, Cleaver said:

> I know that the first demonstration that we had at the courthouse for Huey Newton which I was very instrumental in organizing, the first time we went out on the soundtrucks, I was on the soundtrucks, the first leaflet we put out, I wrote, the first demonstration, I made up the pamphlets.[17]

In September 1968, Newton was convicted of manslaughter in the death of Oakland police officer John Frey, and was sentenced to two to fifteen years in state prison.[18] Also in September 1968, the BPP was added to the FBI's "Black Nationalist" COINTELPRO list. FBI Director J. Edgar Hoover claimed that the party was "the greatest threat to the internal security of the country." By July, 1969, of the 295 authorized "Black Nationalist" COINTELPRO actions carried out, the BPP was the target of 233. At least twenty-eight Panthers were killed as a result. A typical COINTELPRO tactic was to plant undercover informants in party affiliates. Nationwide, the FBI placed sixty-seven informants in the BPP.[19]

One action believed to be COINTELPRO-inspired involved BPP member Ericka Huggins. In May 1969, Huggins was arrested in New Haven, Connecticut, on charges that she conspired with Bobby Seale and seven other party members, including five women, to murder Alex Rackley, a Black Panther from New York. Rackley was tortured to death. Huggins, a BPP member in Los Angeles, had gone to New Haven to start a new party chapter and to bury her Panther husband, John Huggins, a native of New Haven.

Evidence that surfaced during the joint trial of Ericka Huggins and Bobby Seale pointed to a violent FBI informant placed in the BPP as Rackley's probable killer. All charges against Huggins and Seale were dismissed in May 1971, following a mistrial.[20]

Black Panther women were among the survivors of a notorious COINTEL-PRO action against the BPP in Chicago. In the predawn hours of December 4, 1969, police raided a West Side Chicago apartment occupied that night by nine BPP members. The alleged purpose of the raid was to confiscate an illegal weapons cache. Over eighty rounds of police ammunition were fired into the apartment. Only one shot was thought to have been fired by a Panther.[21]

When the shooting stopped, two Black Panthers were dead: Fred Hampton, the charismatic twenty-one-year-old chairman and cofounder of the Illinois BPP chapter, and Mark Clark, twenty-two, a party organizer from Peoria, Illinois. Hampton, who was asleep when the raid started, was shot four times—twice in the head. Evidence indicated that he may have never awakened because he was drugged by an FBI informant—a trusted aide of Hampton's who provided police with drawings of the layout of the apartment. Of the seven Panthers who survived the raid, three were women—Verlina Brewer, seventeen; Brenda Harris, nineteen; and Deborah Johnson, eighteen, Hampton's fiancee, who was eight-and-a-half months pregnant. Many people in Chicago's black community, and BPP supporters nationwide, charged that Hampton—who had forged successful coalitions with white and Hispanic Chicago youth groups—had been assassinated.[22]

The preceding overview summarizes the historical backdrop of the experiences described by the interviewees. Tondalela Woolfolk was among the dozens of Chicago Panthers who left the party after their beloved "Chairman Fred" was killed. Gloria Abernethy primarily served her tenure in the BPP in

Oakland, California, home of BPP national headquarters and party cofounders Huey P. Newton and Bobby Seale.[23]

INTERVIEWS
Tondalela Woolfolk

> Length of time in the BPP: one year (1969)
> Initial location of membership: Harlem, New York City
> Location of longest assignment: Chicago, Illinois

Tondalela Woolfolk was born on September 7, 1950, in Chicago, Illinois, the second of eight children. She lived with her siblings and their Catholic parents in a housing project on Chicago's West Side. Her father, a laborer from Macon, Georgia, had been in the Coast Guard. Her mother was reared in West Virginia before coming to Chicago. At the age of seventeen, she became pregnant and married Tondalela's father.

Tondalela recalled the distinct differences in the personalities and outlooks of her parents:

> My father was an introvert. He had a difficult time dealing with society. He didn't want anyone from the outside in [our house] and he really didn't want us to get out. He monitored our every movement. I felt like he was a dictator. He was the one who gave me grounding in my spiritual development because he was very religious. I loved him. I wanted to please him. I think that's what turned me into a tomboy. I wanted to do everything he held of value, which was a lot of sports—physical kinds of things.

Tondalela's mother, on the other hand, was an outgoing person; having eight children (the youngest, a girl, died on her first birthday) did not stop her from being active in the community.

> My mother was one to be outside the house. She became involved in a block club, was chairman of the PTA at our school, and was on the board of the boys' club because I have five brothers. My father didn't like that because she was outside of the house a great deal.

When Tondalela was still young, her parents separated; her father returned to Georgia. As the second oldest child, Tondalela found that her life changed dramatically.

> I didn't like my mother being a single parent. I had a lot more responsibility. I was always expected to help out around the house, but then I became responsible for meals, and more responsible for my brothers and sisters and their appearance. There was a schism between me and mother. She began to date, and she had friends. I didn't feel like she was as accessible as she had been in the past for me. I was becoming angry with my mother, but we were still close, and I loved her. . . .

Tondalela and her brothers and sisters attended Catholic schools. During this time, she developed friendships with black gang members in her neighborhood. One of her first steps as a political activist came when she helped to form the Black Action Council with some of the gang members. While a student at Providence High School, Tondalela was selected by one of the nuns to participate in an Upward Bound Program which had a study group.

> These kids came from all over the West Side [of Chicago]. Most of us were kind of advanced intellectually and academically. There were lots of ideas and concepts being passed back and forth, and that's when I first heard of the concept of Black Power and about Marxism-Leninism. We were at the age when we were trying on all kinds of stuff, and I was excited to be able to try it on. I started wearing an Afro.

Tondalela's political activism broadened when she became part of a program run by the Ecumenical Institute, a West Side Chicago organization.

> . . . The institute was run by a group of white Protestant ministers and lay people. They said that their mission was to look at the cultural, economic and political conditions [on Chicago's West Side] and make things better. They became a magnet for federal funds, the so-called antipoverty funds, that were coming into the area. They would identify various potential leaders in the community and co-opt them into their program.

High School House was an institute program in which Tondalela became involved.

> . . . High School House was a residential setting that was half white and half black. We were teenagers. We were trained how to be change agents. We were taught that you go into a community, analyze what the problems are, and develop and implement a plan to solve those problems.

High School House students developed a ten-year plan for social change in the world and asked to present their plan before the staff. When the staff refused their request, the students took over a staff meeting. After this "insurrection," High School House was disbanded.

By then an outspoken youth, Tondalela was asked to leave Providence High School during her junior year because of insubordination to a teacher:

> I had a smart mouth and had developed into something of a rebel. I don't remember how the confrontation started, but I remember being in the classroom, and when I refused to apologize to my English teacher [a nun], I was put out of the classroom. . . . Just because she wore a religious habit didn't mean that she was right all the time.

After leaving the school in 1966, Tondalela, then sixteen, went to Riverside,

California, to live with the white, middle-class family of a member of the High School House collective. Mrs. S was a writer, and Mr. S was a creative photographer and inventor.

In Riverside, Tondalela had her first exposure to the Black Panther Party when her host family took her to a political rally.

> There was this feeling of excitement. These black guys [Black Panthers] came in. They were real black and big. They had a lot of pride about them. You got a real sense of seriousness. I found that to be exciting because white people were afraid of them. That interested me quite a bit.

It was also in Riverside that Tondalela first experienced being a black student at a predominantly white school. In Chicago, she had attended "basically black" schools.

> Riverside Polytechnic High School was my first direct exposure to what I call "Leave It To Beaver land." [It] was the first time I was directly exposed to white middle-class folks in their own setting. . . . The only white people I had ever come into contact with had at least professed to be dealing with their racism. Most of the white people I was running into at school in Riverside were acknowledged racists and didn't give a damn whether you knew it. It was very traumatic and very painful.

Tondalela, who had always been a good student, "had never heard of a tracking system" before she attended Riverside Polytechnic, which had such a system. "They had tracked minority students into less challenging academic courses." She was placed in an English honors course at Riverside Polytechnic, but never received a grade above C—which she blames on the racism of the tracking system.

In June, 1968, Tondalela left Riverside.

> I was having some problems at the school dealing with that racism. I would not stand during the "Star Spangled Banner," and I refused to say the Pledge of Allegiance. I didn't think those things had anything to do with me and that they were hypocritical.

After leaving Riverside, "well-meaning adults whom [Tondalela] trusted" urged her to accept an invitation to join a program for inner-city high school students at Yale University in New Haven, Connecticut. Some seventy-five African American, Hispanic, and Native American youths from all over America participated in the program. Tondalela's involvement in the program further honed her politics and activism.

> "Yale was part of a conspiracy to co-opt young political leaders and take them off the streets that summer. . . . There was a Black Power Movement going on

right there on campus because we invited a lot of speakers to come in. . . . They were pushing everyone to make changes from within. We told them the all-American apple pie had worms in it. The humanities core curriculum emphasized Greco-Roman values. The administration was upset when we vocally rejected those values as a smoke screen to hide hyprocrisy, greed and savagery.

I was coming into my own because I was coming into contact with other people my age who were thinking about something other than dating and clothes. That was the good thing that happened to me at High School House in Chicago and also that summer at Yale—meeting those other black kids.

At Yale, Tondalela "hung with" a young black woman who was the Black Panther Party contact in Connecticut. A introduced Tondalela to Ericka Huggins.

I went over to meet Ericka and saw her baby. What completely blew me away was how soft-spoken, thoughtful and intense she was as she talked about the Black Panther Party. She talked about repression and the economic and political roots of the oppression of black people. She talked about losing her husband, John, who was a Black Panther. She talked about what it meant for the party to be the vanguard, how the vanguard draws fire so everybody could know the danger so that they can survive.

Moved by her meeting with Ericka Huggins, Tondalela

spent a lot of time thinking about joining the party. Every other direction and every other endeavor seemed pointless. I didn't like the way things were. The more I thought about it, the more I wanted to do something about it. There was no other choice.

It was then the early months of 1969, and Ericka was in the beginning stages of forming a BPP chapter in New Haven. Tondalela decided she would join the already established party chapter in New York City.

I walked into the Harlem office and said I wanted to be a Panther. They asked why. I said I had met Ericka Huggins in New Haven, and I agreed with her. They gave me this huge stack of Panther papers and told me to go sell them. I got there in May. The New York 21 had already been incarcerated. . . .[24]

I was in the Ministry of Information cadre. The first work was going to the political education classes and selling the paper. You sold the paper out on the streets, in the public, with contact with people in the community. You kind of had your finger on what people were thinking about and what was going on. . . . I was pretty good verbally, and I would sell all my papers in about two and a half hours.

While selling Panther newspapers one day in Harlem, Tondalela "almost got killed."

I remember getting into a heated disagreement with a Muslim brother who had his head shaved. I remember two Panther brothers coming and extricating me from the crowd that had developed because this Muslim guy was saying that he would slice my throat. I guess we had kind of really gotten into it.

Tondalela had grown up in housing projects on the West Side of Chicago in a large, poor family. But that did not prepare her for living conditions in the Black Panther Party.

There was communal living in tenement slums.... You got assigned to one and that's where you were. I wasn't real excited about the living conditions. It was at that point that I learned that the living conditions I grew up in weren't all that bad.

Tondalela lived in the Bronx with another Panther woman, B, and her three young children. The two women worked as state food inspectors "because we had to have some income coming into the house. One of the white radicals [got us the jobs]. We didn't have to do shit for the state of New York."

However, Tondalela and B did use their jobs "to gather resources" for the BPP's Free Breakfast for Children Program:

It was very gratifying to go to one of those grocery stores in our community where they sold substandard products and raked all the money in and never put any money into the community, and force them to put something back. We threatened them with organized boycotts and exposure [by saying that the sisters had a choice of who they slept with].

In addition to her dislike of the day-to-day living conditions of BPP members, Tondalela was also displeased with the nature of sexual relations between "comrade sisters" and "comrade brothers." At the time, many American youth, especially those in radical political movements, engaged in "free love." Sex with multiple partners was common. The Black Panther Party, Tondalela found, was no exception.

Everybody was screwing everybody. The brothers tried to put pressure on the sisters, saying that this was something that they were required to do. B was older than I was. She would say, "Panther pussy is a myth, bullshit. There's no such thing. You are still supposed to be respected."

The whole sex thing in the party was a little out of hand. When D.C. (Donald Cox, a BPP Central Committee member), and some brothers came to New York from California, they would kind of straighten that out a little bit [by saying that the sisters had a choice of who they slept with].

The arrests of the New York 21 caused considerable confusion among the ranks of BPP members in the state, and forced the party to muster enormous political and legal resources for the defense of their comrades.

There was some upheaval going on in New York. The police had raided the Jamaica [New York BPP] branch. They [BPP leaders] sent this brother to stay temporarily with [Tondalela, B and her children]. He was kind of off a little bit. He was a real weapons fanatic. I remember knocking on the door and him pulling this gun on me or something when he opened the door. The paranoia was really intense at that particular point.

The situation was ripe for the FBI to intensify its COINTELPRO campaign against the BPP. "There were a lot of agent provocateurs in the chapter in New York," Tondalela said. She believes she was the victim of one such agent.

I remember we were opening up another crib [for] child care. . . . All of a sudden, S's (Tondalela's coordinator) notebook was missing. Everybody knew it was missing, and we knew there was a traitor in our midst. This sister who was the agent provocateur told me to go into a room and look for the notebook. She was my superior in the organization so I went into the room. There was S's notebook.

It was set up to make it look like I was the infiltrator. I remember being very let down, upset and crying. D.C. told me I couldn't relate to the office or any Panther crib anymore until they got to the bottom of what was going down. . . . I cried for about two or three days. Then D.C. called and said he wanted me to come down to the apartment. That's when he showed me how to take a nine-millimeter gun apart and how to put it together. I guess they finally decided that I hadn't stolen the notebook.

Police intimidation of the New York BPP chapter escalated. One "traumatic" night, several party members were gathered in the apartment that Tondalela shared with B.

We had a walkie-talkie in the room with us. Some brothers doing security had walkie-talkies outside. Everybody was afraid because of what had happened to the Jamaica branch. We didn't know what the police were going to do next . . . it looked like almost every [Panther] weapon in New York was sitting in the crib.

There were disagreements and heated discussions about the authority of the California people in terms of what was happening in New York . . . it became quite painful. We heard gunshots through the walkie-talkie, and I went off. I got behind the sofa. It's almost like B slapped me. She said, "You have to hang on to your presence of mind and not get hysterical or anything like that."

The pigs [Panther term for police] were getting ready to circle the building. There were cars of pigs driving real slow by our building, loaded down [with] so much hardware . . . close to the ground. It was getting real intense. That's when some party members started arguing. It upset me that people would argue and have weapons while we were potentially under siege.

The Panthers subsequently left the apartment, and violence was averted that night. The incident, which had "frightened the shit out of" Tondalela, caused her soon afterwards to leave New York City.

> I had never personally been in real physical danger before in my life. I was shel-
> tered growing up. I wasn't a gang-banger. I didn't know about getting shot at. I
> ... had heard gunfire before. But I'd never been in a situation in which some-
> body was actually going after me with a gun.
>   It was not ... my turf.... [I decided] I'm going to dodge bullets where I
> know all the alleys and I know the people....

She returned home to Chicago, where she joined the Illinois BPP chapter
under the charismatic leadership of "Chairman" Fred Hampton.

> I knew everybody because these were people from my community. I went to
> Providence High School with Deborah Johnson [Fred Hampton's fiancee]. All
> the people who had been in the Black Action Council were now members of the
> Black Panther Party. I knew who I could trust, who I would be under fire with. I
> also knew the physical layout of the area better.

In the Chicago BPP, Tondalela found better organization and more discipline
than she had experienced in the New York BPP, whose leadership, she conced-
ed, "had been kind of decimated" by the New York 21 case.

> ... Fred ... was a strong chairman.... You had to be up at a certain time. You
> had to be where you were supposed to be at a certain time doing what you were
> supposed to be doing. There was more military drill. Fred would call you up at
> three and four in the morning and ask you to recite the Ten Point Platform and
> Program. If you didn't know it, you would be disciplined.... Hampton came
> down on [party members] like a ton of bricks if he discovered they were using
> drugs.
>   Fred didn't have a whole lot of emphasis on violent stuff. He was not into
> nonviolence. He was into self-protection and being strong. His emphasis was on
> building a movement that would tear the structure down and put in another
> more humane, more equitable structure. His emphasis was on program-building.
> That's why the programs were so strong and lasted so long even after he died.

The Chicago BPP also had a different attitude about sexual relations
between men and women, Tondalela discovered. "Fred ... had very definite
ideas about a woman's role in the revolution. It had nothing to do with being
prone." A "comrade brother" whom Tondalela had known from the Black
Action Council "hit on me, but I could say no and not feel judged." In turn,
because Tondalela was an old friend of M, "nobody was going to be messing
with me."

Tondalela did party work and also worked at a restaurant across the street
from the BPP chapter office on Chicago's West Side. She recalled one occasion
on which she and several other Panther women helped provide "security" (protection) for Hampton when he debated a member of the Nazi Party. By this

time, Hampton was convinced that he would soon die because:

> ... his life had been threatened. Fred was always asking, "Why do I have to die?"
>
> [On the way to the debate] ... the sweat was pouring off him ... there was this older white woman on the elevator. She said, "Oh, you're that Black Panther. You should be ashamed of yourself." Fred said, "You old biddy. You should be ashamed of yourself. Here I am twenty-one years old having to give up my life because you sat on your butt and didn't do shit about what was going on in this country."

On November 13, 1969, Chicago Panther Spurgeon "Jake" Winters and two police officers were killed in a shoot-out. A second Panther was wounded and charged in connection with the police officers' deaths. Hampton was out of town at the time of the incident, but police blamed him for it, since he was the key BPP leader in Chicago. Thus, six days later, on November 19, the FBI put Hampton's name on the "Rabble Rouser Index," the bureau's list of "individuals who have demonstrated a potential for fomenting racial discord."[25]

Soon after the debate, Tondalela said, Hampton purged the entire membership of the Illinois BPP chapter "because he felt there were some agent provocateurs and infiltrators. I kind of felt like it was the beginning of the end. I felt awful. .... It was maybe less than a week after that that Fred was killed."

In order to persuade the community of their belief that the police had murdered Hampton and Mark Clark in cold blood, Chicago Panthers arranged for thousands to tour the Monroe Street apartment where the two BPP leaders were killed.[26] Tondalela, like most people who toured the apartment, was stunned at what she found.

> There were bullet holes everywhere. The mattresses were soaked in blood. The blood was what really got me. I was horrified at the violence that was done to Fred Hampton, who was basically a peace-loving, caring individual. They paraded Fred's body afterwards like he was some kind of prize kill or something. It showed their savagery. They had been hunting for this Panther or this lion, something that they were afraid of, and they had killed it.
>
> Until then, it just never occurred to me the lengths that people would go to remain in power. They will try to take you off this planet. They took Fred Hampton's body off this planet. That hurt, the loss of an individual like that in my life. His spirit and my memory of him will never fade away.

Tondalela, like many other Chicago Panthers, left the party. She recalled:

> There was all this shit that was happening between California and New York [Panthers]. There were a whole lot of purgings so it was a confusing period of time. I was not about to become involved in the little sectional controversies over

who was the party and who wasn't the party. I didn't like the leadership. I just did-n't think it was productive or safe for me to be involved at that point.[27]

Meanwhile, in Richmond, California, in the San Francisco Bay Area, police stepped up their harassment of Black Panthers who were selling the party's newspaper and organizing its free breakfast program. BPP member Gloria Abernethy was assigned to work in Richmond, and was among the party mem-bers frequently arrested by police.[28]

Gloria Abernethy
Length of time in the BPP: five years (1968–1973)
Initial location of membership: Sacramento, California
Location of longest assignment: Oakland, California

Gloria Abernethy was born on June 24, 1950, in Sacramento, California, the oldest and only girl of three children born to middle-class parents who both worked. For Gloria, family life was not always harmonious.

> My family was always kind of tumultuous. . . . I think the family prob-lems made me withdraw and do more thinking about the rest of the world.

As she "withdrew," Gloria began to learn more of the history of black peo-ple. With this knowledge came growing political awareness. ". . . I was familiar with the Lowndes County, Alabama, Black Panther Party that formed to deal with voting rights issues in the mid-sixties.[29] I knew people in SNCC, too."

As a high school student, Gloria was involved in several clubs and activities:

> I joined a lot of clubs . . . so I'd have a lot on my record as far as participa-tion. . . . I was in the chemistry/physics club, the French club, spirit club and on the year book.
> I remember going to Berkeley [California] with a high school physics club. Me and this Chinese girl went and hunted down that bookstore that sold "Red Books"[30] and got our first [ones]. A lot of the Asians were real radical, more rad-ical than I was.

Gloria was sixteen and in high school at the time of the BPP's armed march into the California legislature in Sacramento in May 1967.

> I watched it on TV with my dad. I remember I said, "That's it! That's it!" My dad thought it was pretty cool, too. . . . I don't believe anybody in my family ever thought that nonviolence was too rational, even though Martin Luther King was a good man . . . the armed [BPP] demonstration made sense to me.
> When Bobby [Seale] said we have a constitutional right to bear arms, I thought that was right. I learned how the Panthers had started doing the com-munity patrols [of the police] and being there when people were being

harassed. . . . I thought that was good, as compared to nonviolent marching. . . .
It just made more sense to me for where [black people] were in this society; the
disregard the larger community had for our people, knowing you couldn't buy or
rent homes where you wanted to, and the problems in the schools. . . .

1968 was an eventful year for America, one which intensified Gloria's political consciousness:

Martin Luther King Jr. and Robert Kennedy were killed. It was a really highly
charged atmosphere in high school. A lot of my classmates and I were into it. I
was around a lot of Asians. I was always the only black in my classes. I was in
honors classes. . . .

It was in 1968 that Gloria first met members of the Black Panther Party:

I met Emory Douglas, Sam Napier and John Seale at Sacramento State College.
And shortly after that, I attended a meeting with George Murray, who was [BPP]
Minister of Education then. I remember catching the bus to the meeting."

On April 4, 1968, two days before Martin Luther King's assassination,
"Little" Bobby Hutton, seventeen, who was the first person to join the BPP
nationwide, was shot and killed by Oakland police.

I think the biggest catalyst to my joining was when Little Bobby was killed
because he was my age. I felt very confident about my decision. I wasn't scared at
all. It just seemed that it was what I should do, so I did it. . . .

When she joined the BPP, Gloria was finalizing plans to attend the University
of California at Davis.

When my parents found out that I had joined the party . . . I remember my father
saying, "Well, you just get out then." . . . My mother was really upset. So I just
left. What could they do. I thought I'd been the perfect child up till then.

Gloria became a freshman—at U.C.-Davis and in the Black Panther Party.

Everything was focused on the political activity. I guess we did have some social
life, but all of my friends were in the party. So it seemed to me to be fun and
exciting. It was almost like being inside of a movie. There was just so much
excitement, so many different characters and so many things going on—all kinds
of things on the outside that impacted what was going on. To me it was just an
exciting atmosphere, always.

I sold [Black Panther] papers while I was a halfhearted student. Selling
papers, attending meetings and talking to people in the community is mostly
what I did. Then we'd have drills, marches and stuff. C.B. [BPP leader in
Sacramento] would have us marching up and down the street with guns. But I
wasn't there all the time. I was in Davis, and I'd go back and forth.

Gloria's party work caused conflict with her college roommates:

> . . . I had all these Black Panthers coming over, and they [roommates] were these three sweet, middle-class, bourgeois sisters—sorority-type sisters. I know to this day they probably don't want to see me. At one point, C.B., myself and [the roommates'] boyfriends got into a clash. One of the boyfriends ended up getting beat up. So after that they wanted me out. Their mothers told the manager, "She has to go." I felt bad, but they were right. I had to go. . . .

Shortly afterwards, C.B. and several other Sacramento BPP members left the party. " . . . it got down to a core of a few people. Some members went to jail. . . . There were fewer than ten of us by then. It was probably about half men and half women." Eventually, Gloria and most of her comrades in Sacramento were transferred to Richmond [California in the Bay Area].

In Richmond, Gloria found that the black community "had a strong connection" to the BPP because of the Denzil Dowell case.[31]

> The environment in Richmond was very impoverished. . . . North Richmond was just like being in Dodge City [wooden sidewalks and all]. It was really raw. The police were definitely the enemy. They were like a law enforcement posse. Brothers in the community didn't take that much off of them either. The lines were clearly drawn.
>
> There was a lot violence in the community. When we'd sell papers out there, these old people would be sitting on their porches with guns in their laps to protect themselves. Many of the old folks would look forward to our visits and want to talk about their lives, their experiences.

Richmond BPP members worked out of a community center run by a church. Gloria did not like life at the community center, nor the people who ran it.

> . . . D and his wife [who ran the community center] really hated David [Hilliard, BPP Chief of Staff] and the Party. I guess because she [D's wife] thought she should be in the party, but she was white. She was really this super-bourgeois white woman—like a Patty Hearst-type person.
>
> At one point they wanted to kick me out. I found their virulent, unrelenting criticism of the party counterrevolutionary, since they never did anything but make the rank and files' lives miserable.

Gloria subsequently complained to David Hilliard about the couple who ran the community center.

For Gloria, life as a woman in the BPP was essentially the same as it was for a man in the party.

> I think a lot of times, roles [of men and women in the party] were determined by your own inclination and personality. I was more withdrawn and I wasn't ever

very forceful. I would work on preparing papers for mailing and distribution, sell papers, or do whatever. I wasn't really looking to do anything but to fit into the work that needed to be done.

As advocates of socialist revolution in the United States, BPP members studied Marxism-Leninism in their political education classes.

We used to study the "Red Book," the "Points of Liberalism." . . . We also studied Huey's essays and a lot of things I can't remember. . . . The discussions seemed to center on the European philosophers, Kant and Hegel. I got an A when I took a philosophy course after returning to college later.

I thought political education played a big part, at least for me. If someone told me this is the philosophy that we go by, these are the ground rules we go by, then I could always go back to that. At least there were some principles there. . . . It's just like the Bible—you could quote whatever you want in a particular situation. . . . We studied the class struggle, the Chinese Revolution, and tried to mold it to our own experiences as black people, as a black community.

As Gloria studied Marxist-Leninist teachings about class differences,

One thing that kind of jumped out at me was that it seemed like the brothers were always lumpen proletariat [the lowest economic class, and, therefore, the best to Black Panthers], and the sisters were always bourgeois middle class. And I was thinking that if we all came from the same community, how can we have these differences? We're all in the same class, basically.

After FBI Director J. Edgar Hoover's declaration in September, 1968, that the BPP was "the single greatest threat to the internal security of the country," Gloria and her comrades in the Bay Area—like BPP members nationwide—faced increased police repression.

Harassment got to be so regular. Nothing really stands out. They [the police] were just always there, especially before dawn on our way to the breakfast program. I remember police in Richmond stopping us for putting up posters. We were the only ones in the jail. I remember being so tired, I was happy just to go to sleep. They dropped the charges. The arrest was a violation of our First Amendment rights. A party lawyer took care of it. . . .[32]

The police harassment did not affect Gloria's dedication to her party work.

. . . I saw myself as part of a revolutionary struggle—in Vietnam, China, Africa— people struggling against U.S. imperialism. We saw ourselves as one with those people. So whatever their goals were to rid themselves of imperialism or fascism, I just saw myself as connected with that worldwide movement.

The BPP was part of the "worldwide movement" which opposed the war in Vietnam. In the fall of 1969, Gloria attended a major peace march in San Francisco.

> We really didn't want peace for the sake of peace. We really wanted the Vietnamese to win. That was the difference between us and the peaceniks. We weren't against [North Vietnam's] war of national liberation, just the U.S. imperialists' ambitions there.... On the other hand, we saw the brothers that were fighting in that war as victims. There were brothers that had been in Vietnam who became members and leaders in the party. We would send free BPP newspapers to servicemen and prisoners anywhere.

Gloria was later transferred from Richmond to the party's office in West Oakland, where she had "a really good experience."

> It was real different than in Richmond because we were living right in the community, and we had neighbors. We weren't an institution like a church. We actually had a house that was like a center which served as a distribution point for newspapers. It was a center of activity. Everybody would come there.... The community people were so warm.... It was just like being in a family.... The community people ... really respected the party....

While working in West Oakland, Gloria became pregnant. By that time, she and the baby's father had broken up, and he "was with another sister in the party.... but we still had to work together. It was personally difficult."

After Gloria's daughter was born in October, 1970, she ran the West Oakland BPP center for awhile. Huey Newton had recently been released from prison. Gloria recalled one occasion on which he called "a few of us sisters together" to discuss family planning.

> ... Huey ... [said] we needed to start using birth control. I remember getting really upset because we had been talking about abortion and birth control as genocide. I guess before that, everyone was thinking it was okay to just have babies. Most of us were having what we thought (and what turned out to be) our only child.

Being a mother and a Black Panther at the same time was difficult for Gloria.

> After I had the baby, I felt really protective of her. In the beginning, I tried to make our life as "normal" as possible—walks, regular trips to the doctor, etc. After I started working on the paper full-time, there were times when I had to withdraw from her, and let her just be the party's baby. We couldn't live the life we wanted. She couldn't live with me.

Gloria went from West Oakland to work in one of the party's "survival" programs, the George Jackson Free Medical Clinic in Berkeley. Along with another "comrade sister" and Dr. Tolbert Small, Gloria helped in "stockpiling" medicine and equipment for the opening of the clinic.

> ... The vision of the clinic was to provide drop-in care for people that didn't have doctors. The average work day consisted of selling papers, working at the clinic and then sometimes going to work on other projects, like the picket line at Bill Boyette's Liquor Store. We slept about four or five hours and would get up at six o'clock and go back out.

After the Berkeley BPP cadre left the party, Gloria moved to the house where Bobby Seale and other party members lived. For the next two years or so, she worked on the BPP newspaper at party central headquarters in East Oakland.

> I did graphics and layout for the newspaper and flyers, and was in charge of mimeographing. I set that up and maintained the machines and trained other people to do them. Mainly I did them. I guess I had an inclination to do that kind of work from working on the year book in high school. I started doing headlines while I was up at Santa Rosa. I never did any writing, but I contributed in brainstorming sessions for captions and titles. I really liked the Ministry of Culture [the BPP newspaper cadre]. The comrades (Malik, Emory, Ralph, Bennie, and Asali) taught me a lot. I guess that was my niche in the party. That's what I like doing now still.

Content with her work on the party's newspaper, Gloria was unaware of the trouble that had been brewing for some time between Huey Newton and Eldridge Cleaver, head of the BPP's International Section, who lived in exile in Algeria. The trouble, which was promoted by the FBI COINTELPRO campaign,[33] came to a head near Newton's twenty-ninth birthday, February 17, 1971. Gloria recalled:

> We were watching TV. . . . This was the first year [Huey had] been out [of jail], and he was having a big [birthday] celebration. . . . Jim Dunbar had a local talk show program in San Francisco and had a hookup with Eldridge [to talk to Huey] by satellite. . . .
> I can't remember exactly what happened, but the whole thing ended up with Eldridge [and the entire International Section] no longer in the party. . . . The split was that we [those not purged from the BPP] were going more into the community survival programs . . . and Eldridge was going into his revolutionary thing, whatever that was. . . . [To Eldridge] people had put down their guns and they had become soft or something.[34]
> . . . All of us were really in shock. I couldn't believe it. Maybe other people had knowledge that I didn't have. After that I heard comments like, "Oh, well, I knew it was coming. Eldridge was such a fool."

The "split" between Newton and Cleaver devastated the Black Panther

Party, resulting in several violent clashes between Newton's supporters and those of Cleaver. For Gloria, "the worst impact" of the split was the murder of BPP circulation manager Sam Napier.[35]

Sam "had been there from the beginning for me," Gloria recalled.

> We just always remained close. I loved Sam. He was such a hard worker and he was like my idol. That's who I wanted to be like. He would just work, and he'd always say, "There's plenty of time to sleep in the grave." To me, he's still one of the greatest people I've ever known. Sam's death was just like a nightmare in my life. It was the worst thing that happened. But my commitment to the party did-n't change.

While her commitment remained firm, Gloria, however, had begun to take notice of the different ways in which members of the BPP leadership and the rank and file were treated.

> Because of personality or closeness to certain people, some people had more benefits from whatever monies the party had than others. They dressed better, ate better, and lived in better places, while the rank and file were treated poorly. Some people didn't seem to have to do any work, and some people really had to struggle.
>
> I never liked that. I thought we should all be equal. I just think some people are going to naturally go after that. They're going to have material things in life. They're going to have a car, clothes. It never meant that much to me to struggle for that.

Gloria was particularly unhappy with how welfare checks received by some party members were handled.

> Some people had to give their checks to the party, and some kept theirs and spent it on whatever they wanted to. I can remember having to ask to get money back from my check to get clothes for my daughter. That really pissed me off, but I suppressed it.

Nevertheless, Gloria continued overall to have positive feelings about her party work. She mentioned the 1972 to 1973 campaign of Bobby Seale for mayor of Oakland and Elaine Brown for city council as one of the many "good things" that the party was doing.[36]

One party operation that Gloria did not like was the Lamp Post, a bar and restaurant in Oakland which was under the party's management and generated revenue for BPP programs for several years. Party members were assigned to different positions at the Lamp Post.

> I always wanted to stay away from the Lamp Post. I didn't know what it was, but I knew there was something going on there that wasn't right. I didn't know what it was and didn't want to know.

She remembered one occasion when a Lamp Post patron was shot by a BPP member.

> I guess I suppressed a lot of things, but there were hints or shadows of things that just weren't right. My attitude worsened. I guess I disrespected Bobby [Seale] in front of a whole lot of people when he was running for mayor, and so I was sent out to North Richmond. I would no longer be working on the paper or at the Ministry of Culture.

By then, Gloria's faith in the party had started to waiver.

> I was upset, and I started getting afraid for my life. I had never felt like that before. I had always felt that was the safest place I could be [in the Black Panther Party]. I always felt real secure with the brothers and sisters. But after the shootings and . . . the Eldridge thing, people started looking real gangsterish. I felt I had to be very careful.

After watching a 1973 appearance of Newton on William F. Buckley's television show, "Firing Line," Gloria decided to leave the party:

> . . . Huey was going on and on, and I thought he was really evading these questions. Then M told me he [Huey] was on cocaine. I really thought the rules in the party about no drugs were true. . . . I was really naive.[37]

LIFE AFTER THE BLACK PANTHER PARTY, AND CURRENT VIEWS ABOUT THEIR EXPERIENCES

After Tondalela Woolfolk left the Black Panther Party, she remembers,

> I went and stayed in a hotel room. It was very painful because there was no other direction I had set out for myself or thought about. So I had to pull pieces of myself back in and decide what direction I was going to go in and what I was going to do with my life.

Tondalela later worked in the campaign to defeat Cook County State's Attorney Edward Hanrahan, the BPP's main nemesis in Chicago. [Hanrahan, at the FBI's request, issued the order for the police raid in which Fred Hampton and Mark Clark were killed.] Later she attended Nazareth College in Kalamazoo, Michigan, where her mother had moved. Now forty-four, Tondalela works as an affirmative action compliance officer for the U.S. Department of Labor in Grand Rapids, Michigan.[38]

Gloria Abernethy experienced similar disillusionment after she left the BPP. "I was really in shock for about a two-month period, but it seemed like a year," she recalled. "What affected me most was being cut off from your whole life. All principles and everything that you lived for was just gone. For years, I was really messed up."

Gloria later joined other community groups, like the National Committee to

Overturn the Bakke Decision. "They never demanded that kind of commitment [like the BPP]. Joining organizations helped me get a social life again."

Gloria eventually did clerical work and became a draftsman. After returning to college, she became an engineering technician. Today, Gloria, forty-four, is employed as an analyst in Sacramento, California. Her daughter is now twenty-four.[39]

CONCLUSION: ANALYSIS AND IMPLICATIONS

The following analysis summarizes the experiences of Gloria Abernethy and Tondalela Woolfolk in the Black Panther Party. The analysis provides us with a number of insights into some of the typical motives and expectations of women who joined the BPP, and suggests a number of factors which influenced their decisions to leave.

Why They Joined

Although Gloria and Tondalela had very different personal/family circumstances leading to their joining the BPP, they both expressed a deep sense of alienation from the political and social mainstream. Although Tondalela considered herself a very good student, she recalls "feeling really estranged from everything" during her adolescent years.

> I was reading Russian authors, [like] Dostoyvsky, and black authors [like] Ralph Ellison, really depressing things. I really didn't have an opportunity to discuss the ideas I was reading. When I was thirteen and in the eighth grade, I had this intense feeling of alienation."[40]

Gloria, also a top achiever in school, remembers focusing on some serious issues at an early age.

> ... I remember doing some papers in high school about revolutionary leaders like Marcus Garvey, W. E. B. Du Bois, and Malcolm X. I was always really serious, and even at age twelve, I can remember knowing about Nelson Mandela and about the struggles in South Africa."[41]

For both women, family problems seemed to heighten their feelings of alienation.

Tondalela recalled that her mother was persuaded by a high school counselor to allow Tondalela to live at the school's convent for awhile, so that Tondalela would have more time for herself. " ... my home life was unstable. I had too much responsibility for my brothers and sisters, and I really needed time and space to pursue my own studies ..."[42]

Gloria remarked: "My family was so involved in their own domestic issues. We'd all go in our own directions whenever there was a crisis. It wasn't like we were interacting ..."[43]

Additional factors which seem to have significantly influenced both women's decisions to join the Black Panther Party include: extreme *dissatisfaction* and anger about the political circumstances for blacks in America; *disillusionment* with nonviolent strategies; and a sense of *excitement* and romanticism associated with revolutionary struggle in general, and the Black Panther Party in particular.

Regarding the excitement and romanticism of joining the BPP, Tondalela said:

> I have to admit I kind of romanticized the whole thing, to die in the revolution, to die to make things right. . . . At least my life would be for something . . . if that meant that all kinds of power and repression were going to come down on me, fine. Everybody dies anyway.[44]

For Gloria, joining the BPP was:

> . . . a lifelong commitment, but I didn't know how long that would be. I didn't expect to live a long after all. . . . I just thought that [the BPP] was revolutionary. It was just going to be war, and whatever came up, that's what I would do.[45]

Why They Left

A comparison of the experiences which led each woman to leave the party reveals few, but noteworthy similarities. Both women had significant difficulties in leaving, and experienced a deep sense of loss and displacement. Because Gloria's tenure in the party was longer than that of Tondalela's, Gloria may have had a longer and more painful period of adjustment after she left the BPP. Of her period of readjustment, Gloria said:

> What affected me the most was being cut off from your whole life. All principles and everything that you lived for was just gone. And to this day I'm still sorting out what was the good part and what would I have done differently today. But for years, I was really messed up . . . I guess the comradeship, people in the party, and then feeling a part of a larger movement were the things I most valued in the party.[46]

Tondalela also expressed an enormous sense of loss in leaving the party:

> All of a sudden the organization I had devoted my life to was gone. It was like there was this huge void that I was suddenly existing in. So I kind of felt like I was floating out there. I was rudderless.[47]

Both unequivocally expressed no regrets about their involvement in the BPP. When asked if she had regrets about her participation in the party, Tondalela responded, "none whatsoever. I would definitely do it again."[48]

Gloria continued to embrace organizational involvement after her readjustment, although the commitment level was minimal compared to the demands of life in the BPP. However, Tondalela, who had a brief and intense experience in the BPP, completely shunned any organizational involvement.[49]

Both women reflected on two insights they had about their leaving the BPP. First, they said, the principle of "criticism and self-criticism," which was one of the party's most adamantly espoused principles, borrowed from Chinese communist leader Mao Tse-tung,[50] was not faithfully or effectively practiced. In referring to the financial, legal, and political problems arising from Huey Newton's incarceration, release, and subsequent controversial style of leadership, Tondalela reflected:

> I didn't want to spend all my time keeping Huey out of jail. I didn't think that was the purpose of the struggle. At that point I guess Huey was a legend. . . . I can imagine what prison can do. Huey was a casualty and we should have treated him as such. I think it came from a lack of adequate self-criticism. At some point, Huey became a shell of the person who started the Black Panther Party.[51]

Gloria also recalled feelings of confusion created by blatant contradictions between theory and practice exemplified by the BPP leadership.

> I was disillusioned. You couldn't touch the leadership anymore. When we started out, there was criticism and self-criticism and you felt you could really say something to somebody, and that there were principles to base whether this was right or not. But then it wasn't like that anymore . . . I regret that I couldn't take a stand about things that I didn't like and the direction the party was going to.[52]

Second, the lack of critical theoretical analysis and the blind acceptance of revolutionary ideology exported from other struggles contributed to a weak theoretical foundation in the BPP. Consequently, there was no long-range political strategy, which left the organization vulnerable to reactionary responses. Tondalela remarked:

> The most important lesson I learned was that you could not take a theory and apply it to a situation. That's not the way you did things. You did research to find out what the situation was and you formed a hypothesis and you tested it out and you learned about the facts and the reality of the situation. So your theory evolved from reality. You could not take the Algerian revolution or the Cuban revolution and bring [them] to the West Side of Chicago because the dynamics were different and that would be suicide.[53]

Although Gloria thought "we were very innovative," she is in agreement with Tondalela that "we needed to continue to study."

> We should have been more analytical and really examined how closely we wanted to be aligned with Marxism-Leninism and history as it was presented to us. We should have been more analytical and not just swallowed it because it was given to us from progressive forces. We could have improved upon it.[54]

The combination of negative impacts—the FBI COINTELPRO attacks and informant infiltration, drug abuse and "gangsterism," deteriorated or absent leadership, personal fear, poor living conditions, weak family supports, and misplaced priorities—were among the important issues reported by Tondalela and Gloria which influenced their decisions to leave the Black Panther Party.[55]

Regarding the status of women in the BPP, Gloria and Tondalela seem to have had different experiences and observations. These observations are not contradictory, and seem to be at least partially attributed to differences in actual practices and politics among the BPP chapters and branches. Gloria believed that most of the rank-and-file men in the BPP were "more progressive than most men out on the streets. I never felt discriminated against because I was a woman," she recalled. Elaborating, Gloria said:

> In Sacramento, we learned to clean and break down guns. I also took a rifle class at school. I really liked that. I was good, too. I got up to marksman level. In the party, men and women pretty much got the same training. I think a lot of times, roles [in the BPP] were determined by your own inclination and personality. Among the leadership, I couldn't say if there was discrimination based on sex, anymore than in the general community at the time. Within the rank and file, I felt I was respected as a woman. It seemed like it was balanced. We were comrades. Even in sexual relations, things seemed to balance out too.[56]

Tondalela, on the other hand, describes common sexual exploitation in the New York BPP chapter until party representatives from California "would kind of straighten it out...." Her experiences in Chicago were more balanced under Fred Hampton's leadership. However, she said that Fred was frequently overprotective of the "softies."

> ... those who were experienced in street violence more than likely would be in the security cadre. And those of us who were more bookish or studious were in the information cadre. When anything went down on the street Fred made sure that all his softies were under ... cover. I thought it was kind of a bully position to take.[57]

This statement is fairly consistent with Gloria's view that inclination and personality largely dictated one's role or status within the party. In general, opportunities seemed available for those with interests, skills, and inclination for frontline or leadership roles.[58]

Current Political Beliefs

Both Gloria and Tondalela have maintained a "revolutionary" outlook over the years. In fact, similarities in their current political beliefs and attitudes are quite strong. There is a high degree of concern for the lack of current political leadership, quality education for black children, functional means of self-sufficiency, and economic empowerment. Both women have a broad international political perspective. Both women prefer that current progress in addressing these issues be addressed nonviolently. However, they maintain their beliefs in armed struggle as a legitimate reaction to violence and oppression—but only as a last resort.[59]

CONCLUSION

The Black Panther Party represented a vehicle for expressing the critical needs and interests of a significant segment of the black population during a particularly vulnerable period in American history.[60] The party spoke to the primary needs of all human beings—that is, to be safe, free from hunger, cold, poverty, and ignorance. Its strongest doctrine—the right of self-defense—was the guiding principle in the BPP's movement to end police brutality, as well as to feed, clothe, and educate the community. While the BPP had its share of sexually based issues, women made up approximately 50 percent of the organization's leadership, and many women functioned in relatively important and responsible positions.

The experiences of Tondalela Woolfolk and Gloria Abernethy in the Black Panther Party put both women on the edge of personal freedom, for however brief a period of time. Both felt they had found their calling in life, and were willing to pay the ultimate costs to fulfill their aspirations. The men and women of the BPP became their true life heroes. Despite all the hardships and pain, both women, for a time, experienced the liberation of being totally committed and dedicated to a cause. While there may have been a significant loss in the momentum of the two women's political activism over the years, the positive feelings about their experiences and the intensity of their beliefs in and loyalties to the struggle continue.[61]

APPENDIX

Sample Interview Questions
1. Describe what was happening in your personal life just before your decision to join the Black Panther Party (BPP).
2. What political events motivated your desire to participate in the Black Liberation Movement?
3. Describe your experience in the BPP.
4. Describe what was happening just prior to your exit from the BPP.
5. What influenced your decision to leave?
6. How did you feel about leaving the BPP?
7. Describe your experience after you left the BPP.
8. What do you believe is the most serious problem facing African Americans today?
9. Do you believe radical political change will be necessary for achieving social and political justice?
10. Describe your political activity since you left the BPP.

NOTES

1. By revolutionary political movements, we mean those that denounce capitalism and advocate an explicitly socialist ideology. Works by black women who belonged to revolutionary groups in America include four written by former members of the Black Panther Party: Elaine Brown, *A Taste of Power: A Black Woman's Story* (New York: Pantheon Books, 1992); Regina Jennings, "A Panther Remembers," *Essence* (21 February, [1991] 122); Akua Njeri (formerly Deborah Johnson), *My Life With the Black Panther Party* (Oakland, CA: Burning Spear Publications, 1991); and Assata Shakur, *Assata, An Autobiography* (Westport, CT: Lawrence Hill and Co., 1987). See also Angela Davis, *Angela Davis, An Autobiography* (New York: International Publishers, 1988), reprint.

2. John T. McCartney, *Black Power Ideologies: An Essay in African American Political Thought* (Philadelphia: Temple University Press, 1992), pp. 133–47; William L. Van Deburg, *New Day in Babylon: The Black Power Movement and American Culture, 1965–1975* (Chicago: University of Chicago Press, 1992), pp. 155–65; Black Panther Party Platform and Program, October 1966 (hereafter BPP Platform); Huey P. Newton, "In Defense of Self-Defense," *The Black Panther Black Community News Service* (March 7, 1970), p. 12; and also by Newton, *War Against the Panthers: A Study of Repression in America,* Ph.D. dissertation, University of California-Santa Cruz, 1980, pp. 33–37.

3. Henry Hampton and Steve Fayer with Sarah Flynn, *Voices of Freedom: An Oral History of the Civil Rights Movement from the 1950s through the 1980s* (New York: Bantam Books, 1990), pp. 371–72.

4. The term given to women who belonged to the Black Panther Party. Male BPP members were called "comrade brothers."

5. Brown, pp. 3–5, 11, 304, 410–11; Committee on Internal Security, House of Representatives (hereafter Committee on Internal Security, *Staff Study on . . . the Black Panther Black Community News Service,* pp. 7–9, 30, 37.

6. Gloria Abernethy, Sacramento, CA, July 12, 1992, interview by Madalynn C. Rucker.

7. Tondalela Woolfolk, Kalamazoo, MI, June 13, 1992, interview by JoNina M. Abron.

8. Abernethy, interview; Woolfolk, interview.

9. Clayborne Carson, *In Struggle: SNCC and the Black Awakening of the 1960s* (Cambridge, MA: Harvard University Press), 1981, pp. 209–10.

10. BPP Platform; Huey P. Newton, *Revolutionary Suicide* New York: Harcourt Brace Jovanovich, 1973, pp. 110–13; Bobby Seale, *Seize the Time: The Story of the Black Panther Party and Huey P. Newton* (Baltimore, MD: Black Classic Press, 1991), reprint, pp. 59–69.

11. BPP Platform.

12. Newton, *Revolutionary Suicide,* pp. 120–26; Seale, pp. 85–99.

13. Newton, *Revolutionary Suicide,* pp. 146–47.

14. Hampton, p. 368; Newton, *Revolutionary Suicide,* pp. 149–52; Seale, pp. 148–64.

15. Senate Select Committee To Study . . . Intelligence Activities (hereafter Church Committee), Book III, p. 187.

16. Newton, *Revolutionary Suicide,* pp. 171–78.

17. Sister Julia Herve, "Black Scholar Interviews Kathleen Cleaver," *The Black Scholar* 3 December, 1971: 56.

18. Newton, *Revolutionary Suicide,* p. 242.

19. Church Committee, Book III, pp. 187–88.

20. Brown, pp. 160–67, 180; Kenneth O'Reilly, *"Racial Matters": The FBI's Secret File on Black America, 1960–1972* New York: Free Press, 1989, pp. 305–10; "Fascist Federal, State and Local Pigs Conspire to Destroy New Haven Leadership," *The Black Panther* (June 7, 1969), p. 8; and Donald Freed, *Agony in New Haven: The Trial of Bobby Seale, Ericka Huggins and the Black Panther Party* (New York: Simon and Schuster, 1973), pp. 15–17, 316. Besides Ericka Huggins, the other women BPP members arrested in the Rackley case were Francis Carter, Maude Francis, Peggy Hudgins, Rose Smith, and Jeannie Wilson. John Huggins and apprentice "Bunchy" Carter, leaders of the Los Angeles BPP Chapter, were shot and killed by members of US, a black nationalist group that was a rival of the BPP in Los Angeles. According to the Church Committee, the FBI fueled the differences between the BPP and US by sending inflammatory anonymous letters to the two groups.

21. Commission of Inquiry into the Black Panthers and the Police (hereafter Commission of Inquiry), *Search and Destroy* (New York City: Metropolitan Applied Research Center, 1973), pp. vii–ix, 31–39; O'Reilly, pp. 310–16.

22. Hampton, p. 534; Njeri, pp. 39, 42; Commission of Inquiry, pp. 7–10.

23. Woolfolk, interview; Abernethy, interview.

24. Afeni Shakur, "Fascist Courts Try N.Y. Panther 21," *The Black Panther* (February 7, 1970), pp. 10–11. Twenty-one BPP members were arrested in New York City on April 2, 1969, on charges of conspiring to blow up several department stores and a police station and for possession of dangerous explosives. Six of the "21" were women: Rosalind Bennett, Joan Bird, Rosemary Byrd, Delores Patterson, Afeni Shakur, and Sharon Willilams. Thirteen of the "21" were subsequently tried, each charged with twelve different crimes. They were acquitted on all charges in May, 1971, following the longest trial in the history of New York state.

25. O'Reilly, pp. 276, 311.

26. Hampton, p. 537.

27. Woolfolk, interview.

28. Abernethy, interview.

29. Carson, pp. 164–166.

30. The "Red Book," the popular name given to *Mao Tse-tung's Quotations*, is a collection of frequently cited speeches and pamphlets by the late Chinese communist leader. The "Red Book" was highly regarded by many American radical activists in the late 1960s and early 1970s. In the early days of the BPP, party members sold the "Red Book"—primarily to white radicals—to raise money to buy guns. See Seale, pp. 79–85.

31. Dowell, a black man, twenty-two, was shot to death by a white deputy sheriff in Richmond, California, on April 1, 1967. There was considerable conflicting information about Dowell's death reported by eyewitnesses, the coroner's office and the police department. Dowell's family asked the BPP for support in the case. "Why Was Denzil Dowell Killed?" was the front cover story in the first issue of *The Black Panther* (April 25, 1967). Also see Newton, *Revolutionary Suicide*, pp. 137–44; and Seale, pp. 134–47.

32. "Pig Harassment of Richmond Panthers," *The Black Panther* (March 7, 1970), pp. 13, 16. On February 13, 1970, Gloria Abernethy and BPP member Eugene Balthazar were arrested by Richmond police while putting up posters advertising party programs.

33. Church Committee, Book III, pp. 200–207.
34. Newton, *Revolutionary Suicide*, pp. 300–303; Newton, "On the Defection of Eldridge Cleaver from the Black Panther Party and the Defection of the Black Panther Party from the Black Community," *The Black Panther* (April 17, 1971), pp. C–F.
35. Napier was murdered in April 1971, in one of the many violent clashes that occurred between supporters of Cleaver and Newton. See David Hilliard and Lewis Cole, *This Side of Glory: The Autobiography of David Hilliard and the Story of the Black Panther Party* (Boston: Little, Brown and Co., 1993), pp. 322–26.
36. In April 1973, Bobby Seale ran for mayor, and Elaine Brown ran for city council in the municipal elections in Oakland, CA. In a field of four mayoral candidates, Seale finished a strong second, forcing incumbent John Reading into a runoff election in May. Although Seale lost the runoff (Brown also lost), the BPP registered 30,000 new voters, paving the way for the election of Oakland's first black mayor, Lionel Wilson, in 1977. See Rod Bush, *The New Black Vote* (San Francisco: Synthesis Publications, 1984), pp. 323–25.
37. Abernethy, interview. According to the Rules of the Black Panther Party National Headquarters, "Any party member found shooting narcotics will be expelled from this party." See *The Black Panther* (February 7, 1970), p. 18.
38. Woolfolk, interview; Commission of Inquiry, p. 8.
39. Abernethy, interview.
40. Woolfolk, interview.
41. Abernethy, interview.
42. Woolfolk, interview.
43. Abernethy, interview.
44. Woolfolk, interview.
45. Abernethy, interview.
46. Ibid.
47. Woolfolk, interview.
48. Ibid.
49. Abernethy, interview; Woolfolk, interview. Since Woolfolk was interviewed in 1992, she has resumed some organizational involvement.
50. Stewart Fraser, Introduction, *Mao Tse-tung's Quotations* (Nashville, TN: Peabody College International Center, 1967), pp. 258–67.
51. Woolfolk, interview.
52. Abernethy, interview.
53. Woolfolk, interview.
54. Abernethy, interview.
55. Ibid.; Woolfolk, interview.
56. Abernethy, interview.
57. Woolfolk, interview.
58. Abernethy, interview.
59. Ibid.; Woolfolk, interview.
60. McCartney, pp. 187–89; Van Deburg, pp. 9–10, 51.
61. Abernethy, interview; Woolfolk, interview.

From the Inside Out

Survival and Continuity in African American Women's Oral Narratives

9

Gwendolyn Etter-Lewis

O ral tradition in the African American community is a cultural form/practice[1] that has been resistent to the hazards of assimilation. Beginning with slave narratives (both spoken and written, published and unpublished) and continuing to the present, African Americans have persisted in articulating their life stories within and outside their communities. The written text of a slave narrative, an example of oral practice outside the community, was used as a public document to support abolition. White audiences were galvanized and outraged at the candid accounts by slaves and ex-slaves. However, African American life histories/narratives had a much wider dimension. There also was an internal telling created for a kindred audience and situated within the privacy of the family. More than folksy recollections of a distant past, these complex "survival" stories have served a variety of functions for both old and new generations. Thus, the following discussion focuses on selected survival stories/family histories embedded in oral narratives of African American women aged from sixty-one to 101.[2] Issues of social identity and culture maintenance provide a framework for analysis.

THE AFRICAN AMERICAN ORAL TRADITION

Studies and accounts of African American oral tradition have tended to concentrate on folktales[3]; and their respective connections to the African motherland. Data from these studies/accounts are extremely informative and significant. Nonetheless, the oral tradition does not begin and end with folktales. The rich variety of oral narratives in the African American community encompasses a diversity of forms (for instance, riddles, jokes, ghost stories, legends, and so on).

Among these forms are family histories or renderings/tellings of real-life experiences, events, and ancestors, passed down from generation to generation within the same family. I refer to these accounts as "survival stories" because one of the common themes found in all of them is the endurance of the family through times of hardship and prosperity.

Scholars suggest that, well into the last half of the twentieth century, most African American families, contrary to popular stereotypes, were close-knit and functioned according to a strong internal family structure. Their survival as a collective was powerful evidence of their ability to be resistent and resilient.[4] According to Robert Hill, African American families have survived because of several central attributes: "strong kinship bonds, strong achievement orientation, adaptability of family roles, strong religious orientation, and strong work orientation."[5] These qualities were neither accidental occurrences nor desperate attempts to survive, but, rather, well-designed strategies for the maintenance and long-term propagation of the African American family. These central attributes were woven into family structure through a variety of tactics, including oral family histories passed down from one generation to the next. As Alex Haley once observed links to his past, including African ancestors, were embedded in family stories:[6]

> Every summer that I can remember growing up there in Henning, my grandmother would have, as visitors, members of the family who were always women, always of her general age range, the late forties, early fifties. They came from places that sounded pretty exotic to me. . . . And every evening, after the dishes were washed, they would go out on the front porch and sit in cane-bottomed rocking chairs, and I would always sit behind grandma's chair. And every single evening of those summers, unless there was some particular hot gossip that would overrule it, they would talk about otherwise the self same thing. It was bits and pieces and patches of what I later would learn was a long narrative history of the family which had been passed down literally across generations.

What appeared to be empty, habitual behavior (that is, sitting on the front porch everyday after dinner in the summer) was not only a means of socializing, but also a way of passing down and elaborating on the family history. Had this routine not been a consistent practice in Haley's family, he might never have known the "bits and pieces and patches"[7] that he later blended into a fascinating novel that electrified the American public.

LANGUAGE AND IDENTITY

The connection between language and identity (individual and group) is complex and often very subtle. However, when examined within the context of a group, that connection becomes more distinct. Similarly, race/ethnicity as a characteristic of group membership and behavior is equally difficult to define. Edwards argues that ethnicity can be regarded as a "sense of group identity deriving from real or perceived common bonds such as language, race, or religion,"[8] and that it is "an involuntary state in which members share common socialisation practices or culture."[9] While it would be erroneous to insist that *all* African Americans share an identical sense of peoplehood,[10] it certainly is not incorrect to suggest that the "involuntary" nature of ethnic identity makes for a wide net regardless of an individual's personal beliefs or willingness to be included.

Furthermore, Edwards indicates that communicative and symbolic functions of language are separated by the value of language as an "emblem of groupness."[11] In essence, determining meaning beyond words on a page is contingent on a "cultural continuity in which language is embedded, and which is not open to all."[12] Thus, African American families established cultural continuity through ritual behavior (such as sitting on the porch in the summer after dinner, family reunions, modern-day Kwanzaa celebrations and so on). These events, which brought all members of the family together, provided a safe and private context for retelling the past. Words and phrases of family stories were embedded in the bonds of kinship and in the spirit of survival. African American oral family histories are significant not only because of their sociohistorical content, but also because of their function as a means of establishing group solidarity.

In addition, Gumperz emphasizes the importance of language in that "social identity and ethnicity are in a large part established and maintained through language."[13] He explains that "language, ideology, and speaking practices"[14] are intricately bound together by sociocultural and historical factors. In the case of African Americans, our unique ways of speaking (that is, African American English, often referred to as BEV[15]) as well as the specific narrative forms (for instance, dozens, testifying, signifying, and so on) that have survived in our culture indicate the strong role of language within the family as well as the community. Otherwise, without a linguistic means of self-expression African Americans, like any other ethnic group, would lose the capacity to bridge the inevitable gap between generations.

"SURVIVAL" TEXTS

Personal narratives of older African American women have proven to be rich sources of valuable information. Most of the eighty-eight women in my study recalled stories of their ancestors who were either slaves or ex-slaves. These survival texts/stories usually include specific descriptions of how a family survived slavery and other manifestations of overt racism. Elmira, an attorney born in 1908, offered this narrative:

Text 1
Well, the story as my maternal aunt told me ah, she told me one day when I was home on leave from work in Africa. And she said, "You know some of our rela-

tives are in Africa." And she said that in the days of slavery in Kentucky, her father who was my ah, paternal grandfather, and her mother ... And my maternal grandmother's father, belonged to a family who had been given manumission by their owner at his death in his will. And he had left them a certain amount of money so that they could leave the slave state and go to a free area. And at that time, they were organizing passage to ah, Liberia, you remember there was an organization for freed slaves to go and settle in Liberia and they were going to book passage on that ship and go to Liberia and the state of Kentucky told them that the youngest child who was under age could not leave. They would not consent to his leaving. And ah, he couldn't. The state would have to accept his inheritance and he would have to wait. So they went through the agony of deciding whether to leave this child or to give up their plans and face all the dangers of being freed in a slave state. They went on to Liberia and this youngest child who was a boy went up into the Kentucky hills and lived with a family of mountaineers who did not keep slaves. Eventually he grew up, he married a mountaineer girl and they came back to a city in Kentucky. I don't remember the city and my aunt, of course, did not remember. And there he reared his family. And my maternal grandmother was his youngest child. She was a very beautiful girl and one day, as I was told the story, the son of the person who had freed them came back to this city, heard that they were there and came around to look at the family. And told them who he was and he saw Jane, who was the youngest, and saw how pretty she was and said, "I will take this girl and educate her and rear her." And her father said, "No, I will never give her up. She is my child, I'll educate my children." And ah, he [the former master] was rather offended and he left saying, "You better have her ready because I'll be back for her in a week." And ah, the father, Jane's father went to the person who he worked for who was an official in some bank there and said, "Now I'm not going to give up my daughter because I have no confidence in this man rearing this girl and if he takes her, if he attempts to take her I will kill him." And the ah official at the bank said, "Oh no that will cause an uproar. There will be a lynching and there will be all sorts of things. You just go home, keep quiet. I'm gonna give you some money. Tell your family just to take whatever they can carry and I will get you across the river to Ohio which is free territory. And ah you can stay there and carry on your life." So that's what the family did. Jane and the family went to Ohio and I am told that she stayed with the man who was so prominent in the underground railroad, Levi Coffin, for a while. And grew up and one day she met my grandfather, my paternal grandfather and they married and it is from their union that my father, and his brother and sisters were born, four children.... I thought I would like to write about it someday. (36:1, pp. 2–3).[16]

Elmira's lengthy text is crammed with useful information. There are at least three smaller narratives (mini-episodes) embedded in the larger one:

1. the slave family that was freed and resettled in Liberia ("You know some of our relatives are in Africa.")
2. the child who was left behind and grew up in the mountains ("... this youngest child ... went up into the Kentucky hills ...")

3. the ordeal of the youngest child's daughter, Jane ("... and he saw Jane ... and said, 'I will take this girl ...'")

Each of these mini-episodes can be expanded into a full narrative, but at this point simply function as details and support for the core narrative, "some of our relatives are in Africa." In each one of the mini-episodes the family is faced with difficult decisions and ultimately faces life or death consequences ("... I will kill him'." "There will be a lynching."). In the last episode the father is the hero who risks everything to protect his daughter. Even Jane's stay with Levi Coffin could be considered a potential mini-episode.

Some stories were supplemented by artifacts passed down through several generations. Sidney, a full professor of Romance languages, born in 1909, shared her family history through photographs:

Text 2

I am so happy to have this tintype ... of my grandfather standing at attention with his rifle at his shoulder in a Union army uniform. He acquired that in the Civil War when he had watered the horses for the Union Army coming south through Virginia. They took him along as they went on down into the south further as their waterboy. And of course, when they won the war, they brought him back up to Ohio where he finally settled, but they first took him into the army as a regular soldier. So he's proud to be standing there as a Union army soldier in uniform. And my dad, was so proud of his father. ... He'd [grandfather] been a slave and that's how he was selected as a waterboy to go down with the Union Army. ... My grandmother on my father's side ... married my grandfather and they moved to another town in Ohio. [They] set up a kind of a little business, a grocery store, one of the general stores. They worked so hard. My grandfather evidently also stoked the furnaces in the steel mills. And so my father told us that ah, he [grandfather] was so weary and sometimes he'd come out of those hot furnace areas and walk home in the cold nights in Ohio. And he contracted pneumonia which turned into early tuberculosis. And both parents died. And my father lost an older brother also. And so that, at the age of twelve my father was orphaned. (3:1, pp. 5–6)

Sidney provides details about how her grandfather, an ex-slave, eventually migrated to Ohio. Her narrative is infused with pride in the family legacy. Mini-episodes include the following:

1. grandfather's service in union army
2. grandfather's marriage and later life (including work as store owner and steel-worker)
3. grandfather as twelve-year-old orphan

The last episode (No. 3 orphan) functions as both an ending of one mini-episode and the potential beginning of another. The story centers almost exclusively on Sidney's grandfather, with few details about other people in his life. She includes several details about his experience as a waterboy traveling with the Union army, and adds only brief information about his later life. By using this kind of telescoping strategy, Sidney highlights an important occurrence, and shows how this single event (service in the Union army) shaped the entire course of her grandfather's life. The same kind of telescopic structuring can be seen again in the second half of the narrative, when she explains how her father became an orphan ("My grandfather evidently also stoked the furnaces ..."). Cause-and-effect relationships established between events within Sidney's narrative make it an especially compelling story.

Marie, a businesswoman, born in 1919, wanted to reshape the focus of her family histories. Although she was proud of all of her ancestors, she felt that some deserved special recognition:

Text 3

I mention also [my grandmother] because we always talk about the men, and that's because that's what we were **told** about, but my grandmother was my hero. She was born in the north, ah, her father was French. Her mother was part Black and part Indian. And when my grand-dad asked to marry her, her dad blew the roof, and um, ah, but it all worked out, uh, fortunately for us, 'cause we're here. But um, she was really a strong woman, um, she. . . . I didn't know my granddad, he died before I was born, but my grandmother ah, he provided her . . . moderately with you know, decent living conditions and all. . . . Her middle son remained in the north as she did, her home was there, and he had a pharmacy and all of these magazines . . . he would bring her a copy to read, then he'd take it back to the store. And she read every periodical that came out, and retained what it said, and ah, whenever there was a dispute or a discussion in the family when we were all together, I remember, she was the one that usually resolved it, and everyone was willing to accept what she said because she seemed to know what she had retained, what she had read. She died oh, during World War I . . . [she] worked with the ah, volunteer area in the Red Cross, and ah so, and did things like that all her life, I mean she was just ah . . . she had the stamina to get out and do this volunteer work outside [the home]. (52:1, pp. 20–22)

Marie's narrative, unlike the previous texts, is centered around the character traits of her grandmother rather than episodes about past events. There are some potential mini-episodes:

1. the cultural (Native American, black, French) background of grandmother
2. middle son's pharmacy
3. grandmother's position of authority in family
4. grandmother's volunteer activities

However, the seed or kernel ideas (Nos. 1–4) are so briefly mentioned that there are not enough details to provide any indication of their relative importance to the larger whole. Thus, according to the structure of Marie's story, listeners can conclude that her grandmother's thirst for knowledge ("... she read every periodical that came out ...") and position of authority in the family ("... she was the one that usually resolved it ...") were the most important features of this part of the family history.

Other narratives contained only fragments of oral family histories. Zora, a teacher and social worker, born in 1914, recounted only certain aspects of her grandmother's physical appearance and personality:

Text 4
My grandmother on my father's side. She had, she was Carib Indian and so she had hair way down her back. She could sit on it. And she was a very powerful character **according to my father's stories of her.** She was very strong-minded and very anxious that all her children be properly educated and that kind of thing. In those days that was considered quite advanced.... (37:1, p. 9)

Zora did not retell her family history in a chronological manner. Instead, she provided bits and pieces of information about certain family members, especially women. Similarly, Jane, a music composer, also born in 1914, told about special incidents in her family:

Text 5
My grandmother was on the reservation quite a lot and I learned how to do a number of things from her. For instance, I ... learned how to shuck corn, how to make dolls out of apples, and I learned how to braid rugs. In fact, I just learned all of the crafts one normally expects an Indian to do.... I remember so vividly that sometimes I would go out and there were some peach trees ... and I would always want to go and get a peach off from the tree and one year it was too late for me to get peaches off the tree but my grandfather had somehow tied the peaches on the tree so I could pull them off. And they were just darling grandparents. (27:2, p. 36)

Proud of her Native American heritage, Jane fondly recollected specific activities she participated in on the reservation. There were few details, but she associated some activities with the love and affection received from her grandparents ("... my grandfather somehow tied ... they were just darling ..."). Fragmented stories may result from a variety of causes. Some fragments could have been passed down simply as fragments or pieces of part of a story; the narrator could be carefully extracting fragments from a larger whole; some episodes could have been forgotten; and some could have been lost through a multiplicity of life situations (for instance, death, divorce, migration, blended families, and so on). However, the fact that fragments remain with the family is testimony to the internal or within-group importance of African American oral family history.

As the preceding texts indicate, family history connects each generation with the past, preserves events and significant family/personality traits (for instance, commitment to education), traces the specific history of family, and continuously functions as a source of renewal and revitalization for family members. Not all stories have positive outcomes, and not all ancestors are praiseworthy characters; however, lessons for living, surviving, and prospering can be found even in the most dire circumstance of a family's past.

READING BETWEEN THE LINES

The majority of family histories usually related stories of slaves and ex-slaves, their hardships, and their ultimate triumphs over unimaginable difficulties. This common story framework was not formulaic, but varied extensively from family to family. Furthermore, overlap between the stories provided some indication of shared, in-group, discourse strategies and of community/group response to oppressive external conditions.

Examining discourse strategies in particular, we find a number of collective features. Those accounts closest to slavery and the immediate aftermath exhibit some very interesting commonalties. One of the most notable elements is the explicit identification of authority and/or the intimation that the narrator is not the originator of the story. That is, most narrators specify, sometimes more than once, the source of the story:

Text 1:   "... the story as my paternal aunt told me ...", "... as I was told the story ...", "... and I am told ..."
Text 2:   "... that's what we were told ..."
Text 3:   "... according to my father's stories of her."
Text 4:   "my father told us"

The practice of identifying the source gives credit to the original narrator, and simultaneously establishes a relationship between a current narrator and a past or original narrator. In addition, it also ensures some degree of cross-generational continuity. Constantly mentioning the original narrator reinforces memories of that person and subtly validates the time frame of the story.

Similarly, narrators usually establish a kin connection. They explicitly indicate kin relationships at important junctures in the story. Also, narrators situate themselves and/or their generation within the context of the family's past:

Text 1:   "... some of our relatives are in Africa", "... her father who was my paternal grandfather ...", "... and it is from their union that my father, and his brothers and sisters were born ..."
Text 2:   "... my dad was so proud of his father ...", "... my grandmother on my father's side ..."
Text 3:   "... my grandmother was my hero", "... when my grandad asked to marry her ...", "... 'cause we're here ...", "... before I was born ..."
Text 4:   "... my grandmother on my father's side ..."
Text 5:   "My grandmother was on the reservation ... I learned how to do a number of things from her", "And they were just darling grandparents."

Certainly kin relationships are an important part of any family history, but the regularity with which these particular narrators describe such relationships is significant. According to Vansina this kind of "expression of experience"[17] is reflexive, and represents a "stage in the elaboration of historical consciousness."[18] In other words, these connections go beyond remembrance of kin to the preservation of cultural attributes of both the family and group.

Other discourse strategies which also establish links are non-kin connections. Family histories frequently acknowledge relationships to non-kin others, particularly those who offered assistance or otherwise played a positive role in the family's past:

Text 1:   "...belonged to a family who had been given manumission by their owner ...", "I'm gonna give you some money", "I will get you across the river ...", "...she stayed with the man who was so prominent in the underground railroad ..."

Text 2:   "They took him along as they went on down into the south."

Text 3:   "...[she] worked with the volunteer area in the Red Cross."

Even though the example from Text 3 exhibits a different situation (that is, someone in the family being helpful to others), it still illustrates the importance of non-kin relationships. These elements could easily have been omitted from family narratives, but clearly they are retained for a purpose. Although generalizations must be tentative, this may be some indication of that African Americans view themselves as being connected with others and not entrenched in the alienating individualism of Western societies.

Finally, the role and status of women within African American families is described in enlightening detail in many of the family histories. As discussed previously, in several instances women are the originators (family historian) of family stories: "Well, the story as my paternal aunt told me ..." (Text 1). Within various texts in my sample, women are portrayed as:

partners (as opposed to subordinates): "They set up a kind of little business ..." (Text 2)

highly valued family members: "And my maternal grandmother was his youngest child. She was very beautiful.... 'No, I will never give her up. She is my child ...'" (Text 1)

sources of power and authority: "And she was a very powerful character ...", "She was strong-minded and anxious that her children be properly educated ... that was considered quite advanced." (Text 4)

"...my grandmother was my hero ...", "And she read every periodical ... and retained what it said ...", "...she was the one that usually resolved it." (Text 3)

teachers: "I learned a number of things from her." (Text 5)

It is interesting that two of the narrators specify that the above information was provided by male family members. The father in Text 1 was reported to have uttered these words about his daughter, and the father in Text 4 gave this description of his mother. These very positive images of African American women seem to be stark contrasts to present-day anti-female sentiments. How these images may have changed over time or how they may have been negatively influenced by the dominant society is an issue that constantly is being debated. Some would argue that the positive images of women found in African American family histories are merely romantic or idealized, and are unrealistic views of the past. However, several histories of African American women confirm their positive status within the family and the community.[19]

BITS, PIECES, AND PATCHES

The African American oral tradition can be analyzed from a variety of perspectives. On an intimate level, the private retelling of family histories, among family members, holds together past and future generations of African Americans who would otherwise be irretrievably displaced and dehumanized by the divisive effects of racism. Beyond that, structural features of the narratives and internal details (for instance, the role of women, identifying sources of authority, and so on) preserve cultural practices unique to African Americans. Specifically, embedded in the family stories of older African American women we find attitudes and information that provide, in Alex Haley's words, "bits, and pieces and patches" of a shared past that informs the present and future.

NOTES

1. "The expression 'oral tradition' applies both to a process and to its products. The products are oral messages based on previous oral messages, at least a generation old. The process is the transmission of such messages by word of mouth over time . . . ." Vansina. *Oral Tradition as History*, 1985, p. 3.

2. These narratives were selected from a long-range study of African American women's personal narratives. See *My Soul Is My Own* (Routledge, 1993).

3. See the following sources.
    Patricia Jones Jackson, *When Roots Die: Endangered Traditions on the Sea Islands* (Athens: University of Georgia Press, 1987).
    Florence M. Cronises and Henry Word. *Cunnie Rabbit, Mr. Spider and the Other Beef* (Chicago: Afro-Am Press, 1969).
    Ruth Finnegan. *Limba Stories and Storytelling* (Oxford: Oxford University Press, 1969). B. A. Botkin, ed. *Lay My Burden Down: A Folk History of Slavery* (Chicago: University of Chicago Press, 1969).
    Richard Dorson. *American Negro Folktales* (New York: Fawcett, 1967).
    Lorenzo D. Turner. *Africanisms in the Gullah Dialect* (Chicago: University of Chicago Press, 1949).

4. Michigan Humanities Culture Kit, African American Culture, "African American Family Life and Culture Curriculum," by Sylvia Williams.

5. Robert Hill, *The Strengths of Black Families*, 1972. Also see Wade Nobles, "Africanity: It's Role in Black Families," in the *Black Scholar* (May 1974); Janice Hale-Benson, *Black Children: Their Roots: Culture and Learning Styles*

(Baltimore: Johns Hopkins University Press, 1982); "The New Black Family," *Ebony* (August 1993).

6. Alex Haley. "Black History, Oral History and Genealogy," in *Oral History*. David K. Dunaway and Willa K. Baum, eds. (Nashville: American Association for State and Local History, 1984), p. 265.
7. Haley, p. 265.
8. John Edwards, *Language, Society and Identity*. (New York: Basil Blackwell, 1985), p. 6.
9. Edwards, p. 8.
10. See W. Isajiw, "Definitions of Ethnicity," in J. Goldstein and R. Bienvenue, eds., *Ethnicity and Ethnic Relations in Canada* (Toronto: Butterworth, 1980).
11. Edwards, p. 17.
12. Ibid.
13. John Gumpertz, ed. *Language and Social Identity* (Cambridge: Cambridge University Press, 1982), p. 7.
14. Gumperz, p. 8.
15. BEV equals black English vernacular
16. Tape/transcript number, side number, page number.
17. Jan Vansina. *Oral Tradition as History* (Madison: University of Wisconsin Press, 1985), p. 7.
18. Vansina, p. 8.
19. See the following.
    Gerda Lerner, *Black Women in White America: A Documentary History* (New York: Random House, 1972).
    Paula Giddings, *When and Where I Enter: The Impact of Black Women on Race and Sex in America*. (New York: Bantam Books, 1984).
    Jeanne Noble. "The Higher Education of Black Women in the Twentieth Century." In *Women and Higher Education in American History*. John Mack Faragher and Florence Howe, eds. (New York.: W. W. Norton, 1988).
    Linda Perkins. "The Education of Black Women in the Nineteenth Century." In *Women and Higher Education in American History*. John Mack Faragher and Florence Howe, eds. (New York: W. W. Norton, 1988).
    Darlene Clark Hine, Elsa Barkley Brown, and Rosalyn Terborg-Penn *Black Women in America: A Historical Encyclopedia*. Vol. I and II. (Brooklyn, 1993).

Insiders

and

Outsiders

"Hands in the Chit'lins"

Notes on Native Anthropological Research among African American Women

10

Linda Williamson Nelson

As black American women, we are born into a mystic sisterhood, and we live our lives within a magic circle, a realm of shared language, reference, and allusion within the veil of our blackness and our femaleness. We have been as invisible to the dominant culture as rain; we have been knowers, but we have not been known.

—Joanne M. Braxton, 1989:1

We got a hell of an experience. I mean black folks, no matter where you lived, somebody did the same thing.

—R.A.C., Philadelphia informant

On first consideration, anthropological research among one's own people promises much of the certainty and ease of a tender voyage home. After all, the indigenous researcher knows the geographic terrain, the linguistic code, and the social rules. Having so envisioned the experience, I had only to enter the field and begin the work. As I began to gather data for the larger project (code-switching and cultural themes in black women's oral narratives) from which this discussion derives, I heard my own voice unmistakably among those of my informants. This led to my construction of a naïve and all too simplistic concept of endogenous or native anthropology, one that predicted that my insider status would be largely taken for granted as I sought entrance into the homes and lives of my informants. However, the field experience itself, conducted in rural, suburban, and inner-city communities of New York, Philadelphia, and South Jersey, forced me to recognize that the extent to which I could claim insider status would not be consistent from informant to informant and from place to place. The women of this study received me with varying degrees of intimacy, from tepid politeness to sisterly or motherly generosity. Beneath the obvious and sustaining bonds of gender, race, and class[1] lay more subtle features, artifacts of the various microcommunities of our individual enculturation processes, features that either drew us together or set a distance, however slight, between us. I suspected that all that contributed to our social identity, made manifest primarily through our linguistic behavior in the course of the speech event, contributed significantly to the relative ease or difficulty with which I attained access and with which I was able to establish and sustain rapport with individual informants. With each initial encounter with the informants, my identity was constructed through my words. The only identity that I could assume *a priori* was that of black, female researcher, but that did not automatically indicate that I was a trustworthy member of the culture. My status as a member of the culture of the informant was structured during the course of each initial interaction. As I will illustrate in this discussion, all of the interpretive cues within my pronouncements either contributed positively to rapport or distanced me from the informant. In one case of apparent miscommunication, I apparently aliented my informant with an inappropriate reference to the rural location of the informant's home. However, the instances of difficulty cannot be generalized and attributed to one factor, such as informant's perception of class differences or my familiarity with urban as opposed to rural living. In most encounters, I was successful in establishing a comfortable rapport early in the interaction. In a few cases, it was apparent that my identity, as signaled through communicative cues, set me apart from the informant.

The discussion which follows, therefore, is intended to provoke a consideration of native anthropology that concerns itself with what I should like to call "gradations of endogeny." My references below to field experiences among African American women in urban and rural enclaves are intended to demonstrate that, while the sharing of racial, gender, and class membership with informants is my unquestionable qualification for insider status in its broadest sense, each interaction in the field with a new informant revealed the variousness in their individual views of me as a "homegirl," that is, someone who shared their perceptions of reality and had an intimate understanding of their life experiences. I am suggesting that once the researcher begins to recognize such degrees of acceptance, she is, ironically, better able to fully realize the ethnographer's imperative, that is, the communication of the informant's vision of her world and her lifeways. I believe that recognition of gradations of endogeny necessitates a peculiar listening stillness that amplifies one's own idiocultural voice, in all its subtle variations. This, in turn, allows the investigator to claim what Maruyama (1974) would call the polyocular lens which, when taken metaphorically, suggests a peculiar multiangular vision. By looking inward as well as outward at the subject under study, we are able to see ourselves as cultural actors and potential objects of study. This inward focus can provoke our consideration of the ways in which the researcher's identity unavoidably contributes to the kind and quality of the information we gather. Paradoxically, such multifaceted vision can only be fully actualized after we first acknowledge that native status is not a fixed constant with the same intensity from informant to informant and from place to place. Once we recognize such gradations, I will argue, we are better able to make the all-important consideration of the influence of native status on quality of access and immediate rapport, and on the data we gather.

At this point, it is necessary for me to explain that intrinsic to my sampling method were conditions that dictated to a considerable extent the quality of rapport between my informants and me. In choosing informants from a social network, I usually began with friends and relatives, who then gave me names of their friends, sisters, aunts, and mothers. Obviously, the first women that I encountered in a social network were those with whom I was closely or at least casually acquainted. The discussion below, which is intended to argue, in part through reference to field notes, that there are variations in the researcher's perception of her own insider status, admits for examination notes from the interviews with only those informants whom, before the actual life narrative interview, I knew only casually or those whom I knew only through brief, face-to-face meetings or telephone introductions. Obviously, in the cases of those informants with whom I had a close relationship prior to my data-gathering, our prior interactions contributed positively to the rapport-building process at the start of each interview.

Miss Esther,[2] for example, had never met me before our late afternoon meeting at her row home in northeast Philadelphia. Yet when she faced me through the storm door, her greeting was familiar, but ironically so, as she made no attempt to conceal her annoyance with my arrival just at that moment. "I had just put my hands in the chit'lins," she offered peevishly, and with this announcement explained the reason for her perturbance. I was precisely on time for our appointment, but the heavy downpour that afternoon prompted her conclusion that I would not come to see her as planned. Acting on this presumption, she had apparently begun the painstaking task of cleaning chit'lins, a task enacted over and over again in a great many African American households, especially as the holiday season approaches.

In order to understand fully the connection between this description and notions of insider status, the reader must be aware of the ambiguous status of chit'lins in African American communities. "Chitterlings," or as they are almost always pronounced in black communities, *chit'lins* are part of the small intestine of swine. During the period of slavery, these entrails, the feet, and the tails (the "low" parts of the pig) were characteristic of the provisions given to the enslaved Africans. What was actually refuse to the master was transformed by the enslaved into a palatable offering, but only after an extremely long and painstaking cleaning and cooking process, with whatever seasonings were available, the most coveted being cayenne pepper. In recent times, when higher ("higher" on the hog's body, or meats other than pork) cuts of meat have been available to larger segments of the African American population, many of us still eat chit'lins, especially during the winter holiday season. Around the New Year, particularly, it is customary to serve from "low on the hog" (that is, chit'lins, hogmaws, pig's feet) in the recognition of our historic struggle and perseverance, and in the hope for a prosperous New Year. Some blacks, however, eschew all pork, especially chit'lins, for religious reasons as well as for less specifically articulated reasons, sometimes associated with their assimilation into the majority culture and their general desire to cast aside remnants of the earlier period of dire oppression. Because of the ambiguous status of chit'lins, not all blacks who eat chit'lins readily admit to it. And conversely, not all who refuse chit'lins let that fact be known in all contexts. In short, the acceptance or rejection of this particular food can serve as an identity or status maker. Claudia Mitchell-Kernan uses a discussion of chit'lins among two informants to illustrate the black stylistic speech act, "signification." In the process, she also illustrates that one speaker is using "favorable regard of chit'lins" as an in-group marker. In this context, the suggestion of an invitation to eat chit'lins is the occasion for signification: a particular form of subtle insult where the seemingly innocuous denotation of a word forms the outer layer of meaning underneath which lies the implicit meaning and function of the utterance (1971, pp. 69–70). Mitchell-Kernan explains that the informant's half-joking invitation to the researcher and to another acquaintance to return to her home to dine on chit'lins was an instance of signification, for the informant "was, in the metaphors of the culture, implying that Mary (and/or I) were assimilationists [because they did not eat chit'lins]" (1971, p. 71). The fact that the speaker is signifying on Mary and/or the informant becomes clear when Mary rails defensively, disparaging those blacks who criticize others for rejecting chit'lins or other soul food dishes.

This reference is meant to support the basis on which I claim that Miss Esther's unself-conscious announcement of her involvement with chit'lin preparation immediately set me at ease. In the discouse reported by Mitchell-Kernan, the mention of chit'lins was a challenge. In contrast, Miss Esther mentioned chit'lins casually. We can interpret this as a positive aspect of the way Miss Esther viewed this researcher. We can assume that underlying the spontaneity of her front-door greeting were assumptions, or more precisely, presuppositions regarding the cultural knowledge of the researcher.

While I shall, further on, return to the role of common knowledge and presupposition in construction of the life narrative discourse, at this point, I should like to clarify briefly what is meant by presupposition. In a discussion of pragmatics in discourse contexts, Brown and Yule (1983, p. 29) define pragmatic presupposition in "terms of assumptions the speaker makes about what the hearer is likely to accept without challenge." They proceed to further suggest that implicit in such a definition is the notion of common ground, that body of shared cultural knowledge that guides our interpretations of actions and words. John Gumperz (1982) provides further clarification as he offers one of the more explicit explanations of the role of sociocultural knowledge in interpretation of conversations. He states that:

> aside from physical setting, participants' personal background knowledge, and their attitudes toward each other, sociocultural assumptions concerning role and status relationships as well as social values associated with various message components also play an important role. (1982, pp. 156–57)

It should be apparent, first of all, that Miss Esther assumed that I knew what the preparation of chit'lins entailed. While Miss Esther could have likely assumed that almost any African American is familiar with chit'lins, she was not compelled to conclude that I was "one of the folk" who has a positive regard for the food. Her ease and spontaneity suggested that my access was not granted begrudgingly or with the caution with which one receives an outsider. By the end of our meeting, moreover, after the tape recorder was turned off, Miss Esther continued to talk casually about her love of cooking. When the subject returned to chit'lins, as it did, I offered that I loved to eat chit'lins, but I never did learn to prepare them myself. She rose at my announcement and led me to the kitchen, where she demonstrated the process of cleaning chit'lins, where each individual piece is placed, one at a time, under the running tap water for a thorough cleansing.

As I prepared to leave, and repeated my expressions of appreciation for her willingness to meet with me, she repeated what I was to hear over and over again from a number of my subjects: "I believe in trying to help somebody, one of us, if they help themselves, but if you don't try to help yourself, you a lost soul and I don't care to waste no time" (field notes).

Deserving of emphasis here is the distinct indication by Miss Esther and others of a desire to help, based upon ethnic identification; my work was seen as an effort that could ultimately benefit all black people. And just as I see this as my responsibility in large measure, so did a majority of my informants regard their interviews as a contribution to racial progress. Moreover, as one subject, a mental health administrator who was interviewed in her downtown Philadelphia office, remarked as I prepared to leave, "Yeah, girl, white folks always be studying us; we got to help each other, we have to network" (field notes). Aside from her explicit statement of pleasure in helping another African American woman conduct research on African Americans, her black language use at this moment was an index of solidarity. Her use of the Black English Vernacular morphological feature, the durative *be*, was used strategically at that moment. Before this pronouncement, the only ethnic markings of her speech were subtle stylistic intonational contours. The *be* communicated identification on two levels, the one conspicuously articulated, the other her conviction at this point that I was one of the folk, and that she, in turn, could "git down" in the language of the culture.

African American anthropologist John Gwaltney attests to the general willingness on the part of potential subjects to assist in the research of a native investigator:

> Anthropology was seen as a job; a means to privileged status and many people made their contribution to my field project with the specific end of assisting the advancement of a native career. There was a belief that settler[3] field populations were essentially closed to natives and a strong feeling that since the principle of reciprocity did not prevail, assisting the native researcher was an act of racial solidarity and civic responsibility. (1976, p. 236)

Without doubt, virtually all of the women whom I interviewed were willing to contribute to a member's professional development. As expressed by Miss Esther: "I don't have no whole lot of time, but since you are one of us and trying to better yourself, I'll give you my time" (field notes).

In many cases, without my offer of any more compensation than a gift of butter cake, of child care, or a car ride to run errands, I was graciously invited into my respondents' homes and granted generous amounts of time. There were occasions, however, when the actions of the informant or my own reactions within a particular geographical setting prompted me to explore further, subtle notions of endogenous research. Messerschmidt (1981), in his forthright discussion of the influence of pure and applied approaches in the anthropology practiced "at home," refers to the work of the urban-born, insider anthropologist as an "anthropology of issues." Those who choose to return to the communities of their own enculturation are likely to be motivated (as I have readily acknowledged) by their desire to address the social issues that are critical for their people. Such an anthropology, Messerschmidt further clarifies, cannot be defined in terms of only applied work, as opposed to theoretical abstractions. "Rather, it implies a unique and indivisible link between them [application and theory]" (1981, pp. 4–5).

As Gwaltney notes, following Fanon, the natives,

> the poor, powerless and nonwhite ... who are actually saddled with the drudgery and unpleasant realities have a restricted concept of reality and the realm of the possible—what I call the *classical* view—and are obliged by the circumstances of their lives to see it "like it is." (1976, p. 236)

In contrast, what Gwaltney calls the *romantic* cultures are those which "have the power to invent a version of reality which causes them a minimum of discomfort" (p. 236). Because he or she is a member of the group under study, the native anthropologist finds it nearly impossible to see through the *settler's* eyes—academic degrees notwithstanding. When we strive to write about the *classical* view, we are necessarily forging the link suggested by Messerschmidt between theory and application because of the potential disruption to the canon that such a view will bring.

In this sense, any native anthropology coming from a member of an oppressed group can be a revisionist project, one that can rearrange the discursive categories of object and subject, by bringing the voice of observed to the page so that they may speak for themselves. In order to do this, I maintain, we cannot fail to acknowledge that the various corners and large spaces of our own enculturation cause us to view and be viewed by other insiders as either focal or peripheral members of the group.

As we shall see, in the following description of my visit to an informant, my relegation to peripheral status is a consequence of my ignorance of the informant's perception of the area in which she lived.

I drove up the blacktop road to Mrs. Jones's house. On each side, the modest, one- and two-story frame houses stood at the same distance from one another. Clusters of white pine, evergreens, and dwarf pines, divided here and there by willows and birch—remnants of the vast New Jersey Pine Barrens that were cleared for the building of these homes over twenty years before—framed the spacious backyards. In this predominantly black town thirty miles north of Atlantic City, where the post office is the parlor of a converted rancher, most residents know their neighbors well. As I entered Mrs. Jones's house, I was struck by the cool breeze that entered from front and back, and was immediately grateful, as I felt instant protection from the uncommonly warm September afternoon.

After accepting an invitation to sit, my first and irredeemable error was to offer what I intended as a compliment, "How nice it is back here." We were more than five miles from a thoroughfare, and a number of roads I passed coming in through the woods were unpaved, but Mrs. Jone's facial expression immediately told me I had blundered seriously. With indignation and distrust, she retorted, "What do you mean by back here?" The more I attempted to explain my point of view, formed in part by a personal history of living in inner-city New York until relatively recently, and the more I qualified "back here" as meaning grass, trees, quietude, the more she eyed me suspiciously. My unfortunate comment, from the point of view of my informant, served as concrete evidence that shared group membership with one's informants does not protect the anthropologist from errors of interpretation. Although Mrs. Jones is the mother of a personal friend of mine, we had only met for the first time two weeks before the interview. Mrs. Jones's daughter was an older student in a class that I taught a number of years ago, and when I was introduced, she reminded her mother, "Remember, this is my teacher friend." Any attempt to understand the motivations for Mrs. Jones's distrust must also consider my identification as "teacher friend" and not, simply, "friend."

I would strongly maintain that any researcher who returns to the communities of her people to conduct research must expect to confront at least some folk who will reveal their ambivalence toward the homegirl or boy who went off to college and got "the white man's papers." On the one hand, blacks are, in general, fiercely proud of anyone who "gits ovah" but there is also concern over whether or not such educated natives were indeed alienated from their home place. Gwaltney attests to this concern when he considered research techniques that would allow for maximum personal and communal expression of the culture:

> Not wishing to risk being identified as just another of that ubiquitous tribe of homecoming "educated fools," I did not build the use of ... traditional techniques ... into the research plan. "Talking like a man with a paper in his hands" is a local expression for talking nonsense—a characterization I wished to avoid. (1981b, p. xxiv)

In another context, Gwaltney articulates an awareness of the origins of trust and the delicate nature of its establishment in indigenous research. "The fact that some of my informants had known me since the hour of my birth certainly did not prove a hindrance. In other cases I was checked and cross-checked" (1981a, p. 58). Gwaltney also offers that his attempts to gain access to informants who had not known him for a long time was met by very careful scrutiny of the investigator on the part of the potential informant. Many people requested references from reputable members of the community before agreeing to assist. In such cases, a trusted community member's approval of him was "infinitely more valuable than purely professional credentials" (1981a, p. 58).

In the case of Mrs. Jones, my credentials may have been a hindrance. Her agreement to the interview seemed to derive mainly from her daughter's request. In comparison to the average life narrative interview time of one and a half hours, my half-hour interview with Mrs. Jones was conspicuously brief. As the transcription below indicates, speaking into a tape recorder about her life to a virtual stranger, albeit a black female, was inappropriate and not especially comfortable for Mrs. Jones.

After about twenty-five minutes, I began to ask about those individuals in her life who might have provided "word of encouragement, spirit, belief in you? Who were those people who stood behind you?" [I explained that this was a question I was asking all my informants.]

MRS. JONES: I just have to say my mother and father. Then there was a man, he's dead a couple of years now. His name is Mr. Palmer, we call him Brother Palmer as a church member, but my mother and father.

LINDA: Coming up, did you have a lot of women friends that sort of stayed with you and were good pals?

MRS. JONES: Well, she's gone, too. I had two friends. I've had some close friends. . . . Now I don't have anything else to say.

At this point, I thanked her a great deal and prepared to leave.

In the case of women with whom I had no prior relationship, I think that rapport was most dependent upon the enthusiasm of the initial recommendation I received from the woman in her network and then, on the quality of our own face-to-face contact. Given Mrs. Jones's abrupt conclusion of the interview, as well as the brevity of her answers throughout, it was apparent that with Mrs. Jones I failed to establish the kind of rapport that was established with virtually all of the other informants.

When Paul Bohannon and his colleagues went into the Carlson Hotel of San Diego to study the "non-welfare poor," they were still in the society of their enculturation, and there was no language barrier to overcome. Yet they discovered that they still had to spend a great deal of time developing familiarity and establishing trust with informants (Bohannon 1981, p. 35).

In the case of just about half of my informants, I had not entered their homes or met them face to face until the time of the appointment which was set for the life narrative interview. With these women, then, minimal rapport had to be established during the first few minutes of our encounter and sustained throughout in order for a comfortable and meaningful life narrative process to ensue. It was with these women that I was forced to recognize that, while my essential insider status contributed more than anything else to my initial access, solidarity was either established or blocked by my linguistic behavior. In effect, I can in retrospect measure the gradations of endogeny through the effects of the words exchanged with my informants.

The following example is an illustration of the other extreme; in this case we can see where the solidarity achieved through the informant's and the researcher's expressive behavior also contribute to the cohesion and continuity of the life narrative text itself.

Prior to the life narrative interview, I had spent a considerable amount of time with the informant, but our relationship was largely built around the activities of our children, who had formed a friendship in the preschool where they met. Rena and I talked casually during these visits, but never actually shared intimate details of our lives. We lived in the same community, so I walked to her home on the afternoon of our interview. As I was a few minutes early, I was asked to wait in the living room while she finished a counseling session with a client. As a psychiatric social worker, she held a full-time position in a large, city hospital mental health clinic, and maintained a private practice in her home. As I looked through a magazine, my usual, initial feelings of awkwardness in the interview setting were increased by my anticipation of recognizing Rena's client. Fortunately, the client left through a side door. Then Rena warmly beckoned me into her office. After what felt like a rather formal beginning, Rena reached a part in her story about the attention to hair texture and skin color in her family, and the narration was clearly developing around a body of knowledge that was common to both of us as African American women who had reached adolescence before the public affirmation of the beauty of indigenous black features.

RENA: My family is strange. My sister is pretty; one is light. Well, both sisters is pretty . . . well one is light. She has hair down her back and very prominant cheek bones and very slanted eyes and she looks oriental, and as kids, you know a lot of times in black families, it wasn't good to be *black*. It was always good to be mixed. My family always said to my sister, "Oh, you look like a little foreigner." Well, she took that literally and became a foreigner. [Rena was referring to the fact that her sister moved away and married outside her race.]

LINDA: She did, wow! I know just what you mean. Half of the five of us kids, two anyway, my two older sisters are not brown at all, more beige or maybe olive-toned. They look like and take after my mother whose father was white. They often told us "brown ones" how they wish they had our color. Yet I always had the feeling that they didn't mind that much[4] and I, as a little kid, I remember waiting—seriously—for the light side of my under hand, my palms and the color off the soles of my feet, you know, to spread over my whole body (mutual laughter).

The shared knowledge in this context seems to encourage what Susan Kalcik has identified as *serializing*. In her study of the interaction of women in rap (i.e., rap session) discussion groups (1975), Kalcik recognized a type of narrative sequencing or serializing wherein various participants in conversation would string together any number of personal anecdotes. These stories are all related as they appeared to elaborate on a single idea, concept, or experience. Together, the individual kernal stories, as the author calls them, are serialized to form one running piece of discourse. The serializing illustrated above is facilitated by our mutual experience of what Mary Helen Washington has called "that particular aspect of oppression that has affected, for the most part, only women." This Washington offers in response to what she has found to be the absence of a single piece of fiction written by a black male in which he feels ugly or rejected because of the shade of his skin or the texture of his hair (1975, p. xvii).

The next segment of talk with the same informant is again indicative of the way in which cultural solidarity is constructed through the form and substance of the discourse.

RENA: Everybody's family was full of shit! Therefore, we supported each other.

LINDA: Yeah, yeah.

RENA: At times we would spend the night over each other's house. Well, they didn't spend the night over my house cause it wasn't shit to spend the night over my house.

LINDA: Right, right.

RENA: Lee lived on 15th street. Now she had the *House*! Lee's mother ran the speakeasy. We were so naive, we never knew why her mother had all that change. We just thought she always had her apron full of change. There was always people in there giving her money for a drink, so, . . . but we didn't know. You see cause there was always chicken on the weekends and they had *Heat* . . . see. Every weekend her brother say, "Lord, it must be the weekend, cause here come Rena." I say, "Hello," and Miss Hughsey say, "You spending the night?" And we says, "Yes, Miss Hughsey." Me and Sherry, we go to the third floor and we get in the bed . . . (pause, trailing off) because there was heat. . . .

LINDA: Girl, you was living, I know!

RENA: The blankets were heavy and they had chicken in the morning!

LINDA: Hey!

RENA: I never had no chicken wings. We ate breasts and legs, hey, big stuff!

LINDA: Oh, Lord!

RENA: Wit da bread!

LINDA: Lord, Lord (recollecting) that's right, wit the white bread, when the bread gets nice and soft. . . . Oh that's right and smushed up.

RENA: The chicken "samich!"

LINDA: I used to have that chicken "samich" over Ann and Leen's house in the South Bronx where I grew up. Girl, I'm just listening to you and I'm amazed at the parallels, uh, uhm, um, um, um!

RENA: We got a hell of an experience. I mean black folks, no matter where you lived, somebody did the same thing.

LINDA: It's just amazing to me. It really is.

RENA: Uh, uhm, um, um, um!

LINDA: The South Bronx, the coal stove, no heat, spending the night at Ann and Leen's, the great fun talking into the night and eatin' chicken and white bread!

The major distinguishing factors here that mark this exchange for gender and ethnicity are the form and the content. The sequence of turns progresses as a call-response pattern, where the speaker's statements are punctuated by responses from the listener. For Rena's, "I never had no chicken wings, . . ." I follow closely with "Oh Lord!" and Rena says, "Wit da bread!" I say, "Lord, Lord, that's right, wit the white bread." In addition, the subject matter of the exchange, the slumber party or "spending the night," is more typically the experience of adolescent girls. In addition to the call-response stylistic element, the vernacular morphology further enhances cultural meaning. One need only to attempt the preceding discourse on chicken eating in a formalized standard English to recognize the culturally specific value that is added to the truth conditions of the utterances. The act of code-switching toward the vernacular in this context functions rhetorically as an intensifier of cultural meaning and solidarity.

Until now, I have been arguing that the anthropologist who conducts research at home cannot assume that he or she will not face many of the same challenges of gaining entry as the anthropologist abroad. Although the native and the researcher look alike, speak the same language, and share many of the same beliefs and customs, the researcher still approaches the natives to observe them. The ease of access and the quality of rapport are constantly negotiated as the researcher and the informant construct their identities in this intrinsically hierarchical relationship. It is linguistic behavior, more than any other factor, that determines the extent to which the researcher is ultimately regarded as one of the folk.

In the course of this research, however, I recognized that, even in the process of research in one's own community, the social and cultural milieu of the field can also contribute to the complex of cultural variables that influence the researcher's relationship to her subjects. Ironically, my return to the New York City community where I lived most of my life was the occasion for my realization of the impact of environment on the researcher's perceptions of insider status.

At the time of my initial return for the purpose of data collection, it had been nine years since I left Brooklyn and moved to a small-town, suburban community in southern New Jersey. During the time since I moved away, I had made frequent trips back to the city, staying for several days on many occasions. However, these were family trips, for the most part, with my husband and children, and I moved about the city with them. My first field trip to New York was my first occasion to go alone in six years.

The events described below are recounted for their ability to illustrate the stark contrast between my initial arrival and the accompanying feeling of alienation, and my subsequent ease after several days of tenuous reacclimation. When I arrived in Brooklyn that first afternoon, I immediately began to phone the women who had agreed to be interviewed or who I had hoped would agree. My first appointment was for ten o'clock that evening. My enthusiasm on making the contact was tempered by the realization that I would actually be making a trip downtown, in the late evening, alone. Buoyed on by my enthusiasm for the work itself and my anticipation of seeing my first New York informant, a woman I had not seen in ten years, I drove to her home. After finding a parking space, I walked around the corner, combing the area to see if anyone suspicious as nearby. I was certain that my attempt at nonchalance was conspicuous as I strolled past the two men and one woman who were bedded down under cardboard and newspapers on a park bench. Two hours later, when I rose to leave my informant's home, I was measurably more confident, but not yet assured of my ability to negotiate the streets of downtown Brooklyn. I was annoyed by my anxiety since these were the very streets I had traveled alone, regularly, day and night, with little more preparation than a reminder to myself to "just be cool." In short, I had lost much of my street savvy, something I had taken for granted until this disquieting reminder of the inevitable consequences of being away from the inner city for nine years.

After arriving safely, after midnight, at the home of my host, however, I felt a small victory. Tomorrow would surely prove easier. I was to visit a woman who lived only two blocks from where I was staying, which was the general vicinity where I had worked for five years before leaving the city. This next informant lived in an apartment building that was typical for the area. It was quite large, housing approximately one hundred and seventy families in east and west wings that were visible through the outer glass doors. In order to gain entrance, the visitor had to ring an outside bell and wait for the individual to ring back, thereby allowing the outer door to be pushed open. As I approached the building, I hesitated. A disheveled man stood in the outer lobby, glancing about, apparently waiting to walk in behind the first person who gained legitimate entrance. Most city residents, especially those who have lived in such buildings as I had, learn early to avoid entering with suspicious-looking strangers who have not been granted access from a resident. However, a retreat must be subtle, not abrupt and conspicuous, as was my fearful dash to the sidewalk. Before long, I did gain entrance, and made my way without incident to my destination. By the end of the first week of meeting with women throughout Brooklyn and Queens, the ease and naturalness of my response to the environment stood in stark contrast to my earlier anxiety.

It was just after noon when I left my host's home with the intention of walking along the main thoroughfare to search for hot West Indian meat patties. This venture was to be an excursion in search of the best-looking ones, for in recent years West Indians from throughout the Caribbean had settled in and opened up "roti" shops. I proceeded north on the avenue, past a long line of car-leaners, mostly men, who were talking softly and looking around as if to ensure that no passerby would overhear and destroy the privacy of their communion. As I proceeded, I was aware of the return of an appreciable amount of my city sidewalk knowledge. I was confident as I glanced in the shops just long enough to determine if they offered what I was seeking, but not so long as to suggest to the turf-holders backed against parked cars that I would threaten their boundaries. After finding what I was after, I traveled the same path on my return down the avenue. This time, munching the patties, I recalled how commonplace such an occasion used to be, and all the while felt utterly at home. As I proceeded in the direction of the home of my host, a "brother" eased off a car and caught my pace. As he walked alongside me, he said with casual familiarity:

"Hey, like where you bin?"

In response, I smiled, kept walking and said;

"I bin where I always be. I bin around."

He then opened his palm to reveal three quarters and said:

"Like ahm kina short. Kin you hep me out?"

As I maintained my stride and my munching, I responded:

"Wow, man, you shoulda caught me before I hit dese patties! Dis all I got, bro'," I said as I offered him my second pattie (field notes).

This was, indeed, "home-home," the place of my youth, and these were the men I had always known. Even as I saw his eyes on the change purse protruding from my shirt pocket, I "kept cool" and kept moving, neither rushing nor lingering, much more in the casual, but careful way I had always interacted with men on the street before I had moved from the city.

While in the previous illustrations I was constructing a relationship with my informants, in this instance I was establishing a relationship to the field itself. In each case, I recognized the tentativeness and the complexity of insider status. That is, although my subjects and I are black women, and they live in communities that are familiar to me, each contact, indeed each step, into the field revealed the gradations of endogeny.

Joan Cassell (1977) suggests that the ambiguous insider status of the native anthropologist is the inevitable consequence of the observer-observed relationship we have with our informants. In a discussion of peer research among white, middle-class feminists in New York City, Cassell suggests that the behavioral scientist's interest in her research question is often as personal as it is theoretical, and that the researcher has often embarked upon "a symbolic study of him or herself" (1977, p. 413). This is not without risk, Cassell continues, for participant observation among peers does not provide the "clear behavioral, social, and cultural signs" of observer-observed differences and the resulting emotional distance that is more readily acquired in more traditional anthropological research in a distant field (p. 413). Moreover, no matter how emotionally identified the researcher is with the so-called exotic group in a distant field, the investigator is always aware that she does not truly belong. This basic fact does not exist for the anthropologist at home.

I should like to return to my proposal of relative endogeny or gradations of endogeny by suggesting that there are elements intrinsic to all observer-observed relationships that suggest that, even in native or peer anthropological research, the participant observer cannot claim the same measure of belonging as her subjects, who are essentially participants only. Furthermore, as I shall explain more fully, I would postulate that the native researcher's assumption of insider status is more likely when the cultural actors on both sides of the tape recorder are representative of an oppressed minority; regardless of the lines of separation that are intrinsic to the anthropological pursuit, the researcher as well as the observed always and necessarily returns to the status of "other" from the point of view of the larger society. Nonetheless, no matter how sensitive the researcher to the needs of the observed group, the researcher's goals will depart from those of the group. The existential posture of the analyst, or her pursuit of an advanced degree or new insights to enter into the canon, distinguish the indigenous researcher from her subjects. This, I suggest, is so, notwithstanding Messerschmidt's identification of "research at home" as an anthropology that is concerned with social issues affecting the people under study. Cassell's investigation, for example, could surely qualify as an anthropology of issues; she acknowledges having been a participating feminist in the consciousness-raising groups where her actions were dictated by her real-life concerns as middle-class wife, mother, and graduate student. However, at the same time, she was conducting research for her dissertation on the Women's Movement (1977, p. 414).

I would argue that when the researcher's primary reason for gaining access to the group results logically in her leaving the group and taking with her a specific body of data for analysis that is not intended for applied use to meet the group's needs, then the researcher's participation cannot have the same meaning as the participants who are not after data for similar purposes. This qualification is offered as an acknowledgment of those applied anthropologists who expressly set out to investigate a problem identified by the indigenous and to offer a solution to that problem. Hussein M. Fahim (1977) discusses such research that has as its primary objective the advocation of the views and needs of the indigenous Nubians of Egypt after the construction of the Aswan Dam. An even "purer" case of the anthropologist as advocate seems to be John Peterson's (1974) discussion of his work with the Mississippi Choctow Indians.

In his discussion of endogenous research, Magorah Maruyama takes a particularly skeptical view of "exogenously licensed researchers," whom he terms "do-gooders" and self-appointed spokespersons who patronizingly attempt to "speak" for the tribe (1974, p. 318). One of the expressed problems he sees in so-called exogenously licensed, endogenous researchers is what he terms "relevance resonance," that is, the degree to which the purpose of the research converges with the purpose of the people (p. 318). For researchers associated with the academy, he maintains that academic theories are the primary reality, with people and their communities as utility items in service to theorizing. Only the most naive members of the profession would question the legitimacy of Maruyama's claim. It is well known that, especially in the early years of anthropology, studies of the "exotic other" often supported the exploitative work of colonizers. William S. Willis (1974) is relentless, and rightfully so, in his exposure of the historical abuses of an anthropology that complied with white exploitation of colored people worldwide. Maruyama's response to this "academocentricism" (1974, p. 318) that he decries is his participation in research that utilizes members of the community under study to work as data collectors, theorists, focus selectors, hypothesis makers, research designers, and data analysts. In a five-month period, Maruyama formed an inmate research team to study the culture of a California prison (1974, p. 319). While Maruyama unquestionably solves the problem of relevance resonance that he describes—undoubtedly the purpose of his research converged with the purposes or needs of the people—I would not go so far as to foreclose entirely on the possibility that an exogenously trained endogenous researcher could and frequently does simultaneously have as her objectives both the needs of the community under study and her own personal advancement in the academy.

I am arguing however that, in spite of such acknowledged objectives, the endogenous researcher brings to her work one significant characteristic that is not shared by exogenous investigators. When she turns off the recorder and removes the cloak of investigator, she goes home to a community she forever shares with the natives. Their fundamental beliefs as well as their struggles and triumphs are deeply woven into the fabric of her own existence. This profound reality acts as a relentless urging, provoking her continuous attempt to liberate fact from romanticization. Ironically, she cannot hope to accomplish this, as I have argued, unless she is willing to closely examine the community as a system of shared values and beliefs as well as to examine the subtle but significant distinctions among its members.

NOTES

1. It is obvious that it is not possible for me to share class membership with all of my informants. However, in the course of the fieldwork, I realized that the range of economic circumstances within which I have lived from my childhood to the the present time makes it possible for me to identify with the experiences of impoverished, working-class, and middle-class women.

2. I have either changed the names or used the initials of informants to protect their privacy.

3. In the essay cited here, Gwaltney tells the reader that he has borrowed the terms *native* and *settler* from Sartre's introduction to Fanon's *The Wretched of the Earth*: "the use of the terms *native* and *settler* implies that racial distinction which is also reflected in the current inequitable distribution of the strategic resources of the world. *Natives* tend to be poor, powerless and nonwhite while *settlers* tend to be characterized by the arrogance of power and wealth" (Gwaltney 1976, p. 236). These terms appear not only in Sartre's introduction but throughout Fanon's essay as well.

4.   Since the recording of the life narrative with "Rena" which yielded the segment reproduced here, I have had the benefit of a number of initimate conversations with my sisters on the subject of color. These discussions were very painfully revealing of the specific ways in which light skin has been of shifting, uncertain value in their lives. They acknowledge having been granted some privileges emanating from the persistent color prejudice in this society, which places greater value *a priori* on people of color with lighter skin. However, my sisters clearly focused on the ongoing pain of alienation from other African American women who judge them negatively because of their appearance.

An Anthropological Approach to Cambodian Refugee Women

Reciprocity in Oral Histories

11

Lance Rasbridge

S ince the early 1980s, there has been a growing trend in feminist research away from the conception of any examination "on, by, and especially for women" to a more "integrative, transdisciplinary approach to knowledge, one that would ground theory contextually in the concrete realm of women's everyday lives."[1] Earlier feminist perspectives tended to be filled with ethical paradoxes which brought to the fore the question of duality in the research. Much credit for the breakdown of this hierarchical division in researcher/researched has been given to Ann Oakley for her germinal essay, "Interviewing Women: A Contradiction in Terms."[2] Oakley refutes the impassive role of the interviewer and promotes a more interactive and reciprocal approach to feminist research. Similarly, Judith Stacey argues powerfully for heightened "cross-fertilization between the discourses of feminist epistemology and methods and those of the critical traditions within anthropology and sociology."[3] As she notes, the more recent developments toward a critical and self-reflexive ethnography are well applicable to feminist dialogues, particularly those addressing the "experimential."

This paper utilizes an anthropological perspective in approaching life histories of resettled Cambodian refugee women. My methods relied less on formulating questions to these women than on association, "where the focus is on process, on the dynamic unfolding of the subject's viewpoint."[4] After a brief historical sketch of the Khmer Rouge revolution in Cambodia and the lives of Cambodian refugees, I trace the interactive process of trust and reciprocation on which the life history, and all of ethnographic inquiry, is based. Through the use of excerpts from a dozen life histories,[5] I share some of the rich data, and analyze through illustrative passages the emotional plight of Cambodian women through the holocaust and uprooting of which they are survivors.

The research with resettled Cambodian refugees began as a medical anthropological project on infant feeding.[6] Hence the work was women-focused in its investigation of both lactation and the feeding of infants and children, almost exclusively the feminine domain. Some critics have questioned the role and efficacy of a male researcher in this topic; indeed, my role as an "outsider" was doubly compounded, both as a male and as an American. However, my ability to converse in the Khmer language, obviating the need for a third-party translator, aided in developing my rapport with the women in my sample.

Moreover, in my experience, these paradoxes in gender, ethnicity, and even social standing can be advantageous. By being an outsider, I could feign complete ignorance of the subject, particularly breast-feeding, and hence more appropriately ask questions, obtaining details which would not necessarily be provided to a female researcher. Additionally, because I was viewed as an urban American of middle-class background, the refugee women assumed I would know little of breast-feeding practice, since bottle-feeding was seen by these mostly rural Cambodians as the province of the elite. Shostak, in her anthropological biography of a !Kung woman of the Kalahari, similarly speaks to this utilization of "outsiderness" in garnering information "so obvious to them yet so fascinating to me."[7] Of course, this level of rapport can only be reached through much reciprocation, as I will discuss.

Because my research focused on refugee infant feeding practices in the context of intracultural variation and the role of the former urban elite, I collected ethnohistorical data of women's lives in prewar urban Cambodia. Limited ethnographic material of this type exists, and I intended this material merely to serve as an appended backdrop for the larger work. However, the course of the stories always turned quickly to the war years and beyond, with the earlier ways of life about which I inquired being erased from memory. Furthermore, I shortly discovered the blandness of the ethnohistorical approach, which virtually denies personal involvement and interaction in the process.

Given these inadequacies, I subsequently broadened my perspective to that of the life history. As I learned, the oral history can be a highly sensitive tool for probing the innermost depths of cultural systems. In reading the small but powerful life history literature coming from this era,[8] I was motivated to join this voice, albeit in a small way, in educating others to the horror of the Cambodian crisis. I was particularly concerned in presenting the more muted, female voice. Theirs was a voice of special need which was and is frequently overlooked, not just by academics, but by resettlement planners and government agencies.[9]

Frankly, I was motivated more as an advocate, to preserve these stories as a historical testimonial, rather than to add to feminist discourse directly. The Cambodian situation does not neatly reduce to the "colonial model" of gender subjugation frequently applied by feminists to Third World cultures,[10] in that the oppression took place across ethnic and social class lines, to a much greater extent than gender itself. In fact, as history has revealed, women were frequently the subjugators of other women in the Khmer Rouge revolution. Thus, I was not documenting an oppression solely based on gender, but rather an oppression of humanity, and accordingly my viewpoint can be considered that of a "feminist humanist," where the "liberation of women will follow naturally the liberation of people."[11] Empowerment through the oral narrative can help realize this goal.

HISTORICAL BACKGROUND

While the rates of non-European refugees and immigrants to the United States have exploded in recent decades, few individuals or ethnic groups among these multitudes can claim the hardships of the recent past more than the Cambodian refugees. Even among their fellow Southeast Asian refugees, such as the Vietnamese and the Lao, their collective tragedy is unparalleled.

After years of warfare, the ultra-Maoist Khmer Rouge and its leader, Pol Pot, defeated the U.S.-backed Cambodian government and initiated a three-year wave of terror in pursuit of an agriculturally-based economy devoid of Western influence. The cities were forcibly evacuated, and the residents were sent to village communes under maniacal Khmer Rouge control. The family, traditionally the bastion of Cambodian social structure, was devalued in favor of individual allegiance to the State. In fact, the entire Cambodian social structure was turned upside down, with the elite and educated being targeted for elimination, as they were considered corrupting influences in the way of agrarian revolution. The deaths from these purges, together with mortality from starvation, disease, and overwork during this failed social experiment, numbered in the millions.

In late 1978, the Vietnamese invaded and defeated the Khmer Rouge, "liberating" the country and sparking one of the largest refugee exoduses the world has ever seen. An estimated 700,000 Cambodians had already made the perilous trip to refugee camps around the Thai border by the end of 1979. Since that time, approximately 180,000 of these refugees have been accepted for resettlement in the United States, with the flow diminishing to a trickle in recent years. The tragedy continues to the present, as the Khmer Rouge battle for control in the political chaos.

CATHARSIS

Of all the dynamics of interchange which accrue during the refugee life history process, perhaps the greatest lies in catharsis, the "giving back" to the speaker through healing. In the case of Cambodians, they have lived with horrific memories for over fifteen years. While the interviewees vary greatly in their successes in getting over these personal hells, their need to release, to share, is immediately evident through the tears as well as the laughter. The life history encounter offers an appropriate outlet for frequently repressed feelings. As Gail Sheehy writes of her biography of a young Cambodian refugee girl, "the work of writing the book and the healing process become indistinguishable."[12] Having their stories written with the assistance of an American academic provides a sense of legitimacy, as if their shattered lives were not spent in vain.

Similarly, the refugee life history can also be viewed as a tool, at least informally, in documenting social and legal status. In the context of the United States, the refugee frequently encounters a hostile social and economic environment, with very few in the majority population really understanding their plight and the antecedents to flight. In the face of this ignorance and frequent discrimination, the refugee can point to his or her story as qualification for or legitimization of special treatment here. In fact, one woman openly remarked to me that she hoped her story, shared with the American community, would foster more "pity" for her.

At the risk of self-importance, I believe the sensitive researcher does not "take" a life history, but rather encourages and facilitates it, ultimately "giving" a life history back to the speaker. As noted, telling the story can be an empowering experience for the teller, both legitimizing and validating the importance of his or her life.[13] This critical feature widens the role of the researcher well beyond that of the mere academic, and as the reader will see in the following discussion, these women's stories bear a profound influence not just on their resettlement experiences but on the researcher as well.

RECIPROCITY

It is obvious that the researcher is more than an inert recording device. Beyond catharsis for the refugee, what are some of the other issues in interaction and reciprocation? A common perspective in analyzing Southeast Asian social systems is through what is termed the "patron/client relationship." Simply put, under this somewhat formalized cultural construct, there is a conspicuous reciprocation in deed, if not necessarily in kind, for favors granted or services rendered. In my case, I was an American patron, requesting information, sometimes very personal, but supplying a client with a very prestigious product.

Although the product, the written account, was in my mind initially intended for the academic audience, it soon became clear that the refugee highly valued its possession in typed and bound form as a status object. Multiple copies provided to the women in my research were distributed to their American friends. Also, the booklet was frequently displayed prominently to other resettled Cambodians, who may themselves be illiterate in English as well as the native Khmer yet hold a profound respect for academia and literacy. Many of the women expressed gratification that these stories were recorded for their children and the younger generation to read, at least eventually; these stories represent a very real link to the past.

Another product of the life history encounter process, less concrete, was that of mutual obligation: I entered into an informal but binding relationship of assistance. On many occasions our meeting was contingent on my performance of some task that was outside the refugee's sphere of power but within my own. For example, I became a guaranteed ride to the store or a translator at the food stamps office, a relationship that continues to the present. Anthropologists frequently write of this "testing," where those being researched will assay the limits of just what the researcher can (or will) do for them. Here again, having an American patron adds significantly to the Cambodian refugee's status *vis-à-vis* other refugees.

Also, the life history encounter afforded the opportunity for much interactive feedback, in the form of respondents asking back questions that I posed. Hull notes how the roles of anthropologist and subject are reversed at this stage of the enthnographic enterprise, and it marks a critical juncture in the development of trust between the two.[14] By signifying mutuality and friendship, this give and take of information is one of the most gratifying aspects of the fieldwork experience. With this overview of the social context of the life history process, I now turn to an exploration of content.

LIFE STORY ANALYSIS

Beyond the interaction dictated by collaboration in life history encounters, the nature of the text itself can have a profound effect on the process, especially when the respondents are refugees. For one, due to the highly emotionally charged and personal nature of the subject matter, the emotional burden placed on the receiver is profound. Consider this excerpt from one Cambodian's woman's story:

One day at noon I came from the field I was working in to see my brother Sopheap. Sopheap, my father, mother, and sister, everybody was there, so sick. I was so young and so stupid, I did not know anything about death then, I never even saw anybody die. He was laying with tears coming out of his eyes, holding his wife's hand. He tried to speak, but just made like three sounds from his throat. I did not even know he died, but then my father said he was dead. Some people took him to be buried.

It was only two or three days later that my father's sickness got even worse, I think because he was so close to my brother, he loved him so much. Somebody said he should go to the Khmer Rouge hospital, the place where people went to die. And we were all so crazy, we did not know what to do. Everybody was so sick except my sister-in-law and me.

So he was put in this hospital, and I would go to see him every day. I could barely see him, because the lamps they used were so dim. I would ask him if he was OK, and he would say, "I'm hungry, daughter." He would say it like that. So I tried to bring him what little rice there was. And he asked about cigarettes, so I was able to get two cigarettes, just tobacco, really. He wanted to eat fish, he asked about fish a lot. I was even able to get him a little fish, boiled it with a little salt and rice. But when I gave it to him it was already too late, I knew because he said it did not taste good. He only ate three spoonfuls, then stopped and asked for a cigarette, which I rolled in a leaf and gave to him. I saved the other cigarette that I had for later, but I never got to give it to him.

I was working in the field when I asked a Khmer Rouge soldier if he had seen my father that day. He said that he had seen him crawling outside to go to the bathroom, and even my mother was too sick to help him. So I ran back to see my father, and he was still talking like crazy person. He said he was feeling better, but he was not really, it was like *slau chiem*, like strength you get just before you die. But he made me feel better, and he said that I should go back to work, and not worry. The next day he was dead, somebody came to tell me in the field.

So again it was me and my sister-in-law that had to decide what to do, so hard because we did not get support from anybody, and everybody so sick. We did not even tell mother right away. Everybody was so weak except the soldiers, we did not even know how we could bury him. We went to get good clothes to dress him in, like our custom, but there was nobody to bury him. Then we saw the soldiers just take his body away, rolled in a mat, and threw it on an oxcart. They even threw the clothes back, said to keep them. And they took the body away, and we could not even say anything, we just stood there and cried. We do not know what they did with the body.

This level of detail typically emerges from the more general and innocuous only after reaching a high level of trust. After several sessions of many hours spent with this woman, I had proven my level of commitment. The event of recording such tear-filled intimacies marked a change in my relationship with her; I took it upon myself to be her personal advocate in helping her find employment and guiding her through the bureaucratic maze of refugee resettlement.

The emotionality may also encompass the profoundly personal, as evidenced by this passage:

The survivors, including me, ate anything that we could find, including rats, lizards, snakes and wild vegetables just to keep alive. Our stomachs were never full, and the scraps that we did eat were not very nutritious. I became hungry just as soon as I finished my meal. We never had enough to eat, and many more died from starvation and malnutrition. Our hunt for something to eat became more difficult each day as food became scarcer. There were days when we could not find anything to eat at all, and it was at times like these that the sick and weak died. As repulsive as it may sound to well-fed and well-educated Americans, those who did not survive became food for those who did. Unless someone has been in a situation like this, they could not possibly understand the rationale and logic of self-preservation under the most extreme limits. I believe hunger is the cruelest form of torture that exists in the world. Other forms of torture hurt for only a finite time, but the hunger in Cambodia lasted twenty-four hours a day and seemed endless.

For me, on a simplistic level, the weight of receiving such intimate and powerful accounts further instills a sense of obligation, to finish the project and get the information distributed. To promote the circulation of the material both takes the onus off the researcher in sharing the emotional burden with others, while also fulfilling the desire to educate the masses.

Another particularly disturbing type of passage is that detailing what we are beginning to call the "atrocity story." These are the sort of depictions that Haing Ngor, the actor in *The Killing Fields*, prefaces with the following warning to the reader in his autobiography: "It is an important part of the story, but it is not a pleasant part."[15] Here the unspeakable is spoken. In the words of one survivor:

> So they catch me again. This time I think I'm dead, me and four others. Put us far away from the camp. Took two of us away in the afternoon, and I didn't know what they do, but they come back with the heart, with the heart and the string, to tie those people, and I see their arms and hands, blood up to here, so I know those guys are already dead. The next morning about four o'clock they took me and the other guy, took the other guy in the trees, and I just heard one sound, uhh, and after that they took me there, and I see him there. They took the ham chop and chopped him in the back, chopped down all way, he was tied to a tree. All the stomach come out on one side and he still breathing. And I see him and I just shake my head, can't say nothing to him. And he just shake the head to me, and after that they did to me. They tell me to dig the hole for myself, about one and one half yard, and four inches. They tell me to kneel down, hands tied behind my back. They take the shovel and knock me on the back of my head. I hurt in my brain, and I fly straight to the hole. I'm already dead at that time. They took all the string from my hand, took my clothes, and close the ground back.

This victim attributes eventual survival, or more precisely rebirth, to supernatural forces, again a subject touching the innermost depths of spirituality. Here, the distressing details of the atrocity emerged only after the fear of disturbing the listener was surmounted. The mortification surrounding the frank discussion of torture lies with both the teller and the listener. In this case, the refugees were ill at ease, and almost apologetic, in pointing to their fellow Cambodians as the perpetrators, and I was incredulous at the level of perversity and malevolence to which humans could sink.

These excerpts illustrate the extreme depth of emotionality reached in the stories of these refugees. Other writers, notably Patai, also reflect on this issue, questioning morally the "fair exchange" principle in what is ostensibly a one-sided recitation.[16] How is the listener to react to these personal exhortations? I agree with Patai that there are troubling imbalances and innate hierarchies in this research. Nonetheless, I believe that the value in catharsis, the human embrace, is rationale sufficient for life history research. Patai's question, "Is ethical research possible?" remains enigmatic. However, I would ask, Is it not a greater breach of morality on the part of social scientists not to respond to oppression with the tools of research readily within our domain? Of course, the level of oppression in groups such as refugees is greater, and hence the ethical aspects of conducting research is further magnified here. Apart from these larger issues of interpersonal relationships and ethics, these histories do provide feminist scholars with many insights into the cultural domain of Cambodian women, a topic which I now discuss.

CAMBODIAN REFUGEE WOMEN

While the physical and psychological trauma touched all Cambodians refugees, women suffer certain unique fates, by the nature of their roles in traditional Cambodian culture.[17] The most obvious here is the tremendous maternal loss experienced through the deaths of children. In one mother's words:

> When the Pol Pot regime took over Cambodia, I was separated from my children and now all my children are dead. During the communist time there was no store to go to buy any medicine. When all my children got sick and died I went crazy.

The most fundamental aspect of maternalism was brutally wrested from these women. It is difficult to find a Cambodian woman who was not directly touched by this loss.

Another related factor which bears most heavily on women was the breakdown of the family unit, either through forced separation instituted by the Khmer Rouge, or through "reeducation" designed to supplant the mother-child bond with allegiance to the State. As part of the latter effort, the tradition of filial piety, elder respect, was reversed, and children became the objects of fear.

> In our village, the Khmer Rouge had spies, *chlop*, young children, maybe ten or eleven years old, who were taken away from their families, and would come around every night to listen in people's houses.

These antifamily tactics of the Khmer Rouge have left deep and long-lasting psychological scars on Cambodian mothers.

Tragically, but not unexpectedly, these scars were physical as well as psychological. Rape and beatings were all too frequently employed as means of further subjugating women,[18] both during the Khmer Rouge holocaust and in the ensuing era of refugee flight. Here again the unspeakable is spoken, but not always directly, and not just by women. The following is a Cambodian man's observations:

> And then the Thailand army they catch me, and they see a lot of girl, and they try to rape the girls. They had all of us, about thirty people, sit down and they point

gun at us, and they took three girls and tear their clothes out, in front of us. And the girls are too young, and I see that I can't stop it.

Of course, this area of sexual trauma was undoubtedly repressed to some degree in the course of the stories, not only on account of the male collaborator/female narrator gender issue, but also because of the larger Cambodian cultural norms surrounding female sexual modesty.

The violence against women does not always stop upon their resettlement in a country of permanent asylum. As the stressors of acculturation further erode the traditional structure of social relationships, women sometimes become the victims of these frustrations. As one social worker, herself a resettled Cambodian, remarks:[19]

> The most obvious problem I see is violence—I mean family violence, wife and child abuse. Now we are talking about something that is unique for Khmer people. Yes, the woman has not been liberated and she is a second-class person, but the physical harm done to her here in the United States is unlike that in Cambodia. I have seen women with terrible wounds on their faces and arms, teeth missing, and much more. . . . All this is a combination of grief and guilt and somehow there is depression that makes these people violent. This is usually not their nature.

This violence against women is symptomatic of a larger issue in the culture of resettlement. The Cambodian refugee woman has lost a key element of power which she possessed in the traditional context: the role of agricultural laborer, which put her, as a producer, nearly on a par with her husband. One widowed refugee woman lamented:

> My son goes to work every day. In the daytime my children go to school. I stay home by myself and am bored. I just know how to take the bus to go to welfare and to pay the bills.

Traditional roles, where the woman would have a place in the field next to her husband, have been displaced. Sometimes she may go to work here, but with an educational deficit (compared to her husband), work is typically unskilled or simply not available. Moreover, reflective of conditions in the larger cultural milieu, there is latent sexism in much of resettlement programming; few job-training and English classes accommodate women refugees as mothers. Furthermore, the refugee woman has lost her role as provider or nourisher for her family, having now to rely on welfare benefits to feed her children rather than the fruits of her own labor.

Importantly, while the life stories I have recounted illustrate the horrors of the Cambodian holocaust, particularly as they relate to women's experiences, the reader can glean many positive, although sometimes hidden, elements from these histories. Indeed, many refugee women from Cambodia have overcome tremendous obstacles, and have gone on to accomplishments undreamed of even before the war years. Several women spoke of the extreme suffering as a sort of rallying point for survival, and many women told me of heroic acts of compassion displayed, even to the point of endangerment of life. For example, one friend cites a special bond formed with a nonrelative:

> She was from Phnom Penh too. People from Phnom Penh, they loved each other, and tried to take care of each other. Women helped women, like that. I even had one friend who was a farmer person, but she hated the communists like me.

Hence the narratives provide a powerful depiction of the strength of the human soul in the face of such evil.

CONCLUSIONS

This point of survival as strength summarizes the role of the life history in the reciprocal relationship between researcher and refugee. Consider these words from a social service provider:[20]

> Khmer women want very much to survive in this country, but they need confidence in themselves and some positive experiences. Often I do not see either of these needs being met. I believe that even the poor, uneducated women—women who cannot read or write in Khmer language—want to become self-sufficient, but because of their own personal history, the chance of success is very small.

The life history, sympathetically conducted, affords just such an opportunity for women to build confidence by sharing their experiences. This catharsis is a necessary first step in focusing on the reconstruction of life in a foreign and often inhospitable land. Women themselves become the authorities of their life experiences, and the researcher becomes the facilitator of this transition. These women are survivors in the most literal sense of the word, and the life history becomes the documentation of what has been overcome and therefore the foundation for what now can be achieved.

In sum, the life history project with resettled Cambodian women enables them a voice that most likely would have remained silent or at most a whisper. Most of these women are not sufficiently fluent in English to describe the details brought out without the facilitation of a Khmer-speaking facilitator. Furthermore, none of these women currently possesses the skills or the means to write her story without assistance, even in her own language. Outside autobiography in the purest sense, there is necessarily some hierarchical division between the collaborator-researcher and the narrator. To minimize this bias, I reviewed the finished drafts with the women, and allowed them editorial changes, of which very few were made.

A potential area for future development in this area is to have Cambodian women themselves serve as the collaborators with their "sisters," matching the interviewers and interviewees.[21] Of course, in the case of Cambodians, there are very few academics at present with such skills, but this picture will surely change as the younger generation proceeds through the higher education system. While the editors of this volume reflect in the introduction that this matching of gender and ethinicity between the interviewer and interviewee "is more likely to produce an empowering environment for the narrator," this is not always the case for Cambodian and other cultures in which such factors as age grading and elder respect are strongly embedded.[22] Age differentials or social position may weigh even more heavily than gender in influencing the interaction. For example, an older Cambodian of a rural background may not be very forthcoming with a young, academically trained Cambodian-American collaborator, as this would have been a rare association in the past. For these reasons, an "outsider" can potentially obtain the more reliable information.

My own situation as a "double outsider," an American male working with Cambodian females, my aberrancy as it were, together with my role ambiguity as an anthropologist, may even have lessened the elements of intimidation and other forms of bias in the encounter, particularly within this social group, marked by quite rigid intracultural rules of social intercourse.

Extrapolating from a concept Margaret Atwood raises, the paradox of being a "woman writer," questioning whether "woman" and "writer" can possibly be separated in the same person,[23] I do not believe my role as a male researching women's issues makes me a "male feminist." This dyad is antithetical to the holistic, anthropological paradigm. Rather, as an anthropologist sensitive to the reflexivity issues in research, the dyad collapses to that of humanist. In the words of Johnson-Odom, "We must view women's oppression in the context of all oppression. We must challenge a feminist perspective to envisage a human-centered world, in which the satisfaction of human needs, justly met, is a primary goal."[24] In the case at hand, I am an advocate for a particularly needy, yet silent and overlooked group: Cambodian refugee women.

In conclusion, utilizing excerpts from a few life histories, I illustrate several paths by which the elicitor becomes drawn into the interactive realm of the encounter. As Watson and Watson-Franke note, "The anthropologist, let us not forget, is involved in the data-gathering situation no less than his informant."[25] Particularly due to the highly emotionally charged nature of refugees' stories, the anthropologist is ethically bound to a cycle of reciprocation, in kind or deed. Beyond mere catharsis for the refugee, the life history endeavor provides the opportunity to gain a level of friendship and understanding typically not experienced in the research enterprise, by coming to terms with our own humanity.

NOTES

Many thanks to Dr. Rose Jones of Southern Methodist University, Dallas, for her thoughtful critique of this paper, and to the editors and other reviewers.

1. Judith Stacey, "Can There Be a Feminist Ethnography?" in *Women's Words: The Feminist Practice of Oral History*, Sherna Berger Gluck and Daphne Patai, eds. (New York: Routledge, 1991), p. 111.

2. Ann Oakley, "Interviewing Women: A Contradiction in Terms," in *Doing Feminist Research*, ed. Helen Roberts (London: Routledge and Kegan Paul, 1981), pp. 30–61.

3. Stacey, p. 115.

4. Kathryn Anderson and Dana C. Jack, "Learning to Listen: Interview Techniques and Analyses," in Gluck and Patai, eds., p. 23.

5. A more detailed discussion of the methodology employed in the life history project may be found in Lance A. Rasbridge, "Beyond Catharsis: Reciprocity and Interaction through Cambodian Life Histories," *Selected Papers on Refugee Issues II*, MaryCarol Hopkins and Nancy D. Donnelly, eds. (Arlington, VA: American Anthropological Association, 1993). The current work is a development of ideas first presented here. Also, for purposes of this chapter, I also draw from a few life stories published elsewhere; see Note 7 below.

6. For the full account, see Lance A. Rasbridge, *Infant/Child Feeding among Cambodians in Dallas: Intracultural Variation in Reference to Iron Nutrition*. Ph.D. dissertation, Southern Methodist University (Ann Arbor: University Microfilms, 1991).

7. Marjorie Shostak, *Nisa: The Life and Words of a Kung Woman*. (Cambridge, MA: Harvard University Press, 1981), p. 22.

8. For example, see Joanna C. Scott, *Indochina's Refugees: Oral Histories from Laos, Cambodia and Vietnam*. (Jefferson, NC.: McFarland and Co., 1989); John Tenhula, *Voices from Southeast Asia: The Refugee Experience in the United States* (New York: Holmes and Meier, 1991).

9. For a marked exception to this generalization, see Susan Forbes Martin, *Refugee Women* (London: Zed Books, 1991).

10. See Sidonie Smith and Julia Watson, eds., *De/Colonizing the Subject: The Politics of Gender in Women's Autobiography* (Minneapolis: University of Minnesota Press, 1992).

11. Jo Freeman, "The Women's Liberation Movement: Its Origins, Structure, Activities, and Ideas." In *Women: A Feminist Perspective*, Jo Freeman, ed. (Palo Alto, CA: Mayfield Publishing Co., 1975), p. 556.

12. Gail Sheehy, *Spirit of Survival* (New York: William Morrow and Co., 1986).

13. For a similar argument, see Daphne Patai, "U.S. Academics and Third World Women: Is Ethical Research Possible?" In Gluck and Patai, eds.

14. Cindy Hull, "Lessons from the Field," *The Naked Anthropologist: Tales from Around the World*, Philip R. DeVita, ed. (Belmont, CA: Wadsworth, Inc., 1992).

15. Haing Ngor, *A Cambodian Odyssey*, with Roger Warner (New York: MacMillan Publishing Co., 1991).

16. Patai, "U.S. Academics and Third World Women: Is Ethical Research Possible?" p. 142.

17. For a complete discussion of women's roles in traditional Cambodian society, see May Ebihara, "Khmer Village Women in Cambodia: A Happy Balance," *Many Sisters: Women in Cross-Cultural Perspective*, Carolyn J. Mathiason, ed. (New York: The Free Press, 1974).

18. For a summary article on rape as a weapon of war, see Susan Brownmiller, "Making Female Bodies the Battlefield," *Newsweek*, Jan. 4, 1993, 37.

19. Tenhula, *Voices from Southeast Asia*, p. 156.

20. Ibid., p. 156.

21. This "matching," commonly referred to as "native anthropology" or "native ethnography," while potentially empowering to both the researcher and those being researched, is not without a caveat. The researcher must be able to "externalize internal knowledge" while simultaneously "sifting out unique idiosyncracies," skills which require special training and a very different per- spective from that of the "outsider." For a model of this methodology, see Fadwa El Guindi, *The Myth of Ritual: A Native's Ethnography of Zapotec Life-Crisis Rituals* (Tucson: University of Arizona Press, 1986).

22. For a good overview of Asian social structure as it relates to feminist issues, see Elizabeth McTaggart Almquist, "Race and Ethnicity in the Lives of Minority Women," in Freeman, ed., pp. 438–39.

23. Margaret Atwood, "On Being a 'Woman Writer': Paradoxes and Dilemmas," In *Women's Voices: Visions and Perspectives*, Pat C. Hoy II, et al., eds. (New York: McGraw Hill Publishing Co., 1990).

24. Cheryl Johnson-Odom, "Common Themes, Different Contexts: Third World Women and Feminism," in *Third World Women and the Politics of Feminism*, Chandra T. Mohanty, Ann Russo, and Lourdes Torres, eds. (Bloomington: Indiana University Press, 1991), p. 326.

25. Lawrence Watson and Maria-Barbara Watson-Franke, *Interpreting Life Histories: An Anthropological Inquiry* (New Brunswick, NJ: Rutgers University Press, 1985), p. 17.

Like Us But Not One of Us

12

Reflections on a Life History Study of
African American Teachers

Michéle Foster

Increasingly those undertaking field work and conducting oral history are
insiders, members of the subordinate groups they have chosen to study.
Social science reveals a growing trend toward "native anthropology" and
other insider studies, studies by ethnic minorities of their own communities.[1]
Despite this trend, and a large literature on ethnographic and anthropological
method that treats the involvement, role, and stance that researchers adopt *vis-
à-vis* the communities they are studying, most of these references—both the
contemporary work as well as that from earlier periods—deals with research
conducted among others, whether the others are the "natives" in "exotic"
communities in United States society or abroad. This is not surprising.
Traditionally, anthropologists and others undertaking ethnographic and qualitative research have studied the other. Thus, anthropology, even as it promoted cultural relativity, was conceived and nurtured in a colonial world of haves
and have-nots, powerful and powerless, self and other. As the ethnographic
method became more commonplace and studies grew to include more complex industrial and post-industrial societies such as the United States, the
power relationship between researcher and researched remained unaltered.
For the most part, this research is also dichotomized, with the self studying the
other, the powerful the powerless, the haves the have-nots. These days it is
widely acknowledged that all researchers are influenced by their particular
perspectives. Consequently, a distinctive hallmark of the newer literature in
ethnographic theory and method, including recent work in education, is its
self-conscious examination of the subjective nature of the research endeavor.
However, because articles on method tend to focus on the self studying the

other, there are relatively few that discuss the methodological, ethical, and political issues confronting ethnic minorities or the personalities they adopt when they undertake such studies.

It is widely accepted that all researchers, including those of us who are members of ethnic minority groups, are bound by our cultural perspectives. Given that ethnic minorities are first socialized into the values and cultural and communicative norms of their home communities and later, the result of many years of education, into those of the mainstream culture, it is more likely that, unlike our non-native counterparts, we will hold multiple cultural perspectives. This means that as ethnic minorities we have the potential to bring multiple cultural perspectives to our research endeavors. As much as this dual socialization provides an opportunity, it presents an equal danger. In matriculating into the dominant culture, ethnic minorities are schooling in paradigms—new worldviews and ways of knowing and of communicating. Years of schooling teach individuals to rename, recategorize, reclassify, and re-conceptualize their experiences. Once familiar and comfortable ways of knowing, behaving, and communicating may seem strange or unenlightened, or be discounted entirely. New values are implanted, new voices acquired. Moreover, whether intentional or not, the experience of students of color, such as those in many bilingual programs, are typically subtractive, not additive. Like the transition to English, the transition to dominant ways of thinking, valuing, and behaving is often complete and one-way. Thus, although African, Latino, Native, and Asian American researchers may possess certain sociological characteristics that bind us and make us recognizable to our home communities, we may have forgotten or been taught to disregard the belief systems of our birth communities. Moreover, we may have lost the ability to communicate appropriately by using cues that make us recognizable to potential cultural co-members. Absent more important cues, however, these sociological facts may be insufficient for community members to recognize or accept us. More important than the sociological facts may be the political alignments expected of ethnic minority researchers by community members.

Mama Day, a novel by Gloria Naylor (1988), captures some of these tensions. In the book a well-educated young man, known only as Reema's boy, returns home from across the river, where he had gone to be educated, to conduct research among his own people on Willow Spring, a coastal sea island belonging neither to Georgia nor to South Carolina. Armed with notebooks and a tape recorder, the indispensable instruments of an anthropologist, Reema's boy begins questioning relatives and neighbors about a commonly used phrase. Naylor writes:

> And when he went around asking about 18 & 23, there on about "ethnography," "unique speech patterns," "cultural preservation," and whatever else he seemed to be getting so much pleasure out of while talking into his little gray

machine. He was all over the place—What 18 & 23 mean? What 18 & 23 mean? And we told him the God-honest truth: it was just our way of saying something. Winky was awful, though, he even spit tobacco juice for him. Sat on his porch all day, chewing up the boy's Red Devil premium and spitting so there weren't nothing to do but take pity on him as the rattled machine could pick it up. There was enough fun in that to take us through the fall and winter when he had hauled himself back over The Sound to wherever he was getting what was supposed to be passing for an education. And he sent everybody he'd talked to copies of the book he wrote, bound all nice with our name and his signed on the first page. We couldn't hold Reema down, she was so proud. It's a good thing she didn't read it. None of us made it through the introduction, but that said it all: you see, he had come to the conclusion after "extensive field work" (ain't never picked a boll of cotton or head of lettuce in his life—Reema spoiled him silly), but he done still made it to the conclusion that 18 & 23 wasn't 18 & 23 at all— was really 81 & 32, which just so happened to be the lines of longitude and latitude marking off where Willow Springs sits on the map. And we were just so damned dumb that we turned the whole thing around. Not that he called it being dumb, mind you, called it "asserting our cultural identity," "inverting hostile social and political parameters." 'Cause, see, being we was brought here as slaves, we had no choice but to look at everything upside-down. And then being that we was isolated off here on this island, everybody else in the country went on learning good English and calling things what they really was—in the dictionary and all that—while we kept on calling things ass-backwards. And he thought that was just so wonderful and marvelous, etcetera, etcetera. . . . Well, after that crate of books came here, if anybody had any doubts about what them developers were up to, if there was just a tinge of seriousness behind then jokes about the motorboats and swimming pools that could be gotten from selling a piece of land them books squashed it. The people who ran the type of schools that could turn our children into raving lunatics—and then put his picture on the back of the book so we couldn't even deny it was him—didn't mean us a speck of good. (pp. 7–8)

Since 1988, I have been collecting oral life histories of African American teachers. My narrators and I share a number of sociological characteristics. We are all African American, and all except four are women. Though younger than than the majority, I, like them, have been a teacher for most of my professional life. Drawing on my experience conducting this study, this paper addresses some of the issues that arise when researcher and informants are members of the same cultural and speech communities. Its goal is to demonstrate the positive effect that a shared identity can have on establishing rapport and recovering authentic accounts, as well as to illustrate that even members of the same speech and cultural community are differentiated by other equally important characteristics that make the researcher simultaneously an insider and an outsider.

PROBLEM, THEORY, AND METHOD

A review of the sociological, anthropological, and first-person literature on teachers had convinced me that African American teachers largely had been ignored in the literature, and that where they had been portrayed, except in a few instances, their portrayal generally had been negative, not positive. What also intrigued me was that a majority of the negative portrayals were written by outsiders, at a time when the rhetoric of equal opportunity made attacks on segregated schools with all of their attendant shortcomings including African American teachers, legitimate targets. From the twenties through the forties, W. E. B. Du Bois admonished the black community not to confuse the inadequacies of segregated schools with African American teachers, but this warning seems not to have been heeded by white writers.[3] On the other hand, when blacks wrote about black teachers, their descriptions tended to be more flattering and balanced. Though several historical accounts document the fight undertaken by the black community to secure black teachers for their children, both historic and contemporary accounts by black teachers themselves are rare. The negative portryals of black teachers by outsiders, the contrastingly more flattering and well-balanced insider descriptions, and the paucity of black teachers speaking in their own voices made me aware of the need to ascertain how African American teachers viewed their own lives and practice.

Wanting to capture African American definitions of a good teacher, I developed a selection process I have coined "community nomination" specifically for this study. Community nomination means that teachers were selected through contact with black communities. African American periodicals, organizations, and individuals provided the names of the teachers. Building on the concept of "native anthropology" developed by Jones (1970) and Gwaltney (1980),[4] "community nomination" is an attempt to gain what anthropologists call an "emic" perspective, an insider's view, in this case the black community's perspective of a good teacher.

DATA COLLECTION

I tape-recorded the interviews in their entirety. Though I did not transcribe the tapes, I spent many hours reviewing them, because I knew it was critical to capture both what was said and the manner in which it was said.[5] In addition, I built up files of newspaper and magazine clippings, gathered archival data—lesson plans, agendas of meetings, copies of student work and the like—and took notes on numerous other reports.

Eager to secure cooperation, when I spoke with potential narrators I made it a point from the outset to emphasize our shared characteristics. In February 1988, the active phase of my research began with the interview of my first informant. Because there were long periods of time when I was waiting to receive the names of teachers to interview, and lags between initial written contact, subsequent phone conversations, and visits to interview the narrators, there were times when I felt very little was being accomplished. Conversely, at other times when there were several narrators to be interviewed in a short period, each requiring a flight to some faraway city, two or three days of interviews and observations, and a return flight home, the research took on a frenetic quality. One of my biggest challenges was making sure that the teachers would agree to an interview. Since all of the arrangements were made by letter and telephone, there was always a fear that, when I arrived in an unfamiliar city, the teacher would not be there.

Whether claiming insider status by emphasizing our shared characteristics minimized the social distance and ultimately influenced the informants' decision to participate is unclear. Most were flattered to have been selected to be interviewed; only once was an interview refused, and then because of illness. Despite my claims of insider status, however, a number of the teachers were surprised to discover I was black, claiming that I did not sound black over the telephone. Sometimes merely discovering that I was black modified their expectations of the interview that was to take place.

Though, as noted, earlier requests for interviews were rarely refused, negotiating the location of the interview sometimes emphasized my status as a stranger. The majority of the teachers accepted my claims of insider status by inviting me to interview them in their homes. Often I accompanied them, participated in their regular activities, and interacted with their families. Frequently, the teachers picked me up at my hotel, and some even had their friends drive me to the airport. In rare cases, they insisted that I sleep in a spare bedroom rather than waste money on a hotel. While one might see these courtesies merely as instances of hospitality, such extended contact allowed them to test my claims of insider status continuously. Others did not immediately acknowledge my claims to insider status, preferring a more neutral location for their interview, usually their school, but in some cases my hotel room. Whether the interviews took place in homes or classrooms, a meal eaten at home or in a restaurant often preceded the interview. Usually, after the initial interviews were over, the teachers suggested that subsequent interviews be held at their homes. Inviting me to dinner at their homes after a first interview had been conducted at a neutral site occurred frequently enough to suggest that these teachers had felt at ease during our first meeting.

Despite these overt indications of acceptance, there were important characteristics that separated me from individual narrators. Thus, I was both insider and outsider, a Northerner when I interviewed Southerners, an urban resident when I interviewed rural residents, a younger person when I interviewed the older teachers, a woman when I interviewed men. Often I was positioned as an outsider in several dimensions at the same time. These characteristics shaped the interview in some immediately obvious and not so obvious ways. For instance, because I had lived through the turbulent time of the sixties, it was easier for me to identify emotionally with the racial struggles of the teachers who came of age during that same period. Although I had read a lot about the struggles of blacks during the twenties, thirties, forties, and fifties, and had heard a lot about them from my grandparents, who experienced them firsthand, my emotional responses were muted when interviewing older teachers, compared to those I experienced when interviewing my agemates.

Let me give one extended example which illustrates several of these points. When I first contacted Miss Ruby, an octogenarian and the oldest of my narrators, she was delighted that an African American scholar had finally contacted her and wanted to record her sixty year career as a teacher in small South Carolina rural communities. When I finally arrived in Pawley's Island, I called her to get directions to her school, the agreed-upon site of our interview. About a mile, she assured me. Not wanting to be late, I set out for the one-mile walk along Highway 17. Along the way, I was greeted by passersby, who slowed down to wave from automobiles, or was acknowledged by other pedestrians walking along the same highway. After an interminable walk, I finally arrived at the driveway, where Miss Ruby and three other woman greeted me. Chuckling as I made my way up the long drive to the house, Miss Ruby teased that they had not expected a city slicker like myself to be able to walk such a long way, a distance I later discovered was four miles, and one often traveled by African-American residents of this tiny community. This was but the first of many tests that Miss Ruby subjected me to. She scrutinized my behavior as I interacted with her pupils, watched my reactions when the mothers she had asked prepared and served me lunch, and evaluated how I conducted myself when she arranged to have friends transport me around town. Although she had eagerly accepted my invitation to interview her, I remain convinced that these trials were her way of assessing the extent to which I was an insider worthy of her trust and confidence.

During our interviews, when Miss Ruby asserted the fact that during the period when she had attended Avery Institute, in the late teens and early twenties, the students regularly put on Shakespeare plays, I missed the significance of her statement. It was only upon reviewing the tapes and hearing her repeat the claim in marked intonation that I understood its importance to her. Nonetheless, it was not until I had read several books on the schooling of the teachers trained in all-black normal schools that I understood the importance of her claim, particularly her attempts to convey that her own privileged classical and liberal arts education had been a challenge to the social order of the time, which prescribed training in industrial and domestic arts for teachers being prepared to teach in rural black communities.[6]

The difficulty of relating to conditions not particular to my generation also confronted me when Southern teachers proudly recounted the tactics they engaged in as they sought equal wages to whites for comparable work in segregated public schools. Once again, I had trouble fully grasping the significance of these stories, until I read works that underscored how the ideology of white supremacy was in part based on a political economy that dictated blacks not be paid comparable wages to whites for equal work. The point here is that, in much the same ways that African Americans of my generation fault the younger generation of blacks for not being able to appreciate or identify with the struggles of our Civil Rights Movement, initially, my own outsider status made me unable to easily perceive the significance of the racial struggles experienced by many of the older teachers whose eras I had not directly experienced.

The influence of gender is also objectively evident in the interviews. All of the interviews with men show sharply divergent turn-taking patterns from the interviews conducted with the women. In the interviews with women, turn-taking exchanges were much more balanced and evidence much more overlapping speech, and back-channeling indicating co-membership, a phenomena others have described.[7] In the interviews with the men, on the other hand, the turn-taking patterns are uneven, with the men speaking for much longer stretches at a time. To illustrate this point, I present parts of the conversations I had with two teachers, the first female, the second male.

Text 1

I: If you had to describe yourself as a teacher, how would you describe yourself? If you had to characterize yourself as a teacher, how would you?

T: Well, I don't know, I suppose I am caring and sensitive and I'm pretty organized and sometimes creative, and I hope knowledgeable and effective most of the time.

I: Un huh.

T: That's how I see myself.

I: What influenced the kind of teacher you are?

T: You know, I think the things that I've seen through the years in classroom situations and that I've learned from talking with other teachers, and, one course that I remember that is a fairly recent one. Not recent, but within the last ten or twelve years. Teacher effectiveness training kind of influenced me and that was in in-service, a staff development course, something that I took during the summer. But, taught by a very sensitive person who is now a classroom teacher, she was, she tried her hand at county, at a county position and did some training and then she wanted to, she missed the classroom so much herself, but that was ah, it was about being sensitive and active listening and all those kinds of things. That kind of course has influenced me though I think I've always been you know, a sensitive caring teacher. But when I first taught in Cleveland, I remember on one of my evaluations, my department chair said, Oh, you were so militant on some item, and I guess it was my response to a student when he or she had said something, maybe I came down too hard and too aggressively, because I thought that was the kind of thing to do, and that's not even the way I am. But I think at first I may have thought maybe barking at people a little bit or being a little aggressive, and I remember once during that first or second year that a student cried in my class.

I: This was during your first year of teaching in Cleveland?

T: Yes, in Cleveland. Yes, and I, she was making a nuisance of herself and had irritated me and the class, and I don't remember what I said to her but it must have been something that she deserved, and the kids thought that she deserved. Next thing I knew, her head was on her desk and she was really bawling, and I thought well, maybe I came down too hard. And so things I've seen and just hearing people talk about their students and seeing many many things that happen in classes have kind of influenced me. I don't treat anyone harshly, and I think that I can handle most kids and situations by being rather gentle with them and still I can accomplish what I need to. I guess that course and others like that have kind of affected me.

Text 2

I: And so I'm interested in getting some understanding about the kind of teacher you are, how you describe yourself. One of the things I see here is that it says that you are part disciplinarian, part cheerleader.

T: Right.

I: Could you tell me something about that?

T: Well, my demeanor is—I have a very relaxed demeanor, and my personality is very outgoing. I'll smile a lot—kids used to call me "Smiley"—ah, I tend to be, I try to be upbeat, but also, I try to encourage kids, no matter what it is that they can do it. And I always want them to realize that the only thing that separates them from getting ahead is their own motivation. So, I constantly believe that no matter what they say, I respect what they say. And I try to take a negative, and make it into a positive. So, that might be the cheerleader aspect of it, but I have a non—I guess a very serious approach to education, in the classroom, it's only gonna be my way. On the surface. I must convince them that it's much easier for one student to get along with one teacher than for one teacher to get along with thirty-two kids. So, so it's much harder for the kids to change their ways in order to accept me than it is for me to change my ways to accept all thirty-two. So my approach is always to instill discipline number one, because once I have established that as a foundation, then I can lead to some other areas later on, but I do not go anywhere, until I have established my foundation that it's gonna be—if everything works right, one way, at the beginning—accept what I'm trying to do, establish discipline, and then we proceed from that point. So, I pretty much demand that kids accept the rules, respect one another, care about one another, and that learning is two way. I respect them, I demand that they respect me. And I also demand that they respect themselves as well as their classmates.

I: Where did you get your ideas about the kind of teacher you wanted to become? Where did that come from?

T: Many of the people that—I grew up in an area of far North East Washington, where very few of the people were college educated. But they had wisdom beyond a college-educated person. And most of them were workers, but even in our community of workers, the one thing that they all insisted, that people respect one another, and that you would do the right thing. You will achieve, you will try hard to get ahead. So, I guess the basic foundation which I was brought is the fact that you're gonna be respectful, and that you're gonna have some discipline. And I guess that carried me through some very difficult periods of my adolescence. I mean when I went through that period where, you know, rebellion, I had a basic foundation that was strong, you see, and it was that strong foundation that kept me away from alcohol, drugs, being a drop-out, doing mischievous things, being a criminal. My parents instilled in me a great sense of what was right and what was wrong, and also, if you made a mistake, you was gonna have to pay for it yourself. So those kinds of things stayed with me pretty much throughout my young adulthood. And I would also like to say that even as a kid growing, the older kids, the ones that were my models, they even had, despite the fact that they might have had some inadequacy, but they had a sense of respect, that younger people, they would respect younger people, and they would always be willing to help younger people. They would say, "Don't worry about what I'm doing, but I'm not gonna allow you to do certain things." And then, many of them wouldn't allow me to make some wrong turns in my life, and I remember that today, that yes, I wanted to do what was wrong, many times, but hey, they wouldn't allow it. They just wouldn't tolerate it.

These texts illustrate how gender facilitates or contrains the interview. In both texts the teachers are responding to the same questions; how they would describe themselves as teachers and what the influences were on the kind of teachers they became. In the first text, the female teacher speaks 432 utterances over four turns. In the second text, a male teacher speaks 637 utterances over three turns. In response to the same questions, the male teachers speaks thirty-two percent more words over fewer turns, a phenomenon that other African American scholars have noted in their research on cross-gender talk in the black community.

SUMMARY AND COMPARISONS

It is unclear whether the experiences reported here would be the same for outsiders, or for other insiders, for that matter. There is no doubt that the teachers' view of me as an insider influenced their willingness to participate, and shaped both their expectations and responses. There is no guarantee that research conducted by "natives" will be any more objective or less biased than that conducted by outsiders. What we can hope for is that native researchers will offer new insights and alternative ways of thinking, and that including the minority perspective will be a means of creating new paradigms. At the moment, however, it is still the rule rather than the exception to subjugate the voices and distort the realities of ethnic minorities from all groups to fit the requirements of a caste society as well as the needs of popular paradigms.

NOTES

1. For discussions of native anthropology, see John Langston Gwaltney, *Drylongso: A Portrait of Black America* (New York: Random House, 1980); John Langston Gwaltney, "Common Sense and Science: Urban Core Black Observations," in *Anthropologists at Home in North America: Methods and Issues in the Study of One's Own Society*, ed. D. Messerschmidt (Cambridge: Cambridge University Press, 1981), pp. 46–61; Delmos Jones, "Toward a Native Anthropology," *Human Organization* 29(4) (Winter 1970), pp. 251–59.
2. Gloria Naylor, *Mama Day* (New York: Vintage Press, 1988), pp. 7–8.
3. W. E. B. Du Bois, *Chicago Defender*, October 13, 1945.
4. See Note 1.
5. Charles Briggs, *Learning How to Ask: A Sociolinguistic Role of the Interview in Social Science Research* (New York: Cambridge University Press, 1986).
6. James D. Anderson, *The Education of Blacks in the South, 1860–1935* (Chapel Hill: University of North Carolina Press, 1988).
7. Marsha H. Stanback, "Language and Black Women's Place: Evidence from the Black Middle-Class," in *For Alma Mater: Theory and Practice in Feminist Scholarship*, eds. P. A. Treichler, C. Kramarae, and B. Stafford (Urbana: University of Illinois Press) 177–93.

Contributors

EDITORS

GWENDOLYN ETTER-LEWIS is Associate Professor of English at Western Michigan University. She earned her Ph.D. in Linguistics from the University of Michigan and specializes in gender differences in written and spoken language. Dr. Etter-Lewis is the recipient of numerous honors and awards including: a Fulbright to Zambia, 1995; a National Council for Black Studies Fellowship to study and research at the University of Ghana, Leggon, 1994; Council for International Educational Exchange participant in the Faculty Summer Seminar at the University of Zimbabwe in Harare, 1993; Michigan Association of Governing Boards Distinguished Faculty Member Award, 1992; a National Academy of Education Postdoctoral Spencer Fellowship, 1991–1992; NEH Travel to Collections Grant, 1992; NEH Summer Seminar Fellowship, 1991; and a Ford Foundation Postdoctoral Research Fellowship, 1989–1990. Gwendolyn Etter-Lewis is the author of several publications including, *My Soul is My Own: Oral Narratives of African American Women in the Professions* (Routledge, 1993).

MICHÉLE FOSTER is Professor in the Center for Educational Studies at the Claremont Graduate School. Her research interests include the social/cultural context of learning, sociolinguistics, and the ethnography of communication. She has written extensively on African American teachers and is the recipient of several awards including a Spencer Postdoctoral Fellowship and a Smithsonian Faculty Fellowship. Dr. Michéle Foster is the author of numerous publications including her current work on a book of narratives by African American teachers entitled, *Black Teachers on Teaching*.

CONTRIBUTORS

JONINA M. ABRON is Assistant Professor of English at Western Michigan University.

CELIA ALVAREZ is currently Assistant Professor of Women's Studies at Arizona State University West, Phoenix, Arizona.

NANCY P. GREENMAN is a visiting professor in the Department of Anthropology at the University of South Florida. Beginning in 1995, she will be Associate Professor of Education Foundations at the University of Texas at San Antonio.

VALERIE GRIM is Assistant Professor of Afro-American Studies and History at Indiana University, Bloomington, Indiana.

JANNELI F. MILLER is currently a doctoral candidate in Anthropology at the University of Arizona.

SALLY MCBETH is Associate Professor of Anthropology and Multicultural Studies at University of Northern Colorado.

LINDA WILLIAMSON NELSON teachers writing, African American Literature and Anthropology at Richard Stockton College of New Jersey.

LANCE A. RASBRIDGE teaches at the University of Texas, Dallas. His most recent research explores the long-term consequences of refugee resettlement.

ANGELITA REYES is currently an Associate Professor in Women's Studies at the University of Minnesota.

MADALYNN C. RUCKER is program manager for a federal substance abuse prevention program in Sacramento, California, under the administration of the Community Services Planning Council.

JIANLI ZHAO is currently a doctoral candidate at the Graduate Institute of Liberal Arts, Emory University.

in 1965. She authored a booklet on Sacajawea and still serves as consultant for many organizations concerned with the education of American Indian children.

SALLY MCBETH is Associate Professor of Anthropology and Multicultural Studies at the University of Northern Colorado. She holds a Ph.D. from Washington State University and specializes in gender, folklore, multicultural education, and North American Indians. Dr. McBeth is the author of several publications including a book entitled *Ethnic Identity and the Boarding School Experience*.

JANNELI F. MILLER is a doctoral candidate in Anthropology at the University of Arizona. She received her MA in Applied Anthropology from Northern Arizona University. Ms. Miller is a licensed midwife in a home-birth practice in Northern Arizona and has conducted research on the Navajo, Hopi, and Apache reservations and in the Philippines. Her research interests include ethnomedicine, midwifery, women's health, and spiritual aspects of birth, death, and healing.

LINDA WILLIAMSON NELSON is a linguistic anthropologist who teaches writing, African American Literature, and anthropology at Richard Stockton College of New Jersey. The author of many publications on Black English, Dr. Nelson recently began a book-length study of African-American women's life narrative discourse.

LANCE RASBRIDGE completed his dissertation in Anthropology at Southern Methodist University in Dallas. He teaches a course on Southeast Asian History at the University of Texas, Dallas and coordinates the Refugee Outreach Program of Parkland Hospital, Dallas. Dr. Rasbridge's most recent research explores the long-term consequences of refugee resettlement.

ANGELITA REYES, Associate Professor of Women's Studies at the University of Minnesota, earned her Ph.D. in Comparative Literature from the University of Iowa. Her research, writing, and teaching focus on anglophone and francophone African, Caribbean, and African-American literatures in the context of indigenous and comparative historical issues. She has authored several publications including a book entitled *Representations of the Mother-Woman in Postcolonial Women's Writing: Crossing More Bridges*. Dr. Reyes also edited an anthology of contemporary non-western writing, *Global Voices,* and a special issue of *Signs: A Journal of Women in Culture and Society* on "Postcolonial, Indigenous, and Emergent Feminisms."

MADALYNN C. RUCKER is Program Manager for a federal substance abuse prevention program in Sacramento, California under the administration of the Community Services Planning Council. She received her MA in Political Science from Stanford University. Ms. Rucker specializes in adult education and provides advocacy for traditionally underrepresented populations in planning and resource allocation. Her many research interests include women in the Black Power Movement.

JIANLI ZHAO, a Ph.D. candidate at the Graduate Institute of Liberal Arts, Emory University, graduated as an English major from Beijing Second Foreign Languages Institute. She completed her MA in American Studies at Baylor University, Waco, Texas. Ms. Zhao's research focuses on Chinese immigrants in the United States with a concentration on the Chinese community in Atlanta, Georgia.

Index